# The Arab World Facing the Challenge of the New Millennium

*Dedicated to the people of Palestine*

# THE ARAB WORLD FACING THE CHALLENGE OF THE NEW MILLENNIUM

Henry T. Azzam

I.B.Tauris *Publishers*
LONDON • NEW YORK

Published in 2002 by I.B.Tauris & Co Ltd
6 Salem Road, London W2 4BU
175 Fifth Avenue, New York NY 10010
Website: http://www.ibtauris.com

In the United States and Canada distributed by Palgrave Macmillan,
a division of St. Martin's Press, 175 Fifth Avenue, New York NY 10010



ISBN 1 86064 816 9

A full CIP record for this book is available from the British Library
A full CIP record for this book is available from the Library of Congress

Library of Congress catalog card: available

Typeset in Caslon by Dexter Haven Associates, London
Printed and bound in Great Britain by MPG Books Ltd, Bodmin

# CONTENTS


*Figures and Tables* vii

*Preface* xi

1 The Arab world: preparing for a new era of growth 1

2 Challenges and opportunities in the new millennium 13

3 The new economy and its impact on the Arab region 36

4 Arab bond markets: moving from the embryonic stage to the take-off stage 50

5 Arab stock markets: facing up to new challenges 64

6 Drivers of change affecting Arab banks 79

7 Arab currencies: fix or float? 95

8 North Africa 106

9 Levant 136

10 The GCC countries 167

11 The Arab world: a vision for growth 207

# FIGURES AND TABLES

## FIGURES


| | | |
|---|---|---|
| 1.1 | Growth of real GDP (percentage) | 1 |
| 1.2 | Growth of real per-capita income (percentage) | 2 |
| 1.3 | Export growth, 1991–9 (percentage) | 3 |
| 1.4 | FDI (percentage of GDP) | 4 |
| 1.5 | Developing regions' share in FDI, 1999 | 5 |
| 1.6 | Unemployment across regions of the world, 2000 | 5 |
| 2.1 | Corruption Perception Index for selected countries (most corrupt=0, least corrupt=10) | 23 |
| 2.2 | Insurance penetration in Arab markets (penetration rates as percentage of GDP, 1999) | 35 |
| 3.1 | The Internet is the infrastructure of the new economy | 37 |
| 3.2 | E-conomics aggregate supply and demand | 40 |
| 3.3 | Internet usage in the Arab world: why do you use the Internet? | 41 |
| 3.4 | Estimated number of Internet users in the Arab world, 2000 | 43 |
| 3.5 | Growth in Internet usage (April 1999–April 2000) | 43 |
| 3.6 | Projected business-to-business e-commerce expansion ($ billion) | 44 |
| 4.1 | Corporate bond issues in the Arab world, 2000 ($ million) | 50 |
| 5.1 | Arab countries' share of total stock market capitalization, 2000 | 66 |
| 5.2 | Arab stock-market liquidity | 67 |
| 5.3 | Performance of Arab stock markets, 1999–2001 | 69 |
| 5.4 | Net private capital flows to emerging markets | 73 |
| 5.5 | Correlation of Arab stock markets with major indices, 2000 | 76 |
| 6.1 | Distribution of top 1000 banks' tier-one capital by region, 2000 | 82 |
| 6.2 | Arab banks compared to the largest banks of the world by total assets, 2000 ($ billion) | 82 |
| 7.1 | Countries with a fixed or floating exchange rate: 2001 | 96 |

8.1 Tunisia: growth in fixed-capital formation outpaces real GDP growth 125
8.2 Tunisia: consumer pricing index, annual average 126
9.1 Jordan: annual change in the cost-of-living index 140
9.2 Lebanon: gross foreign-exchange reserves 148
9.3 Palestinian territories: consumer price inflation 155
9.4 Arab Syrian Republic: consumer price index, 1985–2000 163
10.1 Oman: CPI inflation 186

TABLES

1.1 Growth rates/ratios for Middle East and North Africa (percentage per year) 3
1.2 Budgetary developments in the Arab countries 6
2.1 Direction of Arab trade (percentage) 17
2.2 The changing management structure 18
2.3 The changing face of Arab capital markets 21
2.4 Tourist arrival by region 27
2.5 Arab countries' defence expenditure (1999 constant prices) 29
2.6 Value of gold reserves in selected Arab countries ($ million) 31
3.1 Mobile telephone market in the Arab region (number of subscribers) 45
3.2 Global growth estimates for the mobile Internet (million) 46
3.3 Speed of connection to the Internet 47
4.1 Treasury bonds issued by Arab countries ($ million) 52
4.2 Long-term sovereign ratings of selected Arab countries, 2000 53
4.3 Corporate bond issues in the Arab world (local currency, million) 55
4.4 Sovereign Arab eurobonds (selected outstanding issues) 61
5.1 Market capitalization of Arab stock markets 66
5.2 Arab stock-market liquidity 67
5.3 Valuation of Middle East stock markets in comparison with other regional stock markets: 2000 68
5.4 Private financial flows to Arab countries ($ billion) 74
6.1 Major indicators of the Arab banking sector, 1998–2000 81

| | | |
|---|---|---|
| 6.2 | Top 15 Arab banks, 2000 | 83 |
| 6.3 | Mergers and acquisitions among banks in the Middle East | 90 |
| 7.1 | Advantages and disadvantages of fixed and floating exchange-rate regimes | 98 |
| 7.2 | Exchange-rate regimes for Arab countries | 99 |
| 7.3 | Inflation trends in selected Arab countries compared to that of the US | 103 |
| 7.4 | Exchange rates, current accounts and foreign reserves of selected Arab countries ($ million) | 103 |
| 7.5 | Assessing risks of devaluation vis-à-vis the dollar for selected Arab currencies | 105 |
| 8.1 | Egypt: main economic indicators | 106 |
| 8.2 | Egypt: summary of national budget operations (EGP million) | 112 |
| 8.3 | Egypt: structure of outstanding domestic debt (EGP million) | 114 |
| 8.4 | Egypt: external debt by type and maturity ($ million) | 115 |
| 8.5 | Egypt: balance of payments ($ million) | 116 |
| 8.6 | Morocco: main economic indicators | 117 |
| 8.7 | Morocco: GDP growth, 1997–2000 | 119 |
| 8.8 | Morocco: current-account balance ($ billion) | 123 |
| 8.9 | Tunisia: main economic indicators | 123 |
| 8.10 | Tunisia: central government budget, 1997–2001 (TD million) | 127 |
| 8.11 | Tunisia: main balance-of-payments indicators | 129 |
| 8.12 | Tunisia: structure of external debt ($ million) | 130 |
| 8.13 | Algeria: main economic indicators | 131 |
| 8.14 | Algeria: GDP growth | 132 |
| 8.15 | Algeria: government budget (AD billion) | 134 |
| 8.16 | Algeria: current-account balance ($ billion) | 135 |
| 8.17 | Algeria: external debt ($ billion) | 135 |
| 9.1 | Jordan: main economic indicators | 136 |
| 9.2 | Jordan: summary of central government budget (JD million) | 142 |
| 9.3 | Jordan: balance of payments (JD million) | 143 |
| 9.4 | Lebanon: main economic indicators | 144 |

| | | |
|---|---|---|
| 9.5 | Lebanon: public finance conditions (LBP billion) | 149 |
| 9.6 | Lebanon: domestic and external debt | 150 |
| 9.7 | Lebanon: balance of payments ($ billion) | 151 |
| 9.8 | Palestinian territories: main economic indicators | 152 |
| 9.9 | Palestinian territories: GDP growth ($ million) | 154 |
| 9.10 | Palestinian territories: fiscal operations of the Palestinian Monetary Authority ($ million) | 156 |
| 9.11 | Palestinian territories: trade balance ($ million) | 157 |
| 9.12 | Arab Syrian Republic: main economic indicators | 158 |
| 9.13 | Arab Syrian Republic: budgets, 1997–2001 (SL million) | 164 |
| 9.14 | Arab Syrian Republic: balance of payments, 1994–9 ($ million) | 165 |
| 10.1 | Saudi Arabia: main economic indicators | 167 |
| 10.2 | Saudi Arabia: budget overview (SR billion) | 173 |
| 10.3 | Saudi Arabia: balance of payments ($ million) | 174 |
| 10.4 | Kuwait: main economic indicators | 176 |
| 10.5 | Kuwait: government budget (KD million) | 180 |
| 10.6 | Kuwait: public domestic debt (KD million) | 181 |
| 10.7 | Kuwait: balance of payments (KD million) | 182 |
| 10.8 | Oman: main economic indicators | 183 |
| 10.9 | Oman: government budget, 1997–2000 (OR million) | 187 |
| 10.10 | Oman: trade balance and current account (OR million) | 188 |
| 10.11 | Qatar: main economic indicators | 189 |
| 10.12 | Qatar: budgets, 1998/99–2001/02 (QR million) | 193 |
| 10.13 | Qatar: balance of payments (QR million) | 194 |
| 10.14 | UAE: main economic indicators | 195 |
| 10.15 | UAE: federal budget (AED billion) | 199 |
| 10.16 | UAE: balance of payments (AED billion) | 200 |
| 10.17 | Bahrain: main economic indicators | 201 |
| 10.18 | Bahrain: government budget (BD million) | 204 |
| 10.19 | Bahrain: current account, 1998–2000 (BD million) | 205 |

# PREFACE

The Arab countries face enormous challenges as they move into the twenty-first century. This book calls on the countries of the region to take a proactive approach when responding to those challenges, rather than be overwhelmed by them. The forces driving the dramatic changes experienced throughout the global economy are clear. Among other things, they include open markets for goods and services, free flow of capital, a heavy reliance on new technology, and the ability to adapt, innovate and compete globally. In the new millennium, the most successful economies will be those that prove most effective in the field of technology, and in delivering quality products to the global market. Brains, not natural resources, will matter most.

Attempts at creating economic co-operation between Arab states have all been brief and unsuccessful, and the lines drawn by the colonial powers in the early decades of the twentieth century remain largely untouched. The Arabs are quick to blame the ex-colonial countries for having divided up the Middle East when they handed over their power to regional governments and for having fostered differences among them; but this cannot be the whole story. Much of the fault lies with the governments of the Arab countries themselves in the post-independence period. This book looks at past and current events in an attempt to understand and explain what needs to be done for the region to have a brighter future.

A new generation of Arab leadership has started to surface in several Arab countries, one that is familiar with the high-tech world, which embraces a global vision, and can reasonably aspire to world-class standards of excellence. With such leadership, countries of the region will be in a better position to promote a common vision based on these values.

On all continents, there are recent examples of countries that have moved beyond economic mediocrity and become pace-setters on the global stage. Obvious examples include Costa Rica in Central America, Ireland in Europe, and Singapore in Asia. While some countries flounder, these nations – all small, all lacking in natural resources, all once written off as potential disasters – have prospered. Learning from their example, the Arab countries too must break from the past, imagine a different kind of future, and then actively strive to reach it.

The Arab countries are going through a period of transition, from having economies in which public sectors have been the dominant players to ones in which the private sector is taking the lead. This necessitates changing the role of the state from that of a 'player', a dominant actor in the economy investing directly in industrial capacity, financial institutions and utilities, towards that of a 'referee', or a regulator in competitive private markets, whose role is to provide a stable macro-economic environment and a level playing field for the private sector. It also necessitates the presence of strong leadership in both the economic and political spheres, leadership which can take bold decisions and put in place a long-term strategy that could see the Arab world into the next millennium.

More rapid economic growth is essential to solve the region's employment problem and achieve prosperity. The Arab countries need to attain rates of growth of per-capita income in excess of 2.5 per cent per year, which, given annual population growth rates of 2.5–3.5 per cent, means aggregate GDP growth of 5–6 per cent well into the first decade of the twenty-first century. To generate the much-needed economic growth that will be adequate to absorb new labour force entrants and reduce the existing high unemployment levels, countries of the region need to intensify their efforts at economic reform and choose the most appropriate economic model. Although economic structures and the pace of growth differ from country to country, the requirements are generally similar throughout the region.

Choosing the most appropriate economic model is not easy, and different models may suit different countries, depending on the level of their financial, economic and political development. Each economic model has its strengths and weaknesses. For example, the American model has been the most successful in creating jobs, but has too wide income inequalities. European countries have been better at combining growth and equality, but at the expense of higher unemployment. The ideal model changes with economic circumstances, and what is considered successful now may be a failure under different circumstances. Furthermore, while the concept of the market economy has now been accepted by many developing countries, most of them still reject market-oriented solutions to social problems.

Today, conditions in the world economy, with the free flow of goods and services across boundaries and fast-changing IT best suit the American model. This model emphasizes flexible and competitive labour and product markets and the maximization of shareholder value. In the 1970s and 1980s, Japan's high-quality training and lifetime employment helped to solve labour shortages and kept wages under control. South Korea's industrial policy during the same period gave evidence of possible gains that could be derived from focused government intervention.

Economic studies suggest that having in place the right ingredients for growth may be even more important than picking the best economic model. These ingredients include changing the role of the state from player to referee, establishing civil societies supported by political and economic reforms, developing the region's human resources, and the formation of a regional economic bloc. Other ingredients of growth also include having in place the right supervisory regime, with good legal and regulatory systems, liberal trade and capital structures, an empowered private sector and a strong leadership to implement all that.

This book offers readily available sources of reference on the region's economies, banking, stock and bond markets, presented in a concise and accessible form. It provides investors, policy-makers, analysts, bankers and other market participants with comprehensive information on Saudi Arabia, Egypt, Jordan, Kuwait, the United Arab Emirates, Qatar, Bahrain, Oman, Lebanon, Morocco, Algeria,

Syria, Tunisia and Palestine. For each country a general overview of its economic performance is given, covering internal and external imbalances, fiscal and monetary policies and growth prospects. The book also provides detailed analysis of such important issues as the new economy and its impact on the region, the drivers of change affecting Arab banks, and the exchange-rate regimes of Arab countries.

I wish to acknowledge the invaluable assistant provided by Ms Lama Nabulsi, who contributed to the research work and the writing up of the manuscript while working as my research assistant, when the two of us were associates with Middle East Capital Group. Without her help, this project would have been very difficult to accomplish.

My appreciation and love to my wife Reem, whose open, stimulating and romantic character has been a breath of fresh air to me and to all those around her. I dedicate this book also to my sons Suhail, Ramzi and Marwan, who are starting to have first-hand experience of the new world in which we live. They are aware that no person, company or nation can become successful without looking forward, and without anticipating the world in which they will operate.

# 1

# THE ARAB WORLD: PREPARING FOR A NEW ERA OF GROWTH

## REVIEWING PAST ECONOMIC PERFORMANCE

According to the *Arab Economic Report* 2000, nominal GDP of all the Arab countries was around $440 billion in 1980, $450 billion in 1990, rising to $599 billion in 1997 and to $650 billion in 2000. Real GDP growth in the Arab region, which averaged around 1 per cent annually in the 1974–1990 period rising to an average of 2.9 per cent annually between 1990 and 2000, had lagged behind other groups of developing countries (figure 1.1).

The total population of the Arab world grew at an average annual rate of 3 per cent between 1980 and 1990, exhibiting the highest population growth-rate in the world. The region's total population reached 220 million in 1990 compared to 135 million in 1980. Population growth in the region slowed down to an annual average of 2.5 per cent between 1990 and 2000, in line with a slowing of population growth in all middle- and low-income countries from an annual average of 2 per cent in the 1980s to 1.6 per cent between 1990 and 2000. This brought the region's total population to 275 million in 2000, double its level in 1980.

**Figure 1.1**
Growth of real GDP (percentage)

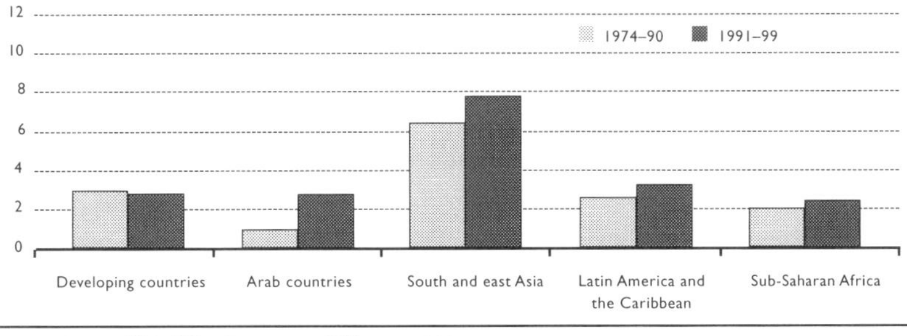


*Source: World Bank,* Global Development and Finance *1999*

Growth in real per-capita income of the Arab countries was the lowest in the world. The region's GDP per capita contracted by 2 per cent annually between 1975 and 1990 compared to an average of 1.2 per cent growth for developing countries as a whole. Per capita real growth was barely positive during the 1990–1999 period at an annual average of 0.6 per cent, far below the performance of other developing countries in Asia and Latin America (figure 1.2).

**Figure 1.2**
**Growth of real per-capita income (percentage)**

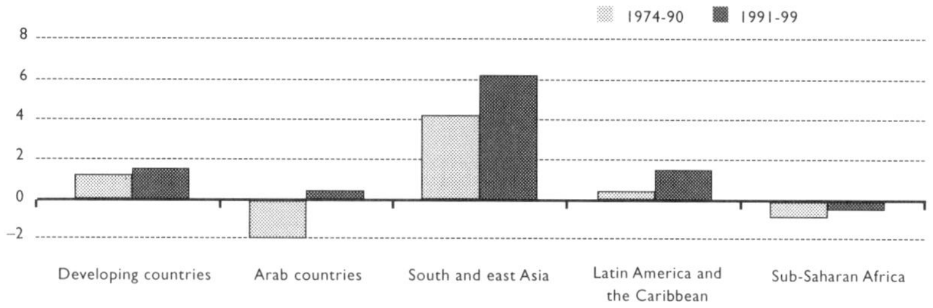


*Source: World Bank,* Global Development Finance *1999*

Signs of a more favourable outlook for the region, emerging in 1997, were dampened by oil prices falling sharply in 1998 before rising again in 1999 and 2000. Real GDP growth for the Arab countries slowed to 2 per cent in 1998 from 3.1 per cent in 1997 but rose to 2.5 per cent in 1999 and 3.2 per cent in 2000. In particular, lower oil prices have had major consequences for the region's oil exporters, which saw their real GDP growth drop from 2.7 per cent in 1997 to 0.5 per cent in 1998. In the six Gulf Co-operation Council (GCC) countries, oil export earnings fell by almost one-third in 1998, causing fiscal balances to deteriorate by 5 per cent to 8 per cent of GDP. The situation was exactly the opposite in 2000, when oil prices and revenues surged, boosting real GDP growth for the Gulf countries to 4.5 per cent. The effect of higher oil prices spread to the non-oil Arab countries, through the rise in remittances from expatriate workers, higher intraregional trade, and a surge in direct and portfolio investments coming from the Gulf region.

The Arab world's non-oil merchandise exports of around $65 billion in 2000 were marginally higher than those of Finland, whose population does not exceed 5.5 million. The progress of Arab countries towards greater integration with the world economy has been slow and lags behind other developing-country regions. The Arab world's total exports including oil accounted for around 3 per cent of the world's total exports that year. The region's export growth averaged only 4.2 per cent per annum between 1991 and 1999, below the 8.7 per cent average annual export growth achieved by developing countries as a group, and below the 6.8 per cent average annual growth in world trade (figure 1.3). Interregional trade has also been low compared to other regions, accounting for less than 10 per cent of total trade since the mid-1980s.

Figure 1.3
Export growth, 1991–9 (percentage)

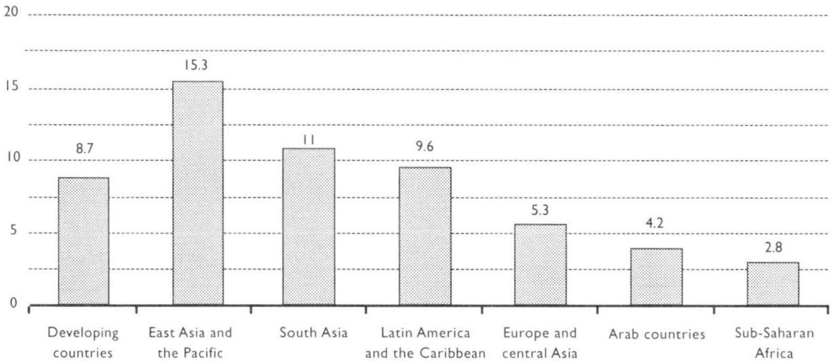


*Source: World Bank,* Global Development Finance *1999*

The majority of the Arab countries have been operating under successive current-account deficits throughout most of the 1980s and 1990s. However, the current-account position of the Arab region improved from a combined deficit of $64.7 billion in 1991 (37 per cent of total exports of goods and services) to a surplus of $12.5 billion and $10.7 billion in 1996 and 1997 respectively (5.5 per cent and 4.5 per cent of total exports of goods and services). The sharp decline in the region's terms of trade in 1998, due mainly to lower oil export revenues plunged the current-account balance back into a $25.8 billion deficit. The current account turned positive in 1999 and 2000, accounting for 1.5 per cent and 5.9 per cent of the region's GDP respectively (table 1.1).

Table 1.1
Growth rates/ratios for Middle East and North Africa (percentage per year)

| | 1990–2000 | 1998 | 1999 | 2000 |
|---|---|---|---|---|
| Real GDP growth | 3.1 | 3.3 | 2.2 | 3.2 |
| Consumption per capita | 1.2 | –0.9 | –0.2 | 1.2 |
| GDP per capita | 0.9 | 1.3 | 0.3 | 1.2 |
| Population | 2.2 | 2.0 | 1.9 | 2.0 |
| Median inflation | | 0.7 | 1.8 | 3.7 |
| Gross domestic investment/ GDP | 21.5 | 21.9 | 22.4 | 22.5 |
| Budget balance | –2.8 | –3.9 | –3.5 | –2.0 |
| Export volume | 4.4 | –11.9 | 12.5 | 6.1 |
| Current account/GDP | –2.2 | –2.7 | 1.5 | 5.9 |
| Memo items | | | | |
| GDP of oil-dominant economies | 2.6 | 0.9 | 1.8 | 3.4 |
| GDP of diversified exporters | 3.9 | 5.5 | 3.3 | 3.2 |

*Source: World Bank Development Prospects Group, February 2001*

The stock of capital held abroad by investors from the region is conservatively estimated at about $800 billion, more than any other region in the world as a percentage of GDP. About half of the capital held abroad is from the GCC countries.

As a percentage of GDP for all Arab countries, investment declined from the mid-1970s until the early 1990s, after which it rose. However, the growth path was lower than that of other developing countries and substantially lower than that of Asia. Private investment of 11 per cent of GDP since 1980 was well below that of other developing countries and has not improved significantly in the past ten years.

**Figure 1.4**
**FDI (percentage of GDP)**

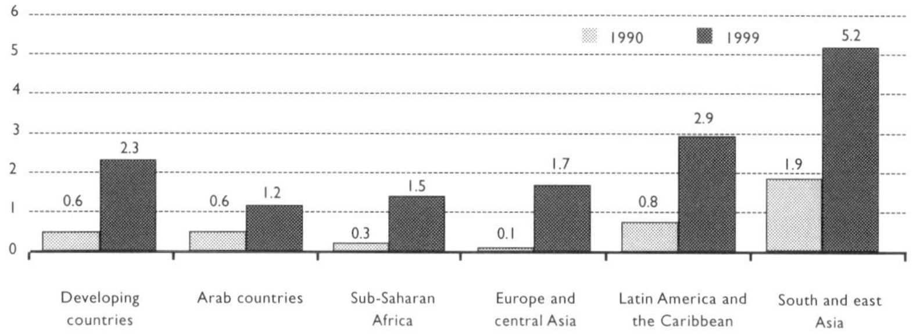


*Source: World Bank,* Global Development Finance *1999*

The region's disappointing performance has been associated with low inflows of foreign direct investment (FDI). In 1980, FDI targeting the Arab region was negative at –0.7 per cent of GNP, rising to $2.8 billion (0.6 per cent of GNP) in 1990, to $5.9 billion (0.8 per cent of GDP) in 1998 and to $7.3 billion in 2000. Yet it remained much lower than in other developing regions, where FDI as a percentage of GDP in 1998 amounted to 2.9 per cent for Latin America, 5.2 per cent for East and South Asia and an average of 2.3 per cent for the developing countries as a whole (figure 1.4).

Moreover, the Arab countries have failed to keep pace with other developing regions in the race towards attracting FDI, and the region's share in total FDI flows to developing countries fell sharply from 11.4 per cent in 1990 to 3.8 per cent in 1998, before rising to 4.5 per cent in 1999 (figure 1.5).

Although accurate figures on unemployment rates in many Arab countries are lacking, all recent estimates point to double-digit figures and an overall unemployment rate of at least 14 per cent (figure 1.6). According to the Arab Labour Organization (ALO), there were an estimated 12 million unemployed people in the Arab world in 2000. The unemployment rates across countries in the region were as follows: 25 per cent in Yemen, 21 per cent in Algeria, 19 per cent in Jordan, 17 per cent in Sudan, 15 per cent in Lebanon and in Morocco, 12 per cent in Tunisia, 9 per cent in Egypt, and 8 per cent in Syria. Although official unemployment figures are

Figure 1.5
Developing regions' share in FDI, 1999

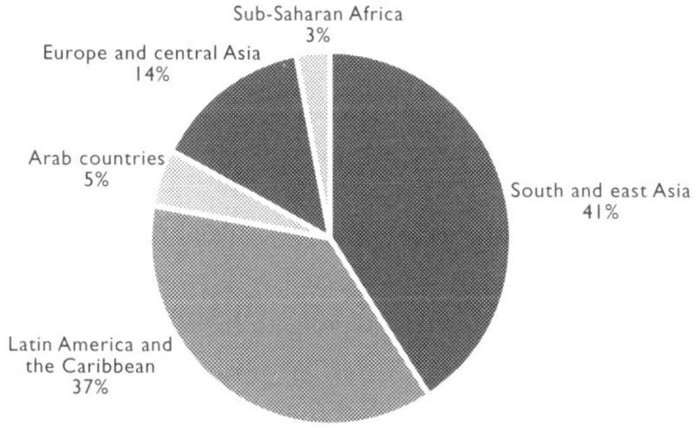


*Source: World Bank,* Global Development Finance *1999*

not available in most Gulf states, unofficial estimates range from as low as 1 per cent to as high as 27 per cent. In 1999, 45.6 per cent of Arab labour was engaged in the services sector (compared to 32.4 per cent in 1985), 35.1 per cent in agriculture (41.7 per cent in 1985), and 19.1 per cent in industry (25.9 per cent in 1985).

Figure 1.6
Unemployment across regions of the world, 2000

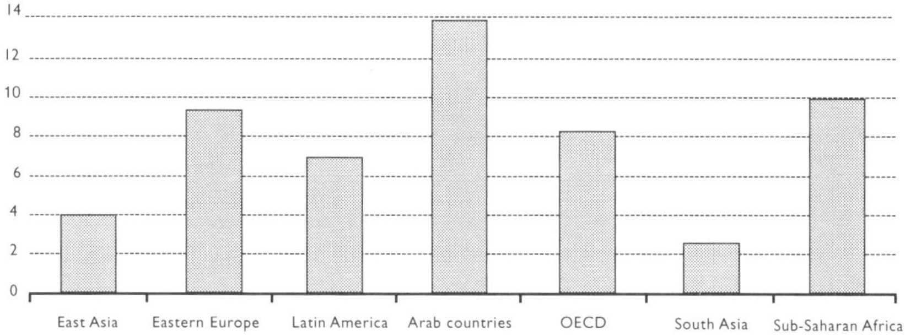


Youth unemployment in particular is a paramount problem, exacerbated by the fact that 50 per cent of the region's population is below the age of 20, which means that large numbers of new entrants to the workforce appear each year. According to the ALO the total Arab workforce has been growing at an annual average of 3.3 per cent over the three-year period 1998–2000, reaching 86.5 million in 2000. The workforce is expected to expand further by 4 per cent per annum to reach 123 million by 2010, at a time when job creation is growing at an average of 2.5 per cent per annum, pointing clearly to an escalation in the current unemployment crisis.

## BUDGETARY DEVELOPMENTS IN THE ARAB WORLD

Faced with widening fiscal deficits in the early 1990s, the Arab governments have been attempting to put their finances in order over the past few years. The oil price shock of 1998 accentuated the vulnerability of fiscal balances in the Arab countries – particularly those in the Gulf region – to the volatility of oil prices, highlighting other structural weaknesses in their budgets. The pursuit of a more balanced fiscal position has been made easy for the GCC governments with higher oil prices in 1999–2001, boosting revenues. Nonetheless, more aggressive efforts to generate stable non-oil revenue sources and compress current spending are called for in order to mitigate the GCC countries' fiscal vulnerabilities. Other Arab countries have their own set of fiscal bottlenecks, such as limited revenue sources, the predominance of a rigid wage bill on the expenditure side, and in particular – in the case of Lebanon – a large interest bill to service a rising public debt.

Table 1.2
Budgetary developments in the Arab countries

| | 1998 | 1999 | 2000 | 2001 |
|---|---|---|---|---|
| **Saudi Arabia** | | | | |
| Expenditure | 50.69 | 48.27 | 54.10 | 68.00 |
| Budget balance | –12.93 | -9.07 | 12.00 | -6.66 |
| Balance/GDP | –9.90% | –6.40% | 7.30% | -4.06% |
| **Kuwait** | | | | |
| Expenditure | 13.04 | 13.15 | 11.77 | 13.94 |
| Budget balance | –1.21 | 4.04 | 4.62 | –5.60 |
| Balance/GDP | –4.80% | 13.80% | 14.10% | –13.50% |
| **Qatar** | | | | |
| Expenditure | 4.50 | 4.30 | 3.94 | 4.23 |
| Budget balance | –0.82 | –0.91 | –0.07 | –0.77 |
| Balance/GDP | –7.30% | –8.90% | –0.60% | –5.00% |
| **Oman** | | | | |
| Expenditure | 5.79 | 5.88 | 6.34 | 7.30 |
| Budget balance | –0.99 | –1.21 | 0.30 | –0.82 |
| Balance/GDP | –7.10% | –7.90% | 1.60% | –4.20% |
| **Jordan** | | | | |
| Expenditure | 2.90 | 2.88 | 2.84 | 3.24 |
| Budget balance | –0.79 | –0.60 | –0.58 | –0.56 |
| Balance/GDP | –9.90% | –7.40% | –7.00% | –6.00% |
| **Lebanon** | | | | |
| Expenditure | 5.16 | 5.59 | 6.93 | 6.62 |
| Budget balance | –2.24 | –2.37 | –3.9 | –3.37 |
| Balance/GDP | –14.00% | –15.00% | –24.00% | –20.40% |
| **Egypt** | | | | |
| Expenditure | 20.80 | 25.30 | 27.00 | 29.20 |
| Budget balance | –0.80 | –3.70 | –3.60 | –3.90 |
| Balance/GDP | –1.00% | –4.20% | –3.60% | –4.20% |

*Source: Several national sources*

Most Arab countries posted improvements in their fiscal stance in the year 2000, with some exceptions. In the Gulf region, higher oil prices of 1999 and 2000 have been accompanied by unprecedented spending restraint, which has resulted in most countries recording a surplus in their 2000 budget for the first time in years. Saudi Arabia's budget showed a surplus of $12 billion in 2000 – the first in 18 years. Revenues surged from $39 billion in 1999 to $66 billion in 2000. Saudi Arabia's commitment to a more prudent fiscal policy stance was further demonstrated with a balanced 2001 budget proposal. However, the actual budget ended up with a deficit of $6.66 billion. In Kuwait, the 1999/2000 budget recorded an impressive surplus of $4 billion, equivalent to 12 per cent of GDP, compared to a budgeted deficit of $6.5 billion. Kuwait was able to turn a budget deficit forecast for the 2000/01 fiscal year into a surplus of $4.6 billion. The 2001/02 budget forecasts a surplus of $5.6 billion.

In Oman in 2000, higher oil and natural-gas export revenues helped transform a budget deficit targeted at $918 million to $300 million surplus. The improvement was even more pronounced in Qatar where the actual deficit for the fiscal year 1999-2000 amounted to only $70 million, compared to the projected $990 million deficit.

In the Levant region, Jordan has successfully reduced its budget deficit from a high of 9.9 per cent of GDP in 1998 to 7 per cent in 2000 primarily through spending restraint. This deficit declined to 6 per cent of GDP in 2001, due to the 16 per cent rise in revenues associated with the introduction of VAT. In Lebanon, government spending soared by over 23 per cent in 2000, while revenues fell by 6.5 per cent, with a resulting deficit equivalent to more than 24 per cent of GDP, compared to a target of 12.7 per cent in the original budget plan. In Egypt, following commendable fiscal performance that brought the deficit down to around 1 per cent of GDP in the mid-1990s, the budget deficit jumped to 4.2 per cent of GDP in 1998/99, due to a 21.5 per cent increase in public expenditure. Spending in 1999/2000 was up by 6.6 per cent while revenues increased by 8.3 per cent, bringing the deficit to GDP ratio down to 3.6 per cent. However, the deficit climbed up again to over 4 per cent of GDP in 2000/01.

The Arab governments' budget proposals for the year 2002 exhibit varying degrees of fiscal restraint. The Saudi Arabian budget is particularly cautious, with expenditure set to decline by 20 per cent on actual expenditures of 2001 and return to a deficit of $12 billion, which will be financed by internal borrowing. This will further increase the domestic debt stock to above 100 per cent of GDP. The Kuwaiti government is increasing spending by 10 per cent, while Oman and Qatar have adopted more expansionary budgets for the fiscal year 2001/02 with spending set to rise by 15 per cent and 14 per cent respectively. These are ambitious spending proposals when set against the expected drop in oil revenues. Jordan's total expenditures are forecast to rise by 10 per cent in 2002's budget – a substantial increase when compared to the previous few years – in order to promote higher economic growth. Lebanon, on the other hand, is planning to cut spending in its 2002 budget in an attempt to address the country's sharply deteriorating fiscal position. The government has apparently chosen to avoid more extreme fiscal austerity measures in order not to paralyse the already strained economy. Despite the need to address a widening deficit, the Egyptian government is planning to boost expenditure in 2002 in order to loosen the current liquidity crunch in the market.

## PREPARING FOR A NEW ERA OF GROWTH AND DEVELOPMENT

The main economic policies needed to attain growth and development are now well known. These include reducing internal and external imbalances, liberalizing trade, accelerating privatization, putting in place an effective financial infrastructure and attracting foreign joint-venture investment. There are other ingredients of economic growth and development that are particularly important to the region. These are: changing the role of the state from a 'player' to a 'referee'; establishing civil societies, empowering the private sector; forming a regional economic bloc; developing the region's human resources. These reform policies and ingredients of growth cannot be implemented without strong leadership, for which the attainment of growth and prosperity is the primary concern.

### *CHANGING THE ROLE OF THE STATE*

Historically, governments of the region have acted as 'dominant players' in their economies, investing directly in industrial capacity, financial institutions and utilities. However, the fiscal constraints of the recent few years and increasing globalization of trade and investment flows have caused a profound shift towards greater reliance on private instruments. This will eventually lead the government to change its role from that of the 'player', direct actor in the economy, towards that of 'referee', or regulator in competitive free markets.

The shift from player to referee signals a change in the instruments of public policy, from direct investment in goods and services towards the regulation of the actions of private investors. Arab governments are called upon to take back-seat roles and act as catalysts, providing a stable macroeconomic environment and preparing the legal and administrative ground for the private sector to participate more actively in the overall development process. Supervision and regulatory functions include enforcing contracts and property rights, clamping down on bureaucracy and corruption, and implementing the rule of law. They also entail putting in place an effective legal system with prudent supervisory frameworks that are rigorously applied. Well-designed regulations can protect the rights of creditors and deposit-holders from the risks of unsound banking practices, open opportunities for medium-sized and small firms, encourage investment, and eliminate unfair trade practices.

The Arab region needs to enforce transparency within individual institutions and in the financial system as a whole. This means clear norms of accounting, reporting and disclosure requirements, a risk-based regime for remedial actions, consolidated supervision, effective corporate governance, and bankruptcy regimes and rules. All these practices should be deeply rooted in a rule of law that applies to all. The spread of transparency will encourage investments and attract foreign inflows from abroad.

## *ESTABLISHING CIVIL SOCIETIES*

Very few Arab societies truly qualify to be described as civil societies. A long, complicated historical process has kept social allegiance closer to the family, tribe or religious sect. Individuals look to these entities for help in times of need and identify with them more than with the state. In a tribe, as in a family, the chief – the father-figure – dictates decisions. These tribal attitudes still prevail today, and explain the autocratic style of the decision-making process, the style of communication and the seniority system. Tribal bias reduces the chances of having a civil service based on merit. Honesty and business ethics are usually compromised in order to promote other members of the same tribe, clan, sect or family.

Civil societies will be established only after political reforms are introduced that call for more accountability; rights of free expression, respect for human rights, and the development of an equitable social security and unemployment compensation scheme. People should be promoted first and foremost on competence and honesty. The educational system should cultivate values and practices that promote allegiance to the state and the country, rather than to the tribe or the family. Arab management will have to cross-breed the advantages of tribalism with modern management techniques. Checks and balances need to be built into the region's political systems through institutions. Democratic practices that fit the social and religious fabrics of the countries should become deep-rooted, and the rule of law should not be compromised.

## *EMPOWERING THE PRIVATE SECTOR*

Private capital in the region has voted with its feet. About $800 billion in Arab capital is held abroad. Private investment as a percentage of GDP has historically been below that of other developing countries. In a world of intense competition for capital, burdensome tax rules and regulatory hurdles are a sure way to deter investors. In certain Arab countries it typically takes several months to complete the formal steps needed to set up in business.

A World Bank study estimates that up to 30 per cent of the average entrepreneur's time in those countries is spent resolving problems with regulatory agencies. The bureaucracy prevalent in the region is a result of the political hegemony of the

Ottoman rule over much of the Arab world for more than 400 years. One of the Ottoman system's greatest legacies is the stamp. In some Arab countries, bureaucrats are obsessed with the act of stamping and signing documents, and as many as 20 stamps can be needed to register a business.

The public sector in the Arab countries remains large. Algeria and Egypt have levels of public ownership comparable to the transition economies of Eastern Europe. Morocco, Tunisia and Jordan have smaller public sectors, but the government-owned enterprise sector is still large compared with Latin America or East Asia. The state is still the largest employer and the largest consumer of goods and services in various Gulf countries. In several Arab countries, governments still own major extractive industries (e.g. oil, gas, phosphates etc), provide the vast majority of infrastructure and utilities, and dominate the financial sector through public commercial banks..

Arab governments have been talking about privatization of public enterprises, but not enough has been done so far. Implementing the privatization plan could help reduce the financial burden of the governments, cut the wage bill of the public sector, and render several public-sector institutions more efficient. Furthermore, the income generated from privatization could be used to retire existing public-sector debt and lower the debt-service bill that is threatening to become a burden on the budgets of some Arab governments.

## *FORMING A REGIONAL ECONOMIC BLOC*

Little progress has been achieved in Middle East integration. Intraregional trade accounts for only 9 per cent of the region's total trade, compared to 60 per cent in Europe and over 35 per cent in Asia. Intraregional trade in Latin America has increased fourfold since 1991, while that of the Arab states has declined in relative importance. The Arab region is characterized by a low degree of differentiation in the structure of trade, with oil, and to lesser extent agricultural products being the main goods traded within the region.

Globalization and regionalization are not necessarily antagonistic, but rather mutually reinforcing. A bolder policy to increase integration in the global market could at the same time favour more dynamic regional integration efforts. The Arab countries need to integrate their economies with the rest of the world, and in doing so they must come together and establish their own regional economic blocs. In today's world, no nation can realize its full economic potential on its own. Only cross-border, regional co-operation will maximize prosperity for each of the member states of the Middle East, as is the case for other regions of the world.

Liberalization of the trade sector could be pursed along two parallel routes. The first is to have each country fending for itself by getting accession to the WTO and/or negotiating separate association with the EU. The second is to have the Arab countries implement regional trade liberalization and arrangements similar to the Arab Free Trade Agreement. However, the pace of implementing this agreement is slow. The world is unlikely to be at a standstill while the Arab countries conclude the free-trade area by 2008. The GCC states have been negotiating a customs union since 1982 without much success.

Aside from issues of economic solidarity, a regional market would reduce excess capacity and duplication, facilitate negotiations with other regional groups, and lead to substantial economies of scale. Because of the small size of the local markets, several industries that may not be feasible in one country would become so at a regional level. Furthermore, the existence of a regional bloc would encourage FDI currently attracted to the region's larger market.

## *DEVELOPING THE REGION'S HUMAN RESOURCES*

Developing the region's human resources is clearly the foundation for the success of any policy or reform programme. An education system designed to produce civil servants as exists in several Arab countries, does not suit the internationally competitive market-place. A country's national competitive advantages depend more on acquired resources than on resources inherited from nature. In the knowledge-intensive world of today, computer literacy and a good working knowledge of the English language have become a must and a prerequisite for success.

A major cause of unemployment in the region is the poor supply of skills – and an oversupply of unskilled workers – resulting from an outmoded educational system that has failed to keep up with the technological requirements of the quickly evolving labour markets. Schools in a number of Arab countries fail to equip students with the skills essential for the future, dumping poorly qualified graduates onto a saturated labour market. In Egypt, Syria and Jordan, more than 50 per cent of the unemployed have secondary or higher education.

In the majority of the Arab countries, the educational system needs to be revamped so that Arab students will be able to acquire skills of international standards. The Arab countries have made significant progress in building a network of schools and universities, offering free education to all citizens. Although the quantity of resources devoted to education is sufficient, the quality needs improvement. Rather than being forced to memorize facts and concepts bearing little relevance to the real world, children should be trained on problem-solving and searching and finding information.

Students must learn to be creative, imaginative and productive; the educational system must encourage debate, in-depth analysis, hard work and independent thinking. These skills are central to the requirements of internationally competitive economies, where workers are expected to solve non-routine problems, adapt to change by a continuous process of learning, and make decisions based on an understanding of the broader context of their companies' priorities.

The basic premise underlying the current educational system is that all of the industrious and good students should attain a university education. However, only one in four – or at best one in three – of secondary-school graduates are university material. To make matters worse, admission to university education is decided on the basis of the candidate's score in secondary-school examinations rather than on scoring in university admission or aptitude tests. This culture and the educational system based on it results in overcrowding of universities. It also means that students who are talented in certain fields, or those who are athletic, creative or imaginative will end up being deprived of a higher education.

## CONCLUSION

To realize the vision of a prosperous future, governments and individuals need to make economics rather than politics their central overriding preoccupation. Research reports about the Arab countries start with politics, and end with economics. This should be reversed, so that economic growth and prosperity become the region's principal concern. With economic systems, as with cars, even the best models need good drivers. What these countries need, therefore, is strong leaderships capable of taking bold decisions that could see the Arab world into the next millennium. The journey from a 'power culture' to a 'performance culture' in the region's business sectors requires courageous leadership, and sometimes mandates a change of leadership.

There has been a general recognition that prosperity depends on liberal economic policies, trade and financial ties with the outside world. Those countries which have been slowest in recognizing this fact are paying the highest price in terms of lost development opportunities. Others are facing a particularly difficult restructuring task, mainly because their economies were highly centralized and protected, and for decades had had minimal exposure to competitive world markets.

Policy-makers should convince the private sector that they are serious in implementing the required reform policies. Credibility is the key to reform, especially in countries that follow a gradual approach. The sustainability of reform policies can foster private-sector confidence by reducing concerns about policy reversal. If a sufficient number of firms delay investing until a more positive assessment can be reached, this could lock the economy into a low-investment, low-growth equilibrium. In contrast, policies perceived as credible, consistent and unlikely to be reversed may turn expectations around and induce private investors to go ahead with their plans, thereby boosting growth and reducing the cost of adjustment.

Countries can choose through the policies they implement whether to be prosperous or poor. Those Arab countries which manage to integrate into the world economy, empower their private sector and change the role of the government from a player to a referee, while maintaining political stability and the rule of law will be winners in today's global markets. On the other hand, those nations which fail to implement reform, or do so only slowly, are condemned to isolation and marginalization.

# 2

# CHALLENGES AND OPPORTUNITIES IN THE NEW MILLENNIUM

During the 1970s, several Arab countries followed socialist ideologies and command-type economies that were in conflict with the free-market policies pursued elsewhere in the region. However, this ideological conflict is no longer an issue with most Arab countries, which now follow free-market policies and implement economic reform programmes that call for a change in the role of the state from player to that of referee.

It is becoming increasingly important for Arab countries to put aside political differences for the sake of common economic interests. The Arab countries are facing a set of challenges, including weak economic growth, high unemployment rates, high internal and external debt levels, and limited export capabilities. All of these challenges require more serious co-operation among Arab countries, for the coming period is one of regional economic blocs. The countries of the region must look at the common challenges and interests that tie them together. Economic co-operation between the Arab countries should not be based solely on the fact that we have a common language and a shared history and culture, but also on the common interests that such co-operation can achieve.

Despite the region's impressive oil wealth, economic growth has lagged behind other regions of the world. The Arab countries' combined GDP rose from $440 billion in 1980 to $650 billion in 2000, an average annual rate of around 2 per cent. Taking average inflation of around 3 per cent for the same period suggests that real GDP growth has been marginally negative over these two decades, compared to an average real GDP growth of 3 per cent globally. Moreover, the region's population has almost doubled from 140 million in 1980 to 278 million in 2000, leading to a marked decline in per-capita income. For instance, per-capita income in Saudi Arabia has fallen from $25,000 in 1981, equal to that of the US at the time, to $7000 in 2000, while per-capita income in the US has risen to $40,000.

Arab leaders have routinely paid lip-service to the concept of regional co-operation over the years, while there has been little progress on the ground. Political rivalries and disagreements and similar production bases have been the main stumbling-blocks to regional co-operation in the past.

## IMPACT OF 11 SEPTEMBER 2001 ON THE ECONOMIES OF THE REGION

The economic impact on the Arab countries of the attack on the US has so far been modest, but the adverse consequences for the region will become more visible in the months ahead. The Arab region, as well as the world at large, has been affected. The tragic events of 11 September were a setback for globalization, affecting cross-border flows of people, goods, ideas and capital. The crisis has changed the way political stability is assessed and increased the risk profile of several countries around the world, including some key Arab countries.

No economic model can predict what the effects of the incidents are likely to be. Previous experience suggests that a disaster such as 11 September often has less impact than predicted at the time of the event. Between August 1 1990, when Iraq invaded Kuwait, and October 1 1990, oil prices jumped from $20 to $40 per barrel. Over that eight-week period, Standard & Poor's of the US stock market dropped by 11 per cent, FTSE of the UK was down 13 per cent, and the French and German stock markets dropped 21 per cent and 25 per cent respectively. All of these markets surged to much higher levels in the months after Iraq was forced to leave Kuwait. During the Gulf crisis, all Arab stock markets suffered, and massive capital outflows from the region were recorded. However, in 1991, the first year after the crisis, those stock markets surged across the board.

A recession was already underway in the US before 11 September, and the attack have made things sharply worse. There are good reasons to expect this recession to be deeper and longer than the average recessions of the past 20 years. This is mainly due to the large scale of investment and borrowing recorded during the late 1990s, and the unusually synchronized nature of this global slowdown, with economies around the world sinking together.

Central banks worldwide have been injecting liquidity in their respective financial markets. In the US, the Federal Reserve brought the Fed funds rate down to 1.75 per cent by the end of 2001, its lowest level in 40 years; the other major central banks in the world have also been lowering their domestic interest rates. Real interest rates – defined as nominal interest rates less inflation rates – on the dollar and the euro are still positive, which suggests that there is still room for interest rates to drop further. Local interest rates in the various Arab countries have been moving down in line with US rates and the trend is likely to continue, meaning lower borrowing costs for businesses in the months ahead.

Markets are now discounting weaker demand for oil associated with a much slower global economy. It is estimated that every 1 per cent loss in expected GDP growth reduces world oil demand by 400,000 barrels per day. Furthermore, oil demand will also be dampened by the drop in airline flights, which make up around 10 per cent of world oil consumption. It is unlikely to see any increase in world demand for oil in 2002, while non-OPEC supply is forecast to increase by 500,000 barrels per day. This puts pressure on OPEC to cut production. Oil prices are likely to trade lower in 2002, dropping to an average of $18 per barrel for Brent crude, compared to an estimated average of $24 per barrel in 2001.

Emerging markets, including those of the Arab region, are likely to receive much less capital flows in the wake of the 11 September attack. The Institute of International Finance (IIF) estimated total net flow of private capital to emerging markets to drop to $106 billion in 2001, from $166 billion in 2000. The corresponding figure for 2002 is put at $127 billion. FDI to the Arab region, which rose to $4.6 billion in 2000, is estimated to drop to $3.5 billion in 2001 and to $2.5 billion in 2002.

Another impact of the 11 September attack on the US has been a surge of anti-Arab sentiment abroad, which has prompted investors from the region to consider trimming their sizeable financial ties to the US. Some are worried that their US assets may be frozen in the global crackdown on terrorism. As much as two-thirds of the estimated $8000 billion that Arab investors hold abroad is thought to be invested in the US or deposited with US banks. Until now, there has been no dramatic shift to move out of the US market or US banks; however, things could take a sharp turn for the worse if the US decides to strike against one or more Arab countries without a justified pretext, or to freeze assets and accounts of alleged suspects without substantiated proof.

The region's stock markets have also been affected by the events of 11 September 2001. Following the attack, all the Arab stock markets adjusted significantly lower, with some losing most of the gain recorded since the beginning of the year. For example, on 9 September 2001 the Saudi market was up 14.4 per cent on its level at the beginning of the year, but ended the month of November up only 4.5 per cent, having lost 10 per cent in the 11 weeks following the attack. Kuwait's market, which was up 32 per cent until 9 September, ended November with an increase of only 23 per cent, a loss of approximately 10 per cent from the high it reached before the attacks. Egypt's stock market, which was down 17 per cent on 9 September compared to its level at the beginning of the year, ended November with a loss of 39 per cent.

The two sectors that have been affected most in the region are air travel and tourism. Unofficial estimates suggest that air travel to and from the region has dropped by around 35 per cent in the three months following 11 September. Many of the major local carriers have cancelled certain destinations, and reduced the number of flights operated. The Arab Carriers Organization estimates the losses of Arab Airlines to exceed $10 billion in 2001. Hotels in Egypt, Jordan, Lebanon and Dubai reported drop in occupancy rates of between 30 and 70 per cent. In excess of 30 million international tourists travelled to the Arab region in 2000, spending around $21 billion. Direct and indirect revenues generated by tourism in the Arab world are estimated at $60 billion, and the losses of these sectors for the region as a whole are expected to reach $10 billion.

The countries of the region that are especially affected by the events of 11 September are Egypt, Lebanon, Syria, Palestine and Saudi Arabia. Egypt's tourism industry and revenues from the Suez canal – which are important sources of current-account receipts – have suffered most. Faced with lower foreign-exchange earnings, a potentially more volatile region and lower growth expectation, the Egyptian pound continues to be under pressure. Lebanon remains very vulnerable to regional geographical developments, which could jeopardize its privatization drive and reduce the ability of the government to service its huge debt burden. Uncertainty in the region would push Syria to delay the liberalization of its economy and to channel more resources towards defence and security.

The Gulf countries in general will be affected indirectly by the events of 11 September through the decline in oil prices and oil revenues. However, most of them have ample government reserves to finance rising internal and external imbalances in 2002. Saudi Arabia may not be able to attract the kind of FDI it has been contemplating, because of the negative reporting on the kingdom by the Western media. The impact of the crisis on Jordan is likely to be manageable, with the visible decline in tourism and hotel industry dampening the otherwise strong economic growth conditions in 2002.

The Palestinian territories will be affected most by the events of 11 September. Israel is now emboldened to take harsher measures against Palestinians in the name of combating terrorism. Equating resistance to Israeli occupation with terrorism would backfire and could reflect negatively on the search for a just and lasting peace in the Palestinian territories. This could lead to a thicker cloud of uncertainty hovering on the region affecting tourism, investment and capital flows to the area.

## COMMON INTERESTS SHOULD DICTATE ARAB ECONOMIC CO-OPERATION

Talk of a common market among the Arab countries started in the 1950s. In 1998, 14 Arab countries established the Arab Free Trade Agreement (AFTA), under which tariffs are to be reduced for participating members by 10 per cent annually, thus establishing a free-trade area by 2007. However, many policy-induced barriers have yet to be tackled, and the long lists of exceptions that various Arab countries have written into their free-trade agreements threaten to make AFTA useless.

The Arab countries' trade performance has also been poor. In 1999, total exports from the Arab world, including oil, reached $163 billion, less than the exports of Hong Kong, which stood at $174 billion that year. The region's non-oil non-mineral exports did not exceed $45 billion in 1999, less than the exports of Finland, a country with a 5.5 million population. More worrying is the low level of intra-Arab trade, which stood at around 8.6 per cent of total trade in 1999 even though AFTA had been in place for two years. The limited size of intra-Arab trade is particularly pronounced when compared to other regional groupings. For example, intraregional trade as a share of total trade stood at 60 per cent in the EU, 40 per cent for the East Asian economies, and 37 per cent for NAFTA countries.

During the 2001 Arab Summit in Jordan, 11 of the summit's final *communiqués* tackled intra-Arab economic co-operation issues, foremost of which was collective support for steps towards developing AFTA. Arab heads of state decided to advance the target date for AFTA to 2005 and to call for the inclusion of services in the free-trade zone. However, time is running out, and Arab governments have to act faster if they are to meet the challenges of globalization. Eleven of the Arab states are already members of WTO, and more are applying for membership, leaving the Arab countries in a situation whereby globalization will precede regionalization, and with no regional economic bloc to take a strong hold in the global economy.

Table 2.1
Direction of Arab trade (percentage)

| | Exports | | Imports | |
|---|---|---|---|---|
| | 1996 | 1999 | 1996 | 1999 |
| Arab countries | 8.7 | 8.7 | 8.9 | 8.6 |
| US | 9.1 | 10.0 | 13.0 | 13.2 |
| Japan | 18.1 | 18.4 | 6.2 | 8.2 |
| EU | 26.8 | 27.2 | 41.2 | 39.0 |
| Southeast Asia | 11.2 | 12.1 | 5.4 | 5.7 |
| Rest of the world | 26.1 | 23.6 | 25.3 | 25.2 |
| Total world | 100.0 | 100.0 | 100.0 | 100.0 |

*Source:* Arab Economic Report, *2000*

Establishing AFTA is only the first step towards forming a strong economic bloc. Alone, AFTA would stand in direct conflict with one of the WTO principles, as it allows the Arab members to discriminate against other non-Arab WTO members by charging higher tariff rates than those imposed on Arab members. AFTA must therefore be followed quickly by the establishment of a custom union, whereby the member countries agree on a unified custom policy towards imports from outside the union. The next step entails forming a common market which, in addition to the free flow of goods and services, allows for the free movement of the factors of production such as capital, labour and technology. The final step is an economic union, similar to the EU, which involves a unified central bank and monetary policy, and a single currency.

The last few years have witnessed some progress in regional co-operation in the Arab world, with an increasing number of joint Arab projects – such as the ongoing construction of a gas pipeline to supply about 12 billion cubic metres a year of Egyptian gas to Jordan, Syria and Lebanon, and the regional electricity grid between Egypt, Jordan and Syria. Such regional projects will give a much-needed boost to Arab co-operation and economic integration. Nevertheless, more needs to be done as Arab countries realize that they will all be more prosperous if they succeed in establishing a viable regional economic bloc.

## THE CHANGING MANAGEMENT STRUCTURE OF ARAB ENTERPRISES

Power cultures have dominated the management of Arab enterprises for a long time. The common features of this culture include a centralized decision-making process, with tasks assigned downward by the chief executive, dedicated staff with extensive experience in their function, a strict hierarchy tempered by heavy doses of paternalism, and a stable environment in which competition is generally regulated. Companies are more likely to provide clients with the kind of goods and services that are available, rather than customized products that meet clients' preferences. Management emphasis has been mainly on size and growth of market share, believing that a large balance sheet over the long haul would guarantee competitive advantage.

Table 2.2
The changing management structure

| Characteristic | Old structure | New structure |
|---|---|---|
| Organization | Pyramid | Horizontal |
| Focus | Size and growth | Maximizing shareholder value |
| Ownership structure | Family | Publicly listed |
| Style | Structured | Flexible |
| Structure | Self-sufficiency | Interdependencies and outsourcing |
| Resource | Physical assets | Information and human capital |
| Operations | Vertical integration | Virtual integration (networking) |
| Marketing | Mass-production and inventory | Mass-customization and build-to-order |
| Products | Internally generated | Selling rivals' products as well |
| Competition | Between enterprises | Between brands, services and products |
| Promotion | Whom you know: 'wasta' | Based on productivity and achievement |
| Financials | Annual | Quarterly |
| Decision-making | Top-down | Bottom-up |
| Leadership | Dogmatic | Inspirational |
| Workers | Employees | Employees who are also shareholders |
| Job expectations | Security | Personal growth, satisfaction and future gains |

In the new economy, Arab enterprises must be willing to accept constant change rather than stability, be organized around networks not rigid hierarchies and depend more on partnerships and alliances rather than being self-sufficient. Companies should be outsourcing skills (back-office operations, research, technology, financial products etc) to outsiders who can perform these functions with greater efficiency – often at lower cost. Outsourcing and partnering are well known by now, but in the new structure they will become more crucial. Managing this intricate network of partners and external relationships will be as important as managing internal operations.

The most profitable enterprise will manage information on markets and clients instead of focusing solely on physical assets. Balance-sheet size will no longer be the criteria for success. Markets will reward efficient businesses that add value. The governing objective of Arab enterprises in the new millennium should be to maximize shareholder value. This necessitates shedding businesses in which returns do not cover the cost of capital, and allocating more resources to those activities that add value over time. Enhanced profitability could also be achieved by controlling – or even reducing – operating expenses through the effective use of modern technology. However, technology should not be an end in itself, but one of the factors that enhances efficiency. The enterprise should not be a showroom to exhibit the latest technological products: the decision to acquire a new system should always be a business decision.

Instead of mass production and selling clients the goods and services that the company produces, an enterprise should allow its customers to demand the kind of product and service they want. Mass customization will produce many individualized products and services. The selling of such products and services on a mass scale is a logical next step in the progress of build-to-order, that is the manufacturing of goods and the provision of services only as and when there is an order from a customer. Competition will eventually force most companies to offer supermarket-style services, in which their clients have access to their rivals' products as well. Competition will be between brands, services and products rather than enterprises.

Companies should strive to attract and retain a high calibre of employees. Such talent would require more than a competitive salary: instead there should be a performance-related system – for example, profit-sharing and stock options – that keeps the best minds engaged. Instead of having civil-service-like employees, mindful of rank and title and rewarded by seniority, the emphasis would be on empowerment, with employees looking for personal growth and promises of future gains rather than security, where the best are given the chance to create and manage businesses.

Each enterprise should have a clear mission statement that spells out in few lines its aims and principles. The mission statement is usually supported by a set of business practices that everyone adheres to – from top management to junior staff. Aligning personal goals with corporate goals should be a priority. Staff need to know where the organization is going, and how visions of the future will shape their destiny. Effective business leadership developed in the West should provide strong pointers for business leaders in the Arab region. However, deep-seated cultural differences have to be recognized and allowed for when formulating management structure of Arab enterprises.

One way to boost the competitive strengths of Arab enterprises in a liberalized global market is through consolidation, both domestic and cross-border. This would reduce operation costs and lead to improved organizational efficiency. Mergers could be used to spread huge technology costs over a bigger base, benefit from economies of scale, reduce the per-unit cost structure, sell products across markets and minimize duplication. Full integration may be needed in order to realize adequate cost savings. Consolidation has to be considered carefully and motivated strategically if it is to be effective. In many cases, protective laws, family ownership and political interference have negative effects on the ability of enterprises to realize the full benefit of mergers.

In the final analysis, what differentiates leading enterprises from the rest is their willingness to take their mission statement seriously, see people and career development as an investment, reward performance through bonuses, stock options etc, measure employees satisfaction and promote from within, maintain full disclosure and transparency, follow a horizontal management structure and adhere to ethics and quality standards.

## CONVERTING ARAB FAMILY BUSINESSES INTO PUBLICLY LISTED COMPANIES

While accurate statistics on family businesses do not exist in the Middle East, it is safe to say that more than 98 per cent of the region's private sector is comprised of family businesses. In Japan, less than 10 per cent of companies are controlled by a single family, compared to 50 per cent in South Korea and Taiwan and between 60 per cent and 70 per cent in Thailand and Malaysia. There are around 1200 companies listed in the Arab stock markets, compared to around 600,000 registered companies of all types. Many of these family-owned businesses are larger and more profitable than publicly listed companies.

In a publicly owned shareholding company, the goal of management is to enhance shareholder value. With family businesses, there are other priorities to achieve beyond shareholder value, which include providing employment for family members, staying away from businesses that require more exposure and transparency, getting into new lines of business that meet the requirements of one of the siblings etc. Several family businesses that have traditionally been involved in trade and property have now expanded their activities to include industry and services. These businesses are facing both internal and external challenges that need to be addressed. Internal challenges include retirement and succession, father–son relationships, sibling rivalry, inter-generational differences, the need to go public etc. External challenges relate to WTO and the onslaught of global competition.

To address these new challenges, family businesses should not be prisoners of the past. They must be willing to respond in new and creative ways to the changes taking place in the market. If they continue to resist change and choose to live on the glory of the past, they risk being taken over by more flexible companies. Interestingly enough, most family companies know the challenges that face them.

It is often not a question of understanding the changes in the market, but rather the willingness to address these changes. The region will face a very painful transition as it moves in the coming few years from pampered local trade regulations to the harsh reality of the WTO and Euro–Mediterranean partnership.

Table 2.3
The changing face of Arab capital markets

| 1970s | 1980s | 1990s | 2000 onwards |
|---|---|---|---|
| – No disclosure | – Demands for disclosure | – Privatization | – Bond issues |
| – Name lending | – Regulatory regimes improving | – Security exchange commissions | – Family businesses going public |
| – External funding restricted | – External funding | – Non-recourse lending | – Restructuring |
| – Poor regulatory and legal structure | – Syndicated loans | – Specialized funds | – Mergers and acquisitions |
| – Commercial bank loans fully collaterized | – Government soft loans | – Islamic borrowing | – Securitization |
| | – Rising equity markets | – Foreign ownership and liberalization | – Full disclosure<br>– Private equity capital |

It is imperative that businesses make practical use of the phase-out grace period offered by WTO to readjust their positions and strength their capability to compete. The Arab countries are in various stages of compliance with WTO requirements. Full compliance by all members is expected by 2005. The grace period offers companies the chance to prepare for competition by becoming outward-looking and by observing required international standards of reporting and specifications of products. They should use this transitional period to introduce advanced management techniques, reduce production costs and develop marketing.

In the Arab world, for a family company to go public carries a social stigma. It is seen in the same light as a company going bankrupt, since it is assumed that the family is incapable of running its business. Furthermore, the idea of going public raises concerns in the area of disclosure and control. It is feared that greater corporate disclosure might reveal considerable private wealth, previously hidden. Another concern is that going public makes it more difficult for future generations to re-establish family identity if the company is owned by 'faceless' investors. There is also the worry that an old rival, or a local or international giant, could take over, with little or no concern for the family's name or needs.

Family companies that are most likely to be successful after going public are those which are transparent and open, and realize the benefit of having the experience and objectivity of other investors. Family businesses that need cash should be encouraged to consider issuing shares and bringing in a new group of investors instead of borrowing, as has been the case so far. Joint ventures are the way forward. It is a natural transition from full ownership of a family business to having a stake in a large company with lots of partners. This spreads the risk and helps the family to gain from its partners' technological capability, knowledge of the international market and management skills.

The future pattern for family companies in the region could be represented by the approach followed by Al-Zamil Group of Saudi Arabia. This group, which has one of the most successful industrial and services companies in the region, decided to go public in 1998 to create the joint-stock company Zamil Industrial Investment Company (ZIIC). The family maintained a 60 per cent stake in the company, offering the rest to other local and Gulf investors. This injected additional capital and allowed the group to expand into the global market. As the region's stock markets gain depth and become well regulated, initial public offerings (IPOs) become a feasible option for family businesses that want to realize the value of their company or to raise additional capital. The facilitators are now in place: investment banks are becoming well entrenched in the region and are able to provide such services as valuation, underwriting and market placement of IPOs.

## CURBING CORRUPTION IN THE ARAB REGION

Recent efforts to fight corruption in several Arab countries suggest that governments of the region have finally started to address an issue that has long tarnished their reputation among international investors and undermined confidence in the credibility of their bureaucracies. In Egypt, anti-corruption campaigns have targeted the ex-Minister of Finance, the head of the customs department and eight other senior officials, a move unheard of in the past. The Moroccan government has also started to crack down on widespread fraud by local government officials. In Libya, the finance minister and 46 senior government officials were recently prosecuted because of a corruption scandal; in Lebanon an ex-minister was prosecuted in 2000. But all these efforts are only the first step in a fight against corruption.

Transparency International, a Berlin-based non-governmental organization that monitors corruption worldwide, found that bribe-taking in many developing countries is widespread, primarily because of low public-sector salaries, greed and the fact that senior public officials and politicians have *de facto* immunity from prosecution. In certain countries, corruption runs so deep that officials give you a receipt for your bribe. Meanwhile, transnational corporations' propensity to pay bribes to public-sector officials is considerable. According to the *BusinessWeek*, the cut for middlemen in certain Gulf countries is between 10 and 40 per cent on military contracts, and 5 and 20 per cent on public works.

Figure 2.1
Corruption Perception Index for selected countries
(most corrupt=0, least corrupt=10)

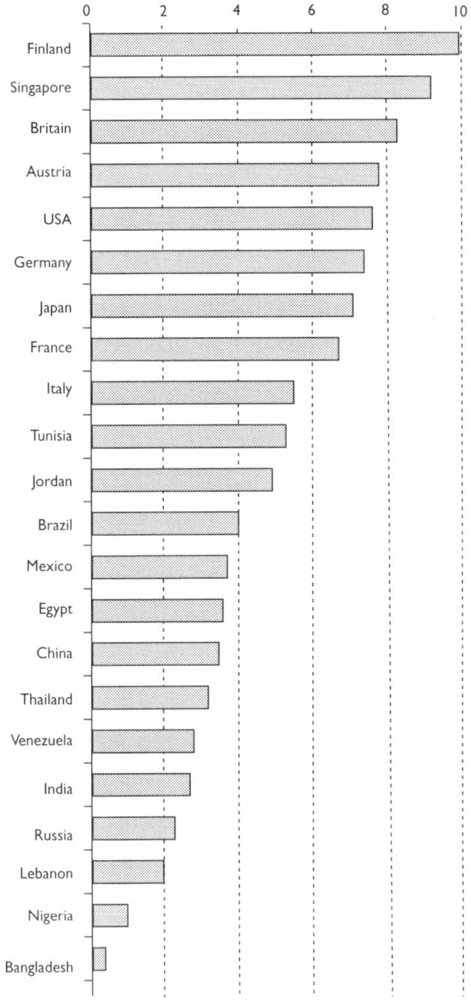


*Source: Transparency International Global Corruption Report 2001*

The Corruption Perception Index (CPI) draws on 14 data sources from seven different institutions: the World Economic Forum, the World Business Environment Survey of the World Bank, the Institute of Management Development in Lausanne, PriceWaterhouse Coopers, the Political and Economic Risk Consultancy, the Economist Intelligence Unit and Freedom House's Nations in

Transit. With the exception of three data sources that relied on expatriates' perceptions, the sources mostly sampled residents, who provided local estimates of the degree of corruption, as seen from their own cultural context. According to the CPI, Finland was ranked as the country that has the least corrupt civil service, with Sweden, Singapore, Canada, Netherlands, the UK and the US close behind. Bangladesh and Nigeria, in contrast, were found to have the highest level of corruption among the 91 countries in the list. Among the Arab countries Tunisia ranked highest at 5.3, just below Italy at 5.5, followed by Jordan, that has seen its rank improve in 2001 to 4.9. Egypt and Lebanon followed with scores of 3.6 and 2.0 respectively.

Although national anti-corruption agencies can be critical in preventing corruption before it becomes rampant, they are difficult to set up and often fail to achieve their goals once they have been established. They do not dare to investigate even the most corrupt government officials, because most of them lack the power to prosecute, and some are poorly staffed.

In order for a country to develop, building the 'hardware' – bridges, airports, computers etc – will not be sufficient. It also needs 'software', which is a measure of the quality of a country's legal and regulatory systems, supported by an efficient and honest civil service, business integrity, ethical code of conducts and a free press that plays the role of a watchdog all the time. Good software includes banking laws, commercial laws and courts, bankruptcy rules, contract laws, business codes of conduct, a genuinely independent central bank, property rights that encourage risk-taking, international accounting standards, laws against conflicts of interest and insider trading, and officials and citizens ready to implement these rules in a reasonably consistent manner.

A transparent and efficient government that can run better-quality software and operating system matters more in the era of globalization and open markets than in a state-controlled economy. The challenge for governments today is to get the quality of their civil service up at the same time that they bring the size of their states down. As countries of the region liberalize further their economies, the role of the government shifts from an active player to that of a referee, the job of which is to define and enforce the regulatory and institutional environment. Privatization of public sector institutions and reduction of military spending will help reduce the opportunity for corruption. In several Arab countries, the legal system is not well prepared to deal with fraudulent behavior related to free-market activities.

Globalization is creating a much higher cost for countries that tolerate corruption. Joining the global economy is equivalent to taking the country public, only the shareholders are no longer the citizens of that country, they now include participants in the international markets. These new players do not just vote once every four years, instead they vote every month and every day through their direct investment, their mutual funds, their brokers and increasingly more directly via the Internet. Corruption for them is just another name for unpredictability. They know quite well that there are alternatives in other countries and other markets and this reduces their interest to invest in countries where corruption is rampant, irrespective of anticipated returns.

A recognition of the need to address ethical issues, and converting that recognition into action, are two different things. If governments and business leaders in the Middle East accept the fact that there is a problem with ethical standards in the region, the first step on a road to improvement is to move business ethics to the top of the agenda. They need then to create a code of conduct based on transparency, rule of law and good governance, and high standard of business practices, all within the context of local culture. Government and business leaders should set the standard to help inspire others to act ethically.

## THE BACKLASH AGAINST GLOBALIZATION IN THE REGION

People in the Arab countries as well as in Europe, Japan and developing countries are worried that the process of globalization and liberalization is gradually robbing them of their culture, language and tradition. They feel they are at a disadvantage when competing with the established multinational companies in a world with no borders. Some voice their discontent by demonstrating against the IMF, World Bank or WTO meetings, others, especially in the Arab region, have opted to do so more discreetly.

There are two ways to make a person feel homeless – one is to destroy his home and render him or her a refugee, the other is to make his or her home look and feel like everybody else's home. Globalization, often considered to be synonymous with Americanization, is generating fears of the latter form of homelessness.

The youth are the most vulnerable to this kind of culture-assault. They associate themselves with anything American, be it fast food, clothes, music, books, movies, software, TV etc. They like these products and want them because of what they are perceived to symbolize: modernity, freedom and creativity. Americanization to them is simply 'cool'. Walking into a McDonald's restaurant in Saudi Arabia or in China is the cheapest trip to the US. It brings to reality the fantasy of living the American way.

It is natural for the only superpower in the world, with an innovative and dynamic economy, to spread its culture. Throughout history there has always been a link between commerce and culture. The entertainment industry including movies, music, software and broadcasting is the US's second-largest exporter after aircraft, and has penetrated all global markets. American films are seen in every country around the globe. *Reader's Digest* publishes in 20 languages; Windows computer programs and MTV can be found in remote corners of China, and the Internet is helping American corporates to spread their reach even further.

It would be naive to think that developing countries can build barriers to stop the spread of globalization. Companies like McDonald's, Nike, Microsoft, Yahoo etc, succeed because they offer people something they want. Given the speed at which satellites and the Internet are widening their reach, almost everyone around the globe will sooner or later be introduced to the American lifestyle and culture. The challenge is to be able to take the good aspects of that culture (individual freedom, creativity, free enterprise, rule of law etc.), refit it into a different frame of reference to make it part of a different culture and pass it on to future generations.

Governments in the Arab region should encourage creativity, freedom of expression and excellence in modern arts. Those who have an obsession with controlling change will end up encouraging it. People, especially the youth, would identify with a different culture as a way of expressing their dissatisfaction with what they have. They want to be part of global trends. There will always be conflicts between globalizers and localizers, between those who eat the Big Mac and those who fear that the Big Mac will eat them.

Expenditures on defence as a percentage of GDP should be reduced from the average of 10 per cent in the region to perhaps 5 per cent, and the balance used to finance educational and cultural activities. Financial aid should be given to students and cultural centres to promote literature and poetry, painting, music, local films and theatrical productions, national heritage and all other forms of cultural activities. Native entrepreneurs wishing to create local cultural industries should have access to funds. Universities should be given endowments to undertake research and teaching in the region's history, art and literature.

Globalization will be sustainable if it is perceived as an efficient way to exchange cultures among people, rather than as a way for one culture to dominate others. Without cultural diversity the world will lose its attraction and cohesion. When people's homes are stripped of their distinctiveness by homogenization, their culture will be undermined along with their willingness to change and evolve. Developing countries need cohesive national communities deep-rooted in history and tradition in order for them to accept change and make tough decisions. If societies feel threatened, insecurities will be magnified, leading to policy inaction and the rise of fanaticism.

## CAPITALIZING ON THE POTENTIAL OF TOURISM IN THE REGION

The 11 September attack on the US and its ensuing ramifications have created adverse conditions for the global tourism industry. Fears of similar attacks were reflected in a sharp decline in air travel, particularly to the Arab region. International tourist arrivals declined across the globe, affecting top tourist destinations. In the Arab region, many hotel reservation cancellations were recorded – especially in package tours. The Arab and Muslim worlds were dubbed by the media in the West as hotbeds of terrorism. Arabs and Muslims travelling in Europe and the US were stereotyped as potential threats.

The future of global tourism in general, and tourism in the Arab region in particular, looks gloomy. However, this conclusion is more probably relevant in the short term. The long-term growth trend of global tourism will not be significantly affected by the attack on the US. There is an unprecedented international co-operation to stem such attacks, which would alleviate fears about air travel. There will also be enhanced incentives by many countries to regain the pace of tourist arrivals.

Table 2.4
Tourist arrival by region

| | Number of tourists (million) | | Percentage change | | Forecasts | |
|---|---|---|---|---|---|---|
| | 1999 | 2000 | 1999/98 | 2000/99 | 2010 | 2020 |
| Africa | 26.5 | 26.9 | 6.1 | 1.5 | 47.0 | 77.3 |
| Americas | 130.2 | 122.3 | 2.3 | 6.5 | 190.4 | 282.3 |
| East Asia/Pacific | 97.6 | 111.7 | 10.8 | 14.5 | 195.2 | 397.2 |
| Europe | 379.8 | 403.3 | 1.7 | 6.2 | 527.3 | 717.0 |
| Middle East | 18.1 | 20.0 | 18.1 | 10.2 | 35.9 | 68.5 |
| South Asia | 5.8 | 6.3 | 10.7 | 9.0 | 10.6 | 18.8 |
| World | 649.9 | 698.3 | 3.8 | 7.4 | 1006.4 | 1561.1 |

*Source: WTO*

World tourism recorded a 7.4 per cent increase in 2000 – its highest growth-rate in nearly a decade, almost double the 3.8 per cent rise in 1999. Strong tourism activity in the year ending the millennium was boosted by healthy global economic growth and special events held to celebrate the new millennium, in addition to other events such as the Olympics, the European football championships, Expo 2000 and the Vatican Jubilee. According to WTO, nearly 50 million more international trips were made in 2000, bringing the total number of international visitors to a record 698 million. Receipts from international tourism also increased by 4.5 per cent to $476 billion. France remained the top tourist destination in the world, attracting 74.5 million tourists in 2000, followed by the US with 52.7 million, Spain with 48.5 million, Italy with 41.13 million and the UK with 24.9 million visitors.

East Asia and the Pacific recorded the highest growth in the number of tourists, at 14.5 per cent. Europe – which accounts for 58 per cent of international tourism – saw an impressive 6.2 per cent rise in the number of tourists, to 403 million. Despite the strong dollar, the US also welcomed millions more international tourists and recorded a growth rate of 8.7 per cent. Africa was largely left out of the tourism boom, with only a 1.5 per cent increase in the number of tourists visiting the region, to a total of 26.9 million, Africa's lowest ever growth rate.

The Middle East anticipated a spectacular increase in tourism activity in 2000, mainly because of the of millennium pilgrimages to the West Bank and the strong attraction of the many historic sites associated with the life of Jesus Christ on the two thousandth anniversary of his birth. However, renewed violence in the Palestinian territories in the third quarter of the year virtually stopped the flow of tourists. In the first nine months of 2000, arrivals were up by as much as 20 per cent, but the region ended the year with a lower – yet still robust – growth rate of 10.2 per cent.

Egypt remains the region's main tourism destination. The country welcomed 5.15 million visitors in 2000, up 15 per cent on the previous year. North-African Arab countries such as Tunisia and Morocco are also prime tourism destinations, ranking second and third in popularity in Africa – after South Africa – attracting 5.06 million and 4.1 million tourists in 2000 respectively. Lebanon recorded strong growth of 11.6 per cent in 2000, with the number of visitors to the country reaching 751,000, following a 12 per cent increase in 1999. Jordan's tourism industry was particularly hard-hit by the regional instability; the number of tourists visiting Jordan reached 1.43 million in 2000, an increase of 5 per cent on the previous year. Tourism revenues have been steadily rising for the past few years, reaching JD564 million in 1999.

While Egypt traditionally accounts for over a quarter of the region's tourism inflow, there are large investments and high prospects of tourism growth in the Gulf region. Led by Dubai, the region is now investing heavily in the tourism sector. Over the past decade Dubai has created a booming tourism sector, attracting visitors from all over the world. According to WTO estimates, tourist arrivals to Dubai totalled 2.48 million in 2000, up by 13.6 per cent on 1999. Other countries in the region, such as Qatar, are following Dubai's lead with heavy investments in luxury hotels and other tourism resources. Qatar attracted 451,000 visitors in 1999, while Oman, capitalizing on its cultural heritage, managed to attract 502,000 visitors. Bahrain relies mainly on the two million or so Saudi nationals who visit the country annually.

Saudi Arabia traditionally attracts the largest number of visitors among the Gulf countries, due to religious tourism. The pace of tourism development is undoubtedly quickening in the kingdom; however, because of religious sensitivity international tourism still has a long way to go. Nonetheless, tourist visa regulations in Saudi Arabia are being eased, conventional tours are now available, and the Supreme Tourism Commission has been set up to develop and enhance the role of tourism in the economy. New regulations introduced in September 2000 will allow Muslims coming for Umra (a tour of religious sites) to gain a one-month visa and travel around the kingdom, instead of being confined to Mecca and Medina. According to WTO estimates, the number of foreign visitors to the kingdom reached 3.7 million in 2000, and are estimated to exceed four million in 2002.

The Middle East has unparalleled historical and tourism assets, yet it is the most underutilized tourist area in the world. However, over the past few years tourism has attracted increasing attention from the Arab countries as its potential for stimulating activity and diversifying the economy is recognized. Arab countries are making vast improvements to their tourism sectors, focusing on infrastructure development and encouraging private-sector participation. Equally important is the need to encourage higher levels of regional tourism. It is estimated that Arab tourists spend around $40 billion annually outside the region, compared to a mere $3 billion within the region. Improving the tourism infrastructure and facilities in Arab countries would divert at least part of this spending to the countries of the region.

## RESOURCES SHOULD BE SHIFTED FROM DEFENCE TO ECONOMIC DEVELOPMENT

According to the report on world defence expenditure by the International Institute for Strategic Studies (IISS), the value of international arms trade fell in 1999, with the value of deliveries estimated at $53.4 billion, compared with $58 billion in 1998. The ranking of the regional markets was unchanged: the Middle East continued to buy more arms than any other region, with Saudi Arabia alone receiving deliveries worth $6.1 billion. However, Saudi military imports in 1999 were down on 1998, when they amounted to $10.8 billion.

As of 1999, 10 countries accounted for almost 75 per cent of global military spending, with the top five accounting for 60 per cent. At $260 billion, the US is by far the largest spender, followed by Russia with $51 billion. Saudi Arabia ranks tenth, spending one-third of its budget on military activities.

Table 2.5
Arab countries' defence expenditure (1999 constant prices)

| | Defence expenditure ($ million) | | Percentage of GDP | | Defence budget ($ million) | |
|---|---|---|---|---|---|---|
| | **1998** | **1999** | **1998** | **1999** | **1999** | **2000** |
| GCC countries | | | | | | |
| Saudi Arabia | 21,303 | 21,876 | 16.2 | 15.5 | 18,400 | 18,700 |
| Kuwait | 3674 | 3275 | 14.3 | 11.1 | 2300 | 2600 |
| UAE | 3056 | 3187 | 6.5 | 6.2 | 3800 | 3900 |
| Oman | 1792 | 1631 | 12.4 | 10.9 | 1600 | 1750 |
| Qatar | 1373 | 1468 | 15.4 | 15.4 | 1300 | na |
| Bahrain | 410 | 441 | 7.5 | 7.7 | 306 | na |
| Subtotal | 31,608 | 31,878 | 12.0 | 11.0 | 27,706 | – |
| More diversified economies | | | | | | |
| Syria | 986 | 989 | 5.8 | 5.6 | 1700 | 1800 |
| Jordan | 559 | 588 | 7.7 | 7.7 | 488 | na |
| Lebanon | 586 | 563 | 3.6 | 3.4 | 560 | na |
| Iraq | 1428 | 1500 | 7.3 | 7.6 | 0 | 0 |
| Yemen | 404 | 429 | 6.6 | 6.7 | 374 | na |
| Subtotal | 3963 | 4069 | 5.2 | 5.2 | 3122 | – |
| North Africa | | | | | | |
| Egypt | 2888 | 2988 | 3.4 | 3.4 | 2500 | na |
| Libya | 1489 | 1311 | 5.5 | 4.7 | 1300 | 1200 |
| Morocco | 1696 | 1761 | 4.6 | 5.0 | 1700 | na |
| Tunisia | 363 | 348 | 1.8 | 1.7 | 351 | 365 |
| Algeria | 3125 | 3086 | 6.5 | 6.6 | 1800 | 1800 |
| Subtotal | 9561 | 9494 | 4.4 | 4.3 | 7651 | – |
| **Arab total** | **45,132** | **45,441** | 7.8 | 7.5 | 38,479 | – |
| **Global total** | **808,671** | **808,546** | 4.2 | 4.1 | – | – |

*Source: IISS*

Military spending by the 16 Arab countries covered in the IISS report amounted to $45.44 billion in 1999, measured in constant 1999 dollars, only slightly higher than its 1998 level of $45.13 billion.

Military expenditure by the GCC countries is typically much higher in both absolute and relative terms than in those of Arab countries without oil resources. Defence budgets in the GCC countries averaged $5.31 billion, almost four times as much as the non-Gulf Arab countries' average of $1.36 billion in 1999. Military expenditure in the Gulf reached $31.88 billion in 1999, accounting for 70 per cent of total Arab military spending. Saudi Arabia's expenditure far exceeds that of any other Arab country, at a total of $21.88 billion in 1999, compared to Kuwait's $3.28 billion – the next largest figure in absolute terms. Among the non-GCC Arab countries, Algeria and Egypt are the biggest spenders, with 1999 figures of $3.09 billion and $2.98 billion respectively.

Despite the increase in absolute figures, average per-capita military spending has declined for the Arab countries as a whole from $549 in 1998 to $535 in 1999 – a drop of almost 3 per cent. However, it remains well above the global average of $221 and NATO countries' average of $388. On a per capita basis, Qatar is by far the region's biggest spender, registering the highest expenditure rise of 1999, by 5.4 per cent to $2156. This is almost double the equivalent figure of Saudi Arabia, where the per-capita figure rose by 1.7 per cent to $1099. Per-capita military expenditure among non-GCC Arab countries falls well below both the regional and global averages.

Military spending as a percentage of GDP for the Arab countries decreased from 7.8 per cent in 1998 to 7.5 per cent in 1999. This compares to a global average of 4.1 per cent. The percentage is highest among the GCC countries, averaging 11 per cent in 1999. In 2000, military spending as a percentage of GDP declined further, in light of the 17 per cent rise in the GCC countries' GDP (nominal). Saudi Arabia topped the GDP league table, spending a total of 15.5 per cent of the 1999 GDP on its military budget, followed closely by Qatar (15.4 per cent) and Oman (11.1 per cent). Military spending as a percentage of GDP for the more diversified Arab countries remained stable at 5.2 per cent in 1999, while the ratio for the North African Arab countries was lower at 4.3 per cent, dragged down by low percentages in Tunisia and, to a lesser extent, Egypt.

As already mentioned, Arab governments prioritize government issues before economic concerns. Reversal of these priorities will help move towards a prosperous future. To facilitate this, more available financial resources should be allocated to development and infrastructure projects and less to defence.

## THE OPPORTUNITY COST OF HOLDING GOLD AS A RESERVE ASSET IN VARIOUS ARAB COUNTRIES

Central banks worldwide have long held part of their reserves in gold. At the end of 2000, gold reserves at central banks and monetary authorities around the world stood at around 950 million ounces, well below the level that prevailed in the 1970s.

Table 2.6
Value of gold reserves in selected Arab countries ($ million)

| | 1996 | 1997 | 1998 | 1999 | 2000 |
|---|---|---|---|---|---|
| Saudi Arabia | 1783.9 | 1522.7 | 1353.5 | 1287.9 | 1283.9 |
| Kuwait | 985.0 | 840.8 | 747.4 | 711.1 | 708.9 |
| UAE | 310.2 | 264.8 | 235.4 | 224.0 | 223.3 |
| Oman | 112.5 | 96.0 | 85.3 | 81.2 | 80.9 |
| Bahrain | 58.2 | 49.7 | 44.1 | 42.0 | 41.9 |
| Qatar | 104.7 | 16.6 | 14.7 | 5.6 | 5.6 |
| Egypt | 942.4 | 804.4 | 715.0 | 680.4 | 678.2 |
| Lebanon | 3575.6 | 3052.0 | 2712.9 | 2581.4 | 2573.4 |
| Syria | 321.9 | 274.7 | 244.2 | 232.4 | 231.7 |
| Jordan | 310.2 | 268.1 | 244.2 | 137.2 | 111.6 |
| Yemen | 19.4 | 16.6 | 14.7 | 14.0 | 2.8 |
| **Total** | **8524.1** | **7206.3** | **6411.5** | **5997.2** | **5942.3** |

*Source: IFS*

Gold reserves held by 11 Arab countries (Bahrain, Egypt, Jordan, Kuwait, Lebanon, Oman, Qatar, Saudi Arabia, Syria, the UAE and Yemen) amounted to 22.5 million ounces in 1991, remained steady at that level until 1994, and then declined gradually to reach 21.29 million ounces in 2000, a drop of 5.5 per cent on reserves held in 1991. This was mainly due to a significant decline in the gold holdings of three countries – Jordan, Yemen and Qatar – while gold reserves of the remaining Arab countries have remained unchanged throughout the 1990s. Lebanon is by far the largest holder of gold reserves in the region, with 9.22 million ounces at the end of 2000, followed by Saudi Arabia with 4.6 million ounces, Kuwait, with 2.54 million ounces and Egypt with 2.43 million ounces. At 62.2 ounces per head, Lebanon has the highest level of gold-to-population in the world.

The amount of gold sold by central banks around the world has outweighed the amount purchased in recent years, and the trend is likely to continue, putting pressure on gold prices to decrease. The price of gold has fluctuated significantly in the past ten years, but the general trend was clearly down. In 1991, gold prices averaged $362.1/oz, fell to $343.8 in 1992, and then climbed back up over the next four years to reach $387.8 in 1996. 1997 was one of the worst years for gold since the price became subject to market forces in 1971, and on 26 November 1997 the spot future gold price closed below $300 (at $296) for the first time since March 1985. Gold ended 1997 at $289.9, although it averaged $331 for the year. The $300 'floor' which had supported gold ever since it first rose above that level in July 1979 had now become a 'ceiling'. The annual average price of gold fell to $279.8 and $279.1 in 1999 and 2000 respectively. Between 1991 and 2000 the price of gold fell by around 23 per cent and closed 2001 at $275 an ounce.

The decline in gold prices recorded in the 1990s has led to a substantial loss in the value of gold held as reserves by central banks around the world. Global gold reserves dropped in value from $340.1 billion at the end of 1991 to $265.2 billion by the end of 2000. For the Arab countries, the value of gold reserves held by central banks and monetary institutions fell from $8.16 billion to $5.94 billion over the same nine-year period. This represents a loss of $2.2 billion (27 per cent), supporting the argument that maintaining reserves in the form of gold is inefficient in comparison to foreign exchange and other assets. In addition, holding reserves in the form of gold also carries a substantial opportunity cost. Traditionally gold earned no return, unlike financial securities such as treasury bills or bank deposits. Although this has changed in recent years with the development of the gold-leasing market, which allows central banks to earn around 2 per cent a year (depending on maturity) on the gold holdings they are willing to lend to the market-place, this is still considerably lower than the return on other assets. Around 118 countries, including several in the Middle East, lend more than 35 per cent of their gold reserves.

Gold reserves have historically been used as a hedge against inflation and as a support for the exchange rate of the domestic currency. Gold is looked upon as one of the few assets not prone to inflationary worries overhanging paper money. The precious metal is liquid, is universally accepted as a means of payment, and provides diversification as a reserve asset. It is also looked upon as insurance against war or the international isolation of a country, especially if accompanied by the freeze of the foreign reserves that the country holds with international banks. In certain cases such as in that of Lebanon, this has become a legacy, making it very difficult for politicians to even discuss the prospects of selling gold reserves.

Recently, however, the reasons to hold gold as a reserve asset have become less convincing. Inflationary pressures worldwide have been subdued, and it has become more difficult to use gold as a means of payment, and in the case of war or international isolation the freeze on foreign reserves will definitely restrict the country's ability to dispose of its gold holdings as well. This, along with the expectation that gold prices will continue to decrease, has convinced central banks around the world to sell more of their gold reserves in favour of income-generating assets.

If the short- and long-term trends for gold prices are heading lower, the Arab country that will be affected most is Lebanon, because of its large holdings of gold reserves, both in absolute terms and relative to the central bank's total foreign reserves. While it is politically sensitive for the country to consider selling its gold holdings, there should be less resistance on the part of the politicians to lease the gold reserves for whatever fee they can generate. This will supplement government's revenues and will allow a small reduction in the country's burgeoning budget deficit.

## THE ARAB INSURANCE MARKET: AN UNTAPPED GROWTH SECTOR

The Arab insurance market is one of the least-developed sectors of the region's financial services industry. Efforts are now being made to rectify this through privatizing social and health insurance, and through mergers between local insurance companies. The free trade in services associated with WTO requires member countries to open up their markets to the activities of foreign insurance and reinsurance companies. By 2005, when the general agreement on services becomes fully applicable, the foreign insurance companies could flood the markets of the region with their great capabilities and sophisticated services, allowing them to greatly reduce the price of the insurance policy and capture a large portion of the local insurance business.

According to the Arab Reinsurance Group (ARIG), gross insurance premiums in the Arab world did not exceed $5.7 billion (an estimated 1 per cent of GDP) in 1998. The ratio remains low compared to 8.8 per cent of GDP for industrialized countries, and 4–6 per cent in the developing countries of Latin America and South Asia. Insurance premiums in Lebanon, one of the more sophisticated markets in the region, averaged $100 per person in 1999, compared to $4000 per person in Switzerland and Japan. Life insurance contributions as a share of total premiums was a modest 15 per cent, against more than 50 per cent in industrialized countries. If the insurance penetration rate was the same as in developed countries, the Arab insurance premium would have reached $50 billion, and would have contributed greatly to the pool of domestic savings available for investment.

Insurance penetration in the Arab region measured by insurance premium as a percentage of GDP ranges from 2.8 per cent in Lebanon and 2.6 per cent in Morocco, to 0.6 per cent in Saudi Arabia and Syria. For the whole region, the average insurance penetration rate is 1 per cent, compared to 8.6 per cent for Asia and North America, and 7.2 per cent for Europe.

Part of the reason for the disparity between the Arab countries and the rest of the world is the fact that insurance in general and life insurance in particular are not sought after by the average Arab citizen. This is the case either because of strong religious beliefs, absence of public awareness of the importance and value of insurance, or because the premiums are high relative to the countries' per-capita income. Growth of the insurance sector has also been hindered by lack of transparency, and with markets being overcrowded by too many small companies. There are 367 providers in the Arab world, with an average premium income of less than $17 million per company. Provision of better services and availability of non-traditional insurance products (e.g. long-term investments and risk-management) take a back seat in an environment where rate-cutting is still the main tool to win business.

The structure of the insurance industry in the Arab world varies from monopoly state-owned insurance sectors (such as Syria, Iraq, Algeria and Libya), to predominantly state-owned insurance companies with several private players (such as Egypt) to markets dominated by private companies but which do not allow foreign ownership (such as Saudi Arabia), and those that are open to both local and foreign members (such as the UAE, Lebanon, Bahrain, Kuwait, Jordan and Morocco).

The premium breakdown by class of business varies from one Arab market to another, but motor insurance remains the dominant class, with around 32 per cent of the total Arab premium. This percentage exceeds 40 per cent in most non-GCC Arab countries. Less than 10 per cent of Arab insurers have shareholders funds in excess of $100 million, and 23 insurance companies out of the 367 are rated by Standard & Poor's, most of them being given investment grades.

Arab insurers retain around 62 per cent of their gross premium, with the balance going to the major international reinsurance companies, compared to 80 per cent for insurers in the industrialized countries. The distribution of insurance products is dominated by traditional channels of agents, brokers and branches, with little co-operation between insurance companies and banks. However, bank assurance business is growing, especially in Lebanon and Morocco, but is still dominated by loan-protection business.

From this low base, the insurance sector now has the potential to expand rapidly as a result of reforms being considered by governments across the region. In the Gulf, the main change has been the move to increase private-sector involvement in health and social insurance. The UAE, for example, has approved the establishment of companies to provide pensions, healthcare and social insurance schemes for nationals. In Saudi Arabia, medical insurance is increasing in response to government spending cutbacks, and is likely to increase further once plans to oblige expatriates to have private health insurance are put into practice.

The most far-reaching reforms to the insurance sector are going ahead in Egypt, where the government has opened the door to full foreign ownership and is anxious to press ahead with privatization of the four public sector firms that dominate the sector.

The main issue at the moment in various Arab countries is consolidation. In Lebanon, this has taken the shape of mergers between some of the smaller players. In Morocco, the changes are taking place at the top end of the market, where the big names in insurance are jockeying for market dominance. The evolution of the Moroccan insurance industry as a leading component of the financial services industry is an example that several other Arab countries could soon be emulating.

As more Arab countries join WTO, the forces of competition at the local level, driven by international companies, will certainly make matters worse for the Arab insurance companies if they fail to position themselves strategically. Countries of the region must restructure their insurance markets to have fewer, stronger insurance companies with regional and international reach. Mergers and acquisitions are the way forward for national insurers to strengthen their capital base, preserve their market shares, and gain a foothold in other markets.

Despite the negative consequences, liberalization of the insurance market in the region is also expected to have positive effects on the insurance industry if the needed improvements are made. The insurance industry has a lot of opportunities to expand, especially in the life and personal classes of insurance. The increasing size of the insurance market in the presence of greater competition would not only improve the level of services, but would bring new insurance products and increase the awareness of the value of insurance. Moreover, increasing insurance-premium income would positively affect the economy if it is invested properly in other economic sectors.

As the new economy takes shape in the Arab world, local Arab insurers have at the outset some comparative advantages over their counterparts from developed nations. These are knowledge and understanding of local customers and of market conditions, established and personal links with holders of large books, control over distribution networks, and established networks with authorities and other insurers. The foregoing strengths will not be adequate in the longer term to counter threats that will come from new entrants unless supported by adequate skills, competences, systems and investments in several areas.

Figure 2.2
Insurance penetration in Arab markets
(penetration rates as a percentage of GDP, 1999)

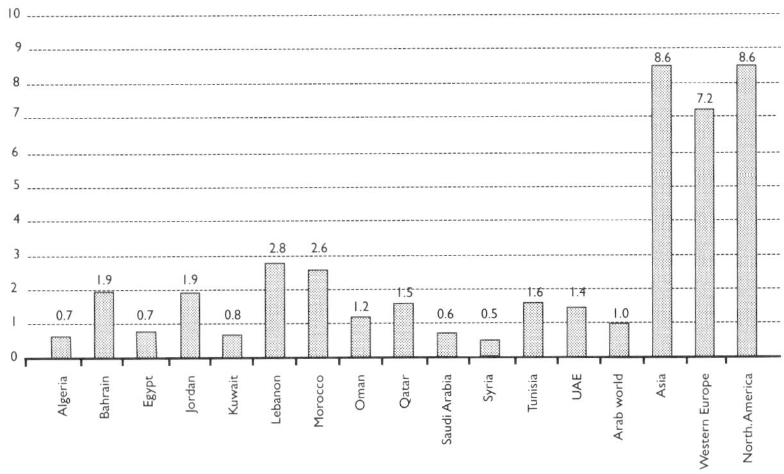

# 3

# THE NEW ECONOMY AND ITS IMPACT ON THE ARAB REGION

## INTRODUCTION

What was unthinkable ten years ago has now become a reality. The whole world is connected through the Internet, with around 200 million people surfing daily, looking for information and entertainment, sending e-mail, trading bonds and stocks, undertaking online banking activities and buying, among other things, books, CDs and airline tickets.

The Internet has grown faster than any communications medium in history. It took only five years for the Internet to reach a penetration rate of 40 per cent in the US market, compared with radio, which took 38 years, and TV, which took 13 years. By 2003, over 500 million are forecast to use the Internet globally, with penetration rates exceeding 70 per cent in the US, 50 per cent in Western Europe and 5 per cent in the Arab world.

The Internet is the basic infrastructure of the virtual or new economy, providing an electronic market-place and a communications channel that has changed the way we live and do business. A number of traditional economic fundamentals have been challenged. The elements of demand, supply, time and distance have become irrelevant for many transactions. Price in the new economy may not be the most important variable. Instead, content, brand recognition, delivery and trust have become better determinants of market demand. Conditions applicable to a perfectly competitive market prevail in the new economy, with similar or identical products (e.g. e-mail), ample information and no barriers to entry or exit. Anyone can open a virtual shop, with little reference to such traditional elements as space, inventory and rent.

The impact of the Internet on the developing countries, including those in the Arab region, could be more powerful than in the West. Countries with high distribution margins, less competition and price transparency are likely to see the biggest gains in efficiency as a result of the Internet. Developing countries will have access to new technologies that had not previously been available to them, without having to develop these technologies at home. It is imperative that policy-makers understand and appreciate the concept of the new economy and the potentials that it offers.

The Arab countries will have to work hard to catch up with the Internet revolution. E-commerce and use of the Internet require a highly-developed telecommunications network, a wide spread of personal computers, and expansion in credit card use. It also requires governments which do not have an obsession with controlling information, and which are ready to embrace the global move. The new economy also requires people with broader skills, who are trained on how to think rather than what to think. It means retraining the workforce and instilling in employees an expectation that in the course of their lives they will have to change jobs at least three or four times. And those who are still studying should be equipped to work in occupations that may not yet exist.

## WHAT CHARACTERIZES THE NEW ECONOMY

The new economy is a virtual market-place brought about by revolutionary advances in communications and computers. It has its own rules and fundamentals that challenge the traditional economic model of basic economics. The infrastructure of the new economy is the Internet, which provides an electronic market-place, a new form of communication and distribution, new software and hardware applications, and a new way of doing business (figure 3.1).

**Figure 3.1**
**The Internet is the infrastructure of the new economy**

Today, the Internet is an integral part of all technology segments: it offers a new information system, a new market-place, a new form of communication and distribution and new software and hardware applications.

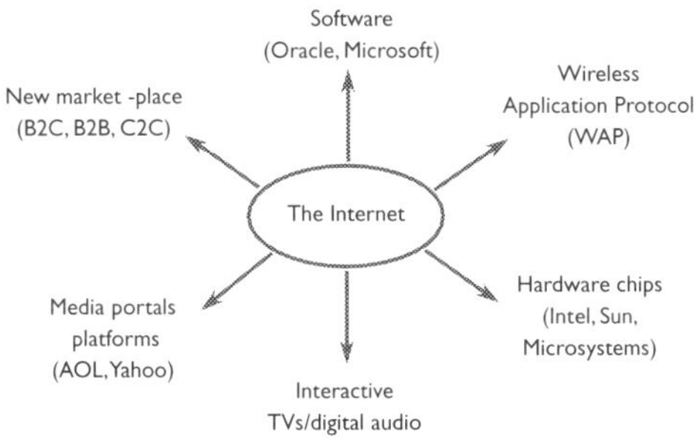


While the new economy will continue to assume rising importance, it will not replace the old economy. In reality there has to be convergence, with the virtual companies embracing the real bricks-and-mortar ones, and vice versa. A traditional company can move into the new economy by using the Internet and provide its services online (e.g. banks extending e-banking services), while Internet companies can acquire old-economy companies (e.g. AOL's takeover of Time-Warner). The most successful business models in the future will undoubtedly be a mixture of virtual and physical, new and old.

The Internet makes the economy more transparent, providing a single market online, making it easier for buyers and sellers to compare prices without the need for an intermediary, at very low transaction and switching costs. Prices of goods (e.g. books, CDs) sold on the Internet are 10–20 per cent less than identical items sold via conventional channels. However, online retailers with the lowest prices do not necessarily receive the most sales, suggesting strongly that brand image and awareness remain important factors online. This is why online companies spend million of dollars on promotion and advertising, aiming for brand supremacy, since technology and information are continually developing.

It is, of course, not only awareness that leads consumers to well-known brands when they shop online: trust also plays a key role. Online buying involves revealing financial and other personal information, while delivery of goods and services bought is often not immediate. Without high levels of consumer confidence in security and delivery guarantees, trust will continue to play a very important role in online buying behaviour.

The rules that govern the new economy differ from those governing the old economy. In the new economy, abundance and supply versatility increase a product's value, while in the old economy, scarcity governs pricing. The concept of infinite expandability is relevant here, where one person's use of, for example, a software program does not reduce its availability to others. This is the inverse of the concept of scarcity on which so much of economic theory is founded.

The new economy is also called the creative economy because is based on talent rather than production, i.e. it is a transformation from manufacturing to designing and using technology, from utilizing resources to processing ideas and information. Companies in the new economy have very high fixed costs but very low marginal ones (the additional costs incurred in producing extra units) once a critical size has been reached. These companies can be profitable if they are able to grasp a large share of the market. Companies which go online first and establish a well recognized brand can benefit from the 'first mover' advantage to establish a permanent dominance in their respective markets.

The infrastructure in the old economy is replaced by the network in the new economy, where fast delivery, product obsolescence and price volatility are normal, in contrast to product durability and price equilibrium in the old economy. In the new economy, price is not the most important variable relating to supply and demand. More significant variables include innovation, accessibility, content, brand recognition, delivery and trust. As mentioned earlier, the new economy has moved closer to market conditions of perfect competition. Textbook laws of profit maximization (marginal revenue equals marginal cost) do not necessarily hold in the new economy.

Unlike markets of the old economy, those of the new economy enjoy demand-side economies of scale, that is, the more consumers a product has, the greater the benefit to each consumer in terms of price and quantity available. For example, the auction site eBay and various providers of business-to-business services use the buying-power of their large consumer-base to extract lower prices from suppliers. This is clearly in contrast with old economy markets, where a surge in demand invariably leads to higher prices. Suppliers in new economy markets are encouraged to price new products low, sometimes offer them free – in the hope of establishing a sufficiently large group of users to attract others and to be able to capitalize on higher advertising revenues.

The dynamics of markets in the new economy can be quite unlike the markets of basic economics textbooks. More traditional markets evolve gradually over time in response to shifting consumer tastes, raw material availability and improvements in productivity. Firms in traditional markets typically concentrate on improving efficiency to gain cost advantage over the competition. In markets of the new economy, there are periods of little or no change as the market becomes locked into one technology, followed by periods of intense and rapid change as a new product becomes dominant. Firms in such markets are less concerned with improving efficiency than with being the first to market 'the next big thing'. Competition between firms is basically about R&D and the introduction of new products.

Dividend-yield has no meaning in evaluating Internet companies. Microsoft and Cisco have never paid a dividend, and AOL, Yahoo and various 'dot-com' companies will also never pay. Dividend-yield on the Standard & Poor's 500 index, already at 1.2 per cent – its lowest ever – will continue to fall as more new-economy companies are added to the Standard & Poor's index. Book value and price-to-earnings ratios are no longer indicative of proper valuation. The NASDAQ index, in which new economy companies are listed, exhibits higher volatility than other exchanges and despite the large decline in share prices from their highs in 2000, the price-to-earnings ratio on the NASDAQ index remains above 60. Investors are learning to live with high daily volatility on the NASDAQ, with increases and decreases of up to 5 per cent.

The accounting profession is looking at ways to evaluate intangible assets better, such as brand name. Price-to-earnings ratios for dot-com companies are very high and are meaningless, since most of them do not generate profits. Positive earning surprises, revenue growth and the price-to-expected earning ratio are better indicators of value for Internet companies.

In evaluating shares of new-economy companies, analysts take into consideration expected growth of earnings in what is usually referred to as PEG (price-to-earning growth). This is expressed as a ratio where price-to-earnings (based on the current fiscal year) is divided by the estimated annual growth of earnings over the next five years. The lower the PEG ratio, the less paid for future earnings, i.e. strong growth in earnings is got at a reasonable price. Companies with a PEG ratio below 1.5 are considered relatively cheap and those above 2.25 are expensive.

The consumer will be the main beneficiary of these developments: competition increases, costs are lowered and technological development and the Internet boost efficiency (figure 3.2). The main advantages for society as a whole will really come if and when the new economy affects the old economy.

Figure 3.2
E-conomics aggregate supply and demand

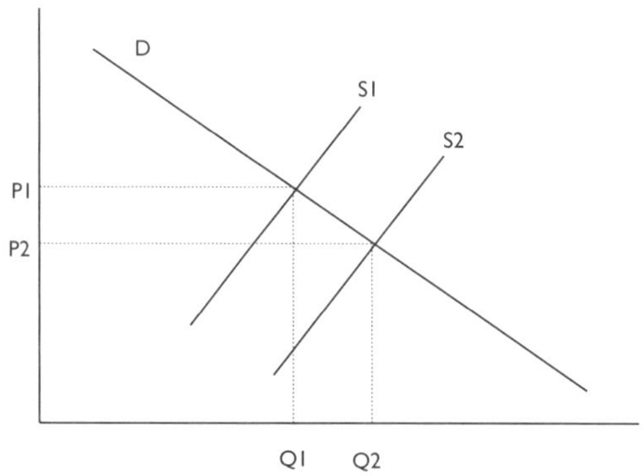


The Internet boosts efficiency and allows firms to produce more at a given price ( i.e. the supply-chain curve shifts to the right from S1 to S2). The long-term equilibrium output would rise (US economy growing at more than 4 per cent annually in the past four years) and prices will fall (core inflation excluding food and energy in the US is below 2.5%).

Old economy companies will experience pressure on margins as a result of lower information costs and increased competition. To boost profits on falling margins, the emphasis will shift to reducing expenditure, outsourcing and capitalizing on economies of scale. This goes a long way toward explaining the increase in mergers and acquisitions recorded among companies worldwide in the past few years. Outsourcing allows companies to consume less of the resources that are in short supply these days – time and management attention – in exchange for resources that are in vast supply – money.

## THE ARAB WORLD: ADJUSTING TO THE NEW ECONOMY

The Arab world has not yet embraced the new economy. Computer illiteracy is still widespread, and even though the use of the Internet has been on the rise, not more than 1 per cent of the total Arab population (2.7 million out of 275 million) were using the Internet in mid-2001. The Arab world online population is, however, expected to reach 8 million by the end of 2005.

Most of those using the Internet in the region do so to send e-mail (59 per cent), browse and search for information (22 per cent) and undertake inter-company transactions (13 per cent), while only 6 per cent use it for e-commerce (figure 3.3). There are hardly any technology, Internet, communication and information-related companies listed on the region's stock exchanges. Instead there are the traditional economy shares of financial institutions, utility companies, natural resources, cement and other service and industry companies. The Arab countries spend less than half of one per cent of GNP on research and development, compared to Israel's spend of 3 per cent.

Figure 3.3
Internet usage in the Arab world: why do you use the Internet?

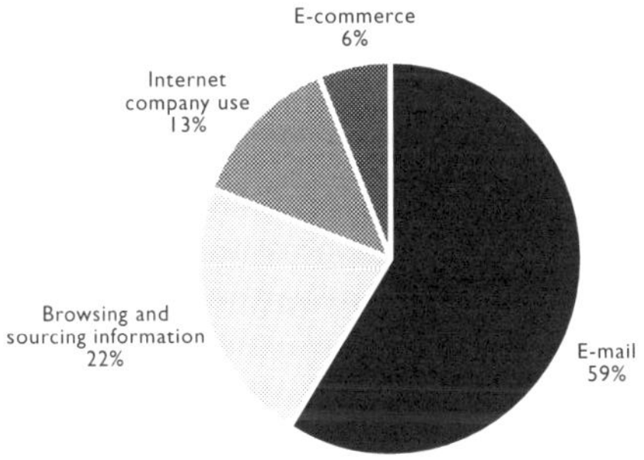


*Source: Aliqtissad Wa Al-Mal, results of a sample survey carried out in 2000.*

An annual survey conducted online in June 2001 by the research unit of Internet Al-Alam Al-Arabi on a sample of approximately 1000 Internet users showed that 9 per cent of users had made at least one purchase in the last year, compared to 4 per cent in 1997. One-third of the buyers made only one purchase. Those who made two or three separate purchases accounted for 26 per cent and 23 per cent respectively. Buyers who made more than three purchases accounted for 18 per cent of all shoppers. Shoppers spent from as little as $1 for subscribing to an entertainment website, to $20,000 on a bundle of PCs and peripherals. Total sums spent by shoppers in the sample throughout the period was $95,000, an average of $1056 per shopper. Software was the most popular item for Internet shoppers. Almost half had bought computer programs during the previous year. Books were the second-most-popular item, bought by 28 per cent of the sample, followed by computers and peripherals (26 per cent), audio CDs and CD Roms (11 per cent) and domain-name registration (10 per cent). Other items bought online were gifts (7 per cent), ready-made wear and travel tickets (5 per cent), site-hosting fees and electronic consumer products (4 per cent) and food products (1 per cent). The majority of online purchases (82 per cent) were made from international vendors, with only 18 per cent of purchases made from the few online vendors available in Arab countries.

Arab vendors and service-providers should move fast to set up online operations to complement their conventional businesses, or face the consequences of a diminishing client-base. Arab governments need to build an infrastructure that supports e-commerce and put in place the appropriate legislation to uphold it. The survey showed that consumers are moving faster than Arab vendors in making the shift to Internet shopping. Amazon was the most popular international vendor among shoppers, while Sakhr was the top Arabic site, with the most purchases. The majority of participants in the survey (48 per cent) said one of the main reasons they decided to shop on the Internet was the availability of consumer products not found in their local markets. Ease of purchase was reported by 45 per cent of the respondents, followed by the convenience of comparing products (32 per cent) and prices (24 per cent).

Respondents, however, did not consider more competitive prices, which generally characterize online consumer products, to be an important reason for buying online. Payments were made by credit cards for 82 per cent of purchases, followed by bank transfers (11 per cent), cash upon delivery (9 per cent) and cheques (3 per cent).

While it is true that the high rates of illiteracy in English (the language of the Internet), poverty, unemployment, cultural constraints and resistance to change are all impediments to the rise of new economy sectors, there are examples from other countries where the IT sector has been able to thrive amidst poverty. India has become a large producer of software, even though there are high levels of poverty, and illiteracy. The $8.6 billion IT industry there is helping the country to integrate in the global economy through information dissemination and communication.

The focus of the region should be on the software part of the IT industry, that is on developing the tools and providing the content and services aimed at local and regional needs. Unlike most productive sectors, a country can utilize and benefit from IT that already exists in the market-place. The market for the application of technology to local and regional needs is starting to take off. For example, Al-Maktoub, the first Arabic e-mail system, which was developed by a Jordanian company, is gaining popularity with 400,000 users and six million page views per month in May 2001. Other well-known sites include Arabia On Line – the leading Arab portal – with 28 million page views per month, Ayna.com, Naseej and MENAFN.

The region needs its own version of the content and services sites found in the US and Europe. To achieve success in this field, Arab firms need to apply existing ideas and not invent them from scratch. They should capitalize on their knowledge of the region, its language, its culture and its local distribution channels to come up with innovative ideas that cater to local needs.

Arab consumers have shown a healthy appetite for the services available on the Internet, and most governments have accepted the fact that the new economy is here to stay. Saudi Arabia, the largest market for personal computers in the region with sales of 430,000 in 2000 out of a total market of one-and-a-half million, launched direct Internet services at the beginning of 1999. Only Libya and Iraq did not offer direct Internet services by the end of 2001.

Figure 3.4
Estimated number of Internet users in the Arab world, 2000

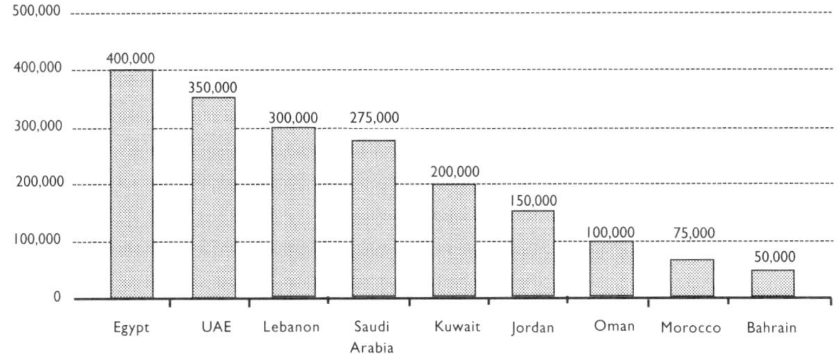


*Source: Jordinvest estimates based on informed sources*

Egypt, which had the second-largest market for personal computers in the region, with sales of 400,000 in 2000, had the highest number of Internet users – 400,000 – accounting for less than 0.6 per cent of its total population. It was followed by the UAE (350,000), Lebanon (300,000), Saudi Arabia (275,000), Kuwait (200,000) and Jordan (150,000) (figure 3.4). The highest increase in Internet users during the period April 1999–April 2000 was recorded in Saudi Arabia (167 per cent), followed by Egypt (112 per cent), the UAE (96 per cent) and Yemen (90 per cent). In the Arab countries, the number of Internet users doubled during 2000 (figure 3.5).

Figure 3.5
Growth in Internet usage (April 1999–April 2000)

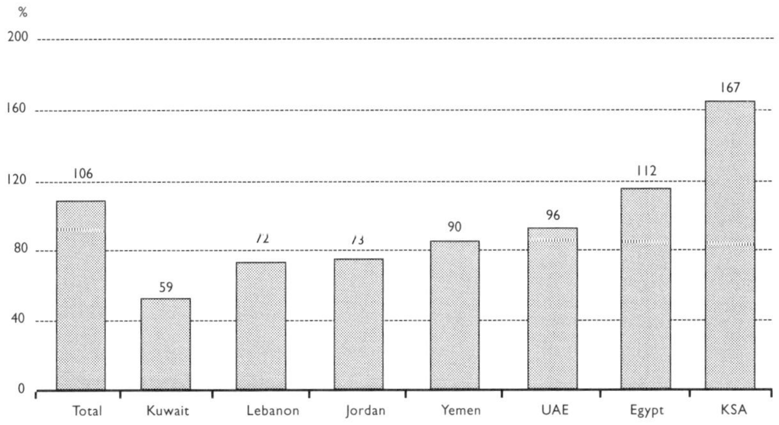


*Source: Dabbagh Information Technology Survey*

The value of e-commerce in the Middle East and North Africa still represents a fraction of that in more developed Western markets (figure 3.6). Nevertheless, it is expected to grow to $1 billion in 2004 from around $100 million in 1999. Middle-East retailers are already offering products on the Internet ranging from books and software to jewellery and beauty items. However, the small number of Internet users in the region, the high cost of personal computers and internet connection, and the fact that many are reluctant to use credit cards over the Internet for business transactions have all dampened the growth of e-commerce in the Arab world.

**Figure 3.6**
**Projected business-to-business e-commerce expansion ($ billion)**

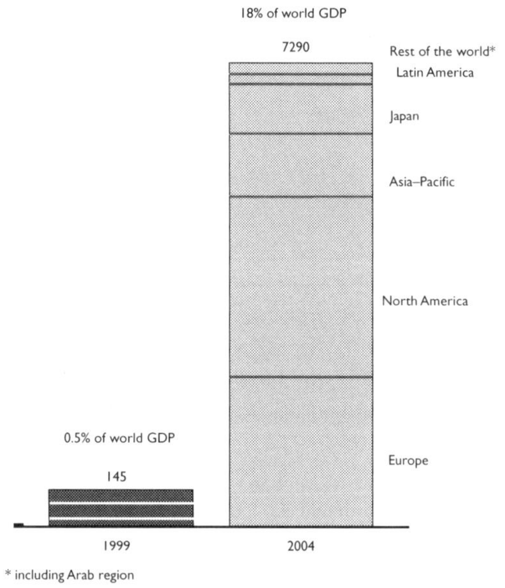


The Internet is making it difficult for domestic Arab markets to be protected from outside competition. This is why Arab firms interested in the export and re-export markets must immediately open their own websites. Such websites, with appropriate links, advertising, proper placement and search-engines, would greatly enhance the role of the region as both a wholesale and a retail market-place. Initially, the website may merely be an information-providing tool, but it can later be extended to include other services.

Domestic banks will be facing competition from the international banking giants providing online Internet banking services to prime customers. Online banks and businesses do not need a local presence, and because the Internet accommodates different languages, this allows international institutions to sell their services and banking products across borders. It is also necessary that business should be conducted more competitively and transparently. If a service or a product is not priced competitively, then the customer can easily go elsewhere at the click of a button.

Most Arab banks have now realized that e-business should be a key component of their future activities, and they have started to invest to capitalize on that potential. If international banks insist that bank-to-bank business be carried out online, then Arab banks will be forced to do their international business the 'e-way'.

## MOBILE TELEPHONY WILL DOMINATE E-COMMERCE IN THE REGION

If the 1990s was the decade of the Internet, the first ten years of the twenty-first century will be the decade of mobile communications. The convergence of IT and the mobile phone is likely to change the way we work, the way we buy goods and the way we communicate with each other. Mobile telephones, still used almost exclusively for voice, are on the threshold of a wave of new service opportunities for businesses and customers. The appeal of the mobile telephone is not difficult to understand. Its portability means that it can be carried everywhere. The growth in the number of mobile users over the past decade has been spectacular. In 1990, there were just over 11 million worldwide, by 2001, almost 400 million with only 180 million having PCs. By 2005, the number of mobile telephones is likely to reach one billion, exceeding the number of fixed-line phones.

**Table 3.1**
**Mobile telephone market in the Arab region (number of subscribers)**

| | 2000E | 2005F |
|---|---|---|
| Algeria | 30,000 | 500,000 |
| Bahrain | 140,000 | 250,000 |
| Egypt | 2,000,000 | 8,000,000 |
| Jordan | 385,000 | 1,300,000 |
| Kuwait | 600,000 | 900,000 |
| Lebanon | 700,000 | 1,800,000 |
| Morocco | 300,000 | 2,500,000 |
| Oman | 220,000 | 800,000 |
| Qatar | 80,000 | 180,000 |
| Saudi Arabia | 1,200,000 | 4,000,000 |
| Syria | 50,000 | 500,000 |
| Tunisia | 200,000 | 1,010,000 |
| UAE | 700,000 | 1,780,000 |
| Palestine | 65,000 | 200,000 |
| Yemen | 24,000 | 800,000 |
| **Total** | **6,694,000** | **24,520,000** |

*E: Estimates based on national and international sources, including International Telecommunications Union (ITU)*
*F: Jordinvest forecasts*

It is estimated that there were around seven million mobile subscribers in the Arab region in 2000, and the number is expected to surge to around 25 million by 2005. The equipment supply sector of the telecommunications industry alone was valued at $4 billion, increasing at the rate of 25 per cent annually. The explosive growth in markets for mobile telephony such as in Jordan (from 100,000 to 650,000 in a year) and Egypt (from 185,000 to 2.2 million in two years), the new mobile networks launching in Syria, Algeria and Yemen, and the privatization moves in Morocco, Lebanon, Oman, Saudi Arabia and Egypt, give credence to the projected rapid expansion of mobile usage in the region. There is a growing demand for new customer services and applications. Because the Arab countries – with few exceptions – have fairly small markets, the only way to achieve the economies of scale required to introduce expensive new technologies and provide good content is to operate regionally. Having a common language, spoken by 275 million people, is an advantage.

Recently, we have witnessed a significant change in the approach of mobile operators. As little as 18 months ago the tactics used to generate new business were based around familiar variables such as cost-per-minute, free voicemail retrieval and signal coverage. Now the focus has shifted to the provision of services that exploit the mobile telephone's unique features, namely personalization and portability. Location, time-specific services, good content that adds value or provides entertainment to the user, and the growing popularity of short messaging services (SMS), are likely to give a big boost to the revenue stream of mobile operators. The value chain is therefore changing from connectivity to application, transaction and content. Those operators in the Arab region who can assume the role of 'content aggregator' are the ones that will dominate the scene.

From retailers to financial-service providers, a large number of organizations are looking to widen their delivery channels to include not just fixed internet but wireless: in essence, allowing users to connect, communicate and transact via the mobile handset. The speed of hand-held wireless data devices is expected to rise from 10kb/s for the current '2G' (or WAP) telephony to three times that speed for the 2.5G technology (or GPRS) and to 2 million kb/s for 3G services (or UMTS).

Table 3.2
Global growth estimates for the mobile Internet (million)

| | 2001 | 2005 |
|---|---|---|
| Total number of mobile phones | 500 | 1,000,000 |
| Total number of mobile phones in the Arab countries | 7 | 25 |
| Number of WAP phones (Global) | 100 | 500 |
| Number of WAP phones (Arab region) | 0.1 | 50 |

*Source: Jordinvest*

When it comes to e-commerce via the mobile telephone, the operators are in a strong position, as they already have a billing system in place and a portal that customers can use for various e-commerce transactions. They are also able to deliver and manage e-services on a user's handset and provide a secure channel through which transactions can be made. The service enables people to place an order – for example, with a fast-food restaurant, a music store, a bookshop or a cinema – and to pick up the goods later. The money transfer will take place simultaneously with the placement of the order but does not require the transfer of credit-card numbers. People will set up an account with a local ISP and provide direct debit instructions when signing up for the service. The actual transaction will then be conducted conventionally through the banking system, with the retailer receiving payment transfer when the order is executed.

Payment security is often cited as the primary obstacle preventing the widespread take-up of mobile commerce (m-commerce). Real-world transactions use face-to-face contact and handwritten signatures to achieve legally binding contracts or to approve financial transactions. A user's private key, central to the security of the infrastructure and the enabling feature for authentication and encryption, can now be stored on the SIM card of a mobile handset. The inherent safety and strength of the SIM card makes it the perfect tamper-proof device for the storage of these keys. Once embedded in the handset, the SIM card gives the user the same functionality and confidentially possible from a PC. With this functionality in place, the ability to conduct secure transactions over the telephone, and to 'sign' for goods electronically becomes a reality. There is also a certification authority, a central and trusted body, responsible for issuing users' key pairs and digital certificates (the online equivalents of a passport). Again, with ultimate ownership of the mobile users' SIM cards and an existing billing infrastructure, the mobile operator is perfectly positioned to accept this role as the central body within the m-commerce universe.

Table 3.3
Speed of connection to the Internet

| | Kb/s |
|---|---|
| **Wireless connection** | |
| 2G (WAP) | 10 |
| 2.5G (GPRS) | 30 |
| 3G (UMTS) | 2000 |
| **Wired connection** | |
| Standard dial-up | 10 |
| Microwave | 400 |
| Satellite | 512 |

To conclude, in order for mobile operators in the region to increase penetration and air-traffic usage and boost revenues, they need to come up with innovate services and attract third-party content-providers to their platform. The trick is to provide time-sensitive information and services relevant to customers on the move that are time sensitive. Mobile operators will succeed if they shift their strategy from being a voice channel to being a transaction distribution channel for goods and services. 2.5G and 3G technology will give mobile operators dominance over e-commerce and allow them to benefit from sizable advertising revenues as they become the main channel of Internet access.

## CONCLUSION

The upheaval generated by the new economy is dramatically altering the power and status of corporations around the world. US-based companies have clearly dominated the digital age, thanks to America's early adoption of the PC. The Internet and other new technologies grew from the PC, and most North Americans access the Internet through their office or home computers. But the stationary PC is giving way to hand-held information appliances, and the mobile is clearly the portal of the future. Today, Europeans and Japanese are ahead of the Americans in mobile telephony. Europe has a single wireless standard, GSM, while the US continues to use three. Europeans are quickly replacing their desktop telephones completely with mobiles. Meanwhile, Japanese students have permanent Internet connections.

The Arab world is still lagging behind other advanced and developing countries in the creation of an information-based new economy that generates high economic growth. Ownership of PCs is low, while other prerequisites such as the availability of qualified labourforce, high Internet penetration rates, widespread credit-card usage, and an efficient delivery mechanism are still lacking. However, several Arab countries and local businessmen have been trying to catch up with the global boom in IT business. To a large extent their success will depend on their ability to find qualified staff, keep abreast of technological developments and attract enough users. According to US-based research group IDC, demand for skilled IT personnel in the US market will exceed supply by at least 350,000 people annually in the coming few years, leading to substantial demand for foreign workers. This will put additional pressure on countries of the region to retain qualified staff in the IT field. Running out of IT workers today is like running out of iron ore in the industrial revolution.

Other prerequisites of success include having in place venture-capital funds willing to take equity stakes in start-up businesses in the region. These newly formed companies should thrive to establish a link-up with foreign operators that can offer clear advantages in terms of technology transfer and market penetration. The region also needs to have in place the right legal and regulatory framework to facilitate the growth of IT industries. Politicians should focus on nurturing technology-driven growth, rather than traditional issues of income redistribution and budgetary expenditures on projects. More resources should be allocated to research and development, and college scholarships should be increased for engineering, computer science and other 'high-tech' fields that have not been attracting enough Arab students.

The Arab countries need to pursue a regional vision in order to be able to compete internationally. One key advantage is that of the common language, which if used wisely will allow new economy companies to have a large Arabic-speaking regional market. Several efforts in the IT field are being duplicated in, among others, Dubai, Jordan, Egypt, Lebanon and Bahrain. Those Gulf countries which do not have the human resource talent to build a viable IT industry should concentrate on being a centre for financing ventures in new economy sectors. Lebanon, Jordan and Egypt are able to provide much cheaper cost-based centres in which new economy companies can operate. Dubai – with its advanced Internet City – could serve as a cross-border platform for online procurement and regional e-business. Furthermore, the Arab countries should have a common trade area in information communications.

# 4

# ARAB BOND MARKETS: MOVING FROM THE EMBRYONIC STAGE TO THE TAKE-OFF STAGE

## INTRODUCTION

Bond markets in the Arab region are still in the early stages of development, with total values of corporate bond issues at around $5 billion in 2000, compared to the total capitalization of Arab stock markets of $175 billion. Of the outstanding $5 billion in corporate bonds, Eurodollar bonds account for around $3 billion and the balance of $2 billion is issues on local currencies (figure 4.1). Both the primary markets – where new securities are issued – and the secondary markets for bonds are illiquid. Bond trading makes up less than 1 per cent of total trading on the region's stock exchanges. Investors – typically banks, social security and insurance companies – tend to hold bonds to maturity. Getting a competitive quote on a corporate bond listed in Jordan or Morocco, for example, could take days, while in the eurobond market it would take seconds.

**Figure 4.1**
**Corporate bond issues in the Arab world, 2000 ($ million)**

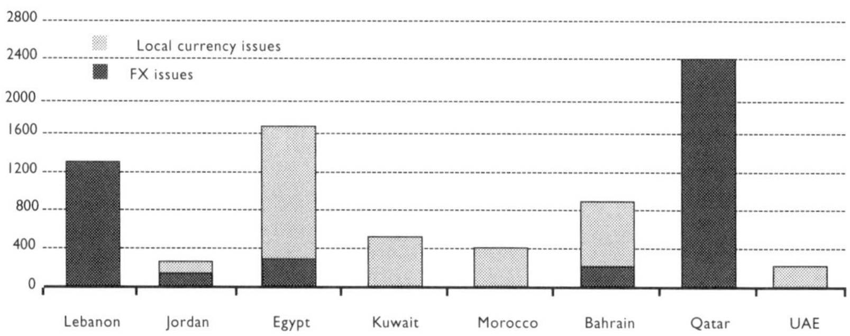

However, the bond markets in the region are likely to gain added depth and versatility in the coming few years, as the need increases for long-term capital borrowed at a fixed rate. This will complement the region's fast-developing equity markets and provide a fresh source of financing for private and public projects. It will also encourage the creation of new risk-management instruments such as interest-rate futures and options, while adding to the scope of central banks to conduct monetary policy through open-market operations. From the borrower's point of view, bond finance increases the flexibility of debt-management and allows for terms and conditions different from those available in the loan market.

Borrowers are able to access funds that are more suitable to the financing of large and capital-intensive projects. Bonds typically have a longer maturity than bank loans and amortize in one bullet payment. Furthermore, the majority of bonds have a fixed coupon that many companies prefer, as it facilitates longer-term financial planning and protects them from unanticipated interest-rate changes. Bonds also provide local investors with the option to diversify their portfolios away from equities into fixed-income securities. For banks, the issuance of bonds provides the opportunity to generate new sources of funds of longer maturities at fixed rates.

The emergence of bond markets is linked to financial liberalization. Until the late 1980s, the banking systems in several Arab countries were repressed by extensive controls on interest rates and credit allocation. In recent years, reforms have dramatically transformed the financial environment in the region giving a boost to the development of bond markets. Several prerequisites for the development of bond markets in the Arab region are now in place. Investment banks have been established at national and regional levels to act as intermediaries between borrowers and investors, and provide underwriting and placement capabilities. International rating agencies are also beginning to position themselves in the region, and several regulatory reforms have been introduced although much more needs to be done in this respect. Standards of reporting are improving, yet most Arab countries are still way behind Western financial markets when it comes to revealing information.

## WHY HAVE A GOVERNMENT BOND MARKET?

There has been a huge increase in government bond markets in the region in the last 10 years. Nearly all the major Arab countries issue treasury bills and bonds, with a total of $87 billion of government bonds outstanding by the end of 2000 (table 4.1). The trend began in the mid-1980s, when several Arab countries started operating under deficit budgets financed mostly from local funds. Saudi Arabia, Kuwait, Oman, Egypt and Lebanon have particularly active government bond markets, with discount facilities adding liquidity to these instruments. However, most of the bonds issued in the region have maturities ranging between two and five years with only Saudi Arabia and Egypt issuing government bonds with maturities reaching seven years.

Table 4.1
Treasury bonds issued by Arab countries ($ million)

| Country | Bonds outstanding 2000 |
|---|---|
| Jordan | 363 |
| Lebanon | 15,911 |
| Egypt | 22,800 |
| Tunisia | 2865 |
| Algeria | 1660 |
| Morocco | 8808 |
| Yemen | 645 |
| Saudi Arabia | 25,250 |
| Oman | 2019 |
| Kuwait | 5776 |
| Bahrain | 700 |
| **Total** | **86,796** |

*Source:* Unified Arab Economic Report, *Arab Monetary Fund, 2001 and other national sources*

Governments of the region should create local bond markets even if the borrowing requirements of the public sector are low and there is plenty of liquidity through bank savings. Government bonds help to establish a benchmark for pricing of corporate bonds; the yields on these bonds serve as reference-points in the derivative markets and are used as discount rates to value equities and appraise investment projects.

Various steps should be taken to support a viable government bond market. These include establishing a legal framework for security issuance, and a regulatory environment to foster market development. There must also be a viable market structure encompassing efficient and safe custody, clearing and settlement procedures, removing any tax or other regulatory impediments which may hamper trading in government securities, and promoting other money and market risk-management instruments such as repurchase orders and interest-rate futures swaps. Strengthening the demand for government securities involves building the potential investor base through removing regulatory distortions, eliminating below-market-rate funding through captive-investor sources, and implementing appropriate rules and regulations on the participation of foreign investors in the domestic market.

Equally important is the method of trading in government bonds. This can be done through the stock exchange or over the counter but both forms need to be regulated. There are advantages and disadvantages associated with each form; there is some degree of international agreement that trading through the stock exchange is more efficient and encourages wider participation if accompanied with prompt and assured settlement. Many countries go as far as to offer calendars of likely future issues, published well in advance, with much background information on the market. Others have also set up a system of primary dealers (mainly from licensed banks) entrusted with the tasks of selling government bonds in the primary market and acting as market-makers in order to generate liquidity in the secondary market.

In developed financial markets with many government bonds unsold, the main buyers are usually institutional investors who want first-class security and a guaranteed return. Such investors have varying requirements: banks prefer shorter-maturity bonds, while pension funds and insurance companies, for example, want at least part of their portfolios invested in longer-maturity bonds. Where an investment fund industry exists or is starting up, there will be an appetite for bonds with maturities of all yields. It is therefore important and advantageous for governments to offer products satisfying demand across the range of maturities.

To encourage the development of bond markets in the Arab region, countries and corporates should be rated. Arab private and institutional investors are reluctant to invest in unrated bonds, whether Arab or otherwise. Credible rating agencies have now started to carry out periodic credit analysis on Arab countries and Arab incorporated companies, providing investors with reliable up-to-date information.

Ratings add value to borrowing entities because they offer independent confirmation of their creditworthiness. Many such entities in the region – especially banks – have already recognized this and have agreed to allow rating companies to perform the required due diligence. This does not constitute investment recommendation, but provides investors with an objective assessment of a borrower's ability to meet reliably its obligations, thus assisting investors in making investment decisions. Ratings are likely to promote the differentiation of interest rates based on risk, thereby assisting in the efficient allocation of resources. Markets and companies are encouraged to improve their financial structure in order to procure a better grade and thereby lower their cost of borrowing. Ratings lead to greater transparency and investor protection, and improve the reporting and disclosure of financial information.

Table 4.2
Long-term sovereign ratings of selected Arab countries, 2000

| | Moody's | Standard & Poor's |
|---|---|---|
| Bahrain | Ba1 | nr |
| Egypt | Ba1 | BBB– |
| Jordan | Ba3 | BB– |
| Kuwait | Baa1 | A |
| Lebanon | B1 | BB– |
| Morocco | Ba1 | BB |
| Oman | Baa2 | BBB– |
| Qatar | Baa2 | BBB |
| Saudi Arabia | Baa3 | nr |
| Tunisia | Baa3 | BBB– |
| UAE | A2 | nr |

*Ratings below Baa3 from Moody's, and BBB– from Standard & Poor's are below investment grade; nr: not rated*

*Source: Moody's Investors Service, Standard & Poor's*

Six Arab countries have an investment-grade rating from Moody's. The UAE has the highest rating of A2, followed by Kuwait (Baa1), Oman and Qatar (Baa2), then Saudi Arabia and Tunisia (Baa3). Egypt, Bahrain and Morocco were given a sub-investment credit rating of Ba1, followed by Jordan (Ba3) and Lebanon (B1) (table 4.2). Standard & Poor's assigned an investment grade rating of BBB– and above to Kuwait, Qatar, Oman, Egypt and Tunisia, while Jordan, Morocco and Lebanon were given a speculative-grade rating.

## CORPORATE BOND MARKETS

The success of a corporate bond market will be affected by several factors, including macroeconomic conditions, standards of reporting, financing alternatives and the market's infrastructure components (e.g. regulations, trading systems and rating agencies). Although standards of reporting for companies in the Arab region have improved – especially for those which are incorporated or publicly trading – yet more is needed to enhance the transparency of companies which are planning to enter the local bond market. Without full disclosure, no reputable investment bank would be willing to underwrite a bond issue for a local company.

The presence of excess liquidity in the domestic-banking system should not be a reason to delay the development of a local bond market. The argument that banks can provide all the capital that companies need, is not always true. A viable local bond market would provide 'patient capital' – that is a new source of long-term financing for corporate borrowers – that would help reduce their over-dependence on short-term lending from banks. The shortage of medium-to-long-term funds has been identified as a significant impediment to industrial growth and financial development in the region.

The East Asian financial crisis of 1997 highlighted the importance of maintaining diversified funding sources. Before the crisis broke, there was no reason to question the three decades of solid regional economic growth, largely financed through the banking system. There was no need for a back-up source of financing, as long as the ratio of non-performing loans to bank assets remained low. The need for a 'spare tyre' became evident when the financial crisis hit the region, pulling its economies down with it. The crisis was less severe in Singapore and Hong Kong where viable bond markets existed.

Sweden had a developed corporate bond market with a variety of non-banking funding sources, so that the crisis that hit Swedish banks in the early 1990s when property prices there collapsed did not impact companies' borrowing ability. In contrast, the Thai and Indonesian financial systems mainly had banks as financial intermediaries, with the corporate bond market virtually non-existent, so the crisis there has taken much longer to be resolved, leading to a protracted credit 'crunch'.

A developed bond market would help provide local institutions, which are the major sources of long-term funds ( pension funds, insurance companies, social security etc) with attractive investment outlets denominated in local currencies. From the borrower's point of view, bonds increase the flexibility of debt-management and allow for terms and conditions different to those available from the commercial banks. Bonds give corporate borrowers the chance to maintain their credit limits with banks and provide them with an alternative long-term funding source not readily available in the local loan market. Banks typically like to lend for fairly short periods because their sources of funds are short. Furthermore, the majority of bonds have a fixed coupon, which many companies prefer, because they facilitate long-term financial planning and protect borrowers from a sudden surge in interest rates.

Several prerequisites for the development of a corporate bond market in the Arab region have recently been put in place. Investment banks have been established to act as intermediaries between borrowers and investors, and to provide underwriting and placement capabilities. There has been a limited issuance of government bonds that has helped to establish a benchmark for pricing corporate bonds. These are basically priced by charging a premium over the corresponding government bond yields according to the creditworthiness of the issuing corporate borrower.

In most Arab countries, corporate-sector financing has mainly been in the form of loans solicited directly from banks. Yet reforms which encourage greater issuance of debt securities to finance public- and private-sector activities indicate that this market is likely to grow significantly in the near future. One reason for this is the capital adequacy requirements and exposure limits imposed on bank lending. These new regulations will force banks to be more careful in their allocation of capital and are likely to raise the cost of loans for borrowers. This will encourage corporate borrowers to switch from banks to domestic debt markets to meet their long-term financing needs.

Table 4.3
Corporate bond issues in the Arab world (local currency, million)

| Issuer | Date | Currency (years) | Amount (million) | Maturity (years) | Yield (per cent) |
|---|---|---|---|---|---|
| **Kuwait** | | | | | |
| Commercial Facilities Company | Dec. 92 | KD | 7 | 5 | 9.500 |
| Kuwait Real Estate Bank | Dec. 93 | KD | 15 | 5 | 7.125 |
| Kuwait Real Estate Bank | May 94 | KD | 20 | 3 | 6.500 |
| Kuwait Investment Projects Company | Oct. 94 | KD | 12 | 5 | 8.250 |
| National Investment Company | May 96 | KD | 8.25 | 5 | 8.500 |
| Commercial Facilities Company | Dec. 97 | KD | 15 | 5 | 8.000 |
| Commercial Bank of Kuwait | Oct. 98 | KD | 25 | 5 | 8.125 |
| National Industries Group | Feb. 99 | KD | 35 | 2 | 7.875 |
| Kuwait Real Estate Bank | Sep. 99 | KD | 20 | 3 | 7.500 |
| **Total** | | KD | 157 | | |
| Value in \$, assuming \$1=KD0.31 | | | 507 | | |

| Issuer | Date | Currency | Amount | Maturity | Yield |
|---|---|---|---|---|---|
| | | (years) | (million) | (years) | (per cent) |
| **Bahrain** | | | | | |
| Bahrain Commercial Facilities Company | Jul. 94 | BD | 7 | 3 | Libor+2.000 |
| Aluminum Bahrain | Oct. 94 | BD | 100 | 7 | Libor+0.750 |
| Bahrain International Bank | Sep. 95 | BD | 60 | 3 | Libor+1.750 |
| Bahrain International Bank | Jun. 96 | BD | 60 | 5 | Libor+1.370 |
| Bahrain Commercial Facilities Company | Dec. 97 | BD | 7 | 3 | Libor+2.000 |
| **Total** | | BD | 227 | | |
| Value in $, assuming $1=BD0.38 | | | 597 | | |
| **Egypt (TB=treasury-bill rate; DR=discount rate;** *=floating rate note) | | | | | |
| Victoria United Hotels* | Apr. 95 | EGP | 21 | 7 | TB182+0.75% or 12.000 |
| Egyptian Arab Land Bank | Dec. 95 | EGP | 10 | 5 | 12.000 |
| Citibank* | Mar. 96 | EGP | 200 | 5 | TB91 |
| Egyptian American Bank | Jun. 96 | EGP | 200 | 5 | 10.750 |
| Egyptian Arab Real Estate Bank* | Sep. 96 | EGP | 90 | 7 | DR less 1.500 |
| American Express Bank* | Sep. 96 | EGP | 300 | 5 | TB91 |
| Avintis Pharma* | Dec. 96 | EGP | 30 | 5 | TB182+0.250 |
| Egyptian British Bank* | Dec. 96 | EGP | 100 | 5 | TB91+0.250 |
| Arab African International Bank* | Mar. 97 | EGP | 300 | 5 | TB91+0.250 |
| Egyptian Arab Land Bank | Apr. 97 | EGP | 40 | 7 | 10.500 |
| Commercial International Bank* | May 97 | EGP | 300 | 5 | TB182 + 0.125% or 9.000 |
| Industrial Development Bank* | May 97 | EGP | 150 | 5 | TB91+0.250 |
| National Societe Generale Bank* | Jun. 97 | EGP | 150 | 5 | TB91+0.250 |
| Arab Banking Corporation - Egypt* | Oct. 97 | EGP | 125 | 5 | TB91+0.375 |
| Middle East Modern Lighting Company | Dec. 97 | EGP | 50 | 7 | 11.000 |
| Egyptian Engineering Real Estate Inv. | Feb. 98 | EGP | 40 | 3 | 10.000 |
| Egyptian Financial Company* | Feb. 98 | EGP | 30 | 5 | TB91+0.750 |
| Orascom Projects & Tourism | Jun. 98 | EGP | 80 | 7 | 11.500 |
| Arab Steel Factory | Jul. 98 | EGP | 250 | 7 | 11.000 |
| Industrial Development Bank* | Nov. 98 | EGP | 150 | 7 | TB91+0.750 |
| Orascom Construction Industries | Feb. 99 | EGP | 280 | 7 | 11.000 |
| Lakah | Apr. 99 | EGP | 400 | 7 | 11.000 |
| Commercial International Bank | May 99 | EGP | 300 | 5 | 10.250 |
| Mega Investment & International Trade | Jun. 99 | EGP | 200 | 7 | 11.250 |
| Delta Sugar | Jun. 99 | EGP | 80 | 7 | 11.000 |
| Industrial Development Bank* | Jul. 99 | EGP | 200 | 7 | DR less 1.500 |
| Export Development Bank of Egypt | Oct. 99 | EGP | 113 | 10 | 11.000 |
| Egyptian Company for Mobile Services | Oct. 99 | EGP | 340 | 8 | 12.250 |
| Orascom Projects & Tourism | Jan. 00 | EGP | 100 | 7 | 12.870 |
| **Total** | | EGP | 4856 | | |
| Value in $, assuming $1=EGP3.44 | | 1412 | | | |

| Issuer | Date | Currency (years) | Amount (million) | Maturity (years) | Yield (per cent) |
|---|---|---|---|---|---|
| **Tunisia** | | | | | |
| Tunisia Kuwait Development Bank | Oct. 98 | TD | 20 | 10 | 8.000 |
| Bank Tunisia For Economic Development | May 99 | TD | 50 | 8,10 | 6.500 |
| **Total** | | TD | 70 | | |
| Value in $, assuming $1=TD1.46 | | | 48 | | |
| **Morocco** | | | | | |
| Credit Immobilier et Hotelier | Jun. 97 | MD | 300 | 2 | 10.500 |
| Credit Immobilier et Hotelier | Oct. 97 | MD | 280 | 10 | 10.000 |
| Credit Immobilier et Hotelier | Aug. 98 | MD | 350 | 5 | 8.000 |
| Credor | Jan. 98 | MD | 200 | 3 | 8.600 |
| Taslif | Sep. 98 | MD | 30 | 3 | 8.000 |
| Banque Nationale de Developement Economique | Dec. 98 | MD | 200 | 5 | 7.950 |
| SOFAC | Feb. 99 | MD | 150 | 3 | 8.000 |
| Wafasalaf | Apr. 99 | MD | 150 | 3 | 7.700 |
| Union Bail | Jun. 99 | MD | 100 | 4 | 7.600 |
| Banque Morocaine du Commerce et de l'Industire | Aug. 99 | MD | 450 | 5 | 6.500 |
| Diac Salaf | Sep. 99 | MD | 166 | 5 | 7.300 |
| Marco Leasing | Sep. 99 | MD | 107 | 3 | 7.100 |
| Credit Immobilier et Hotelier | Sep. 99 | MD | 200 | 5 | 6.750 |
| Banque Nationale de Developement Economique | Sep. 99 | MD | 100 | 5 | 6.750 |
| Credor | Nov. 99 | MD | 256 | 3 | 6.240 |
| Credor | Nov. 99 | MD | 144 | 5 | 6.460 |
| BMCI Leasing | Nov. 99 | MD | 122 | 5 | 6.440 |
| Maghrebail | Dec. 99 | MD | 200 | 5 | 6.150 |
| Acred | Jan. 00 | MD | 122 | 3 | 6.630 |
| List includes only bonds with maturity of 3 or more years and value exceeding MD100 million | | | | | |
| **Total** | | MD | 3627 | | |
| Value in $, assuming $1=MD9.72 | | | 373.1 | | |
| **Jordan** | | | | | |
| Citibank, Amman | Sep. 00 | JD | 5 | Sep. 03 | 7.500 |
| Middle East Complex for Engineering Electronics and Heavy Industries | Jul. 00 | JD | 5 | Jul. 05 | 9.750 |
| The Jordanian Hotels and Tourism Company | Jun. 00 | JD | 10 | Jun. 07 | 10.000 |
| Jordan Worsted Mills Company | May 00 | JD | 7 | May. 05 | 9.250 |
| Zara Investment Company | Dec. 99 | JD | 10 | Dec. 04 | 10.000 |
| Cairo Amman Bank | Sep. 99 | JD | 10 | Sep. 02 | 9.380 |
| Jordan Cement Factories Company | Jun. 98 | JD | 10 | Jun. 03 | 9.200 |
| Union Chemicals for Vegetables and Oil Industrie | Mar. 99 | JD | 3.5 | Mar. 04 | 9.500 |

| Issuer | Date | Currency (years) | Amount (million) | Maturity (years) | Yield (per cent) |
|---|---|---|---|---|---|
| International, Industrial, Commercial and Tourist Investment Company | Oct. 99 | JD | 7 | Oct. 05 | 10.500 |
| International Tobacco and Cigarettes Company | May 98 | JD | 3.5 | May 03 | 11.000 |
| **Total** | | JD | 71 | | |
| Value in $, assuming $1=JD0.709 | | | 100 | | |
| UAE | | | | | |
| BMW US Capital Corporation | Nov. 99 | AED | 350 | Nov. 02 | 6.710 |
| Abbey National Mortgage Bank | Jun. 00 | AED | 400 | Jun. 05 | 8.500 |
| National Bank of Abu Dhabi | end 99 | | NA | | |
| (three bonds linked to the price of crude oil, the Nikkei 225 index) | | | | | |
| **Total** | | AED | 750 | | |
| Value in $, assuming $1=AED3.67 | | 204 | | | |
| **Total local currency issues in $ million** | | | 3242 | | |

In many Arab countries, a large number of companies are owned and managed by families. Although these enterprises are invariably in need of long-term funds to expand their operations, the original shareholders are often reluctant to finance these needs through a public equity offering, as this would result in a dilution of their ownership of the enterprise. Once its financial condition is rendered more transparent, the use of the bond market by the companies as an alternative to equity finance should provide a viable source of medium- and long-term funds, while allowing the original shareholders to maintain their equity stakes.

The Egyptian bond market is relatively the most advanced among its neighbouring countries, with 30 corporate bonds outstanding by the end of 2000, worth around EGP4.8 billion ($1.4 billion) (table 4.3). Hoechst Orient was the first market entrant with an issue of EGP30 million ($8.7 million) in May 1994, and Victoria United Hotels Company followed suit in April 1995 with an issue of EGP21 million ($6.2 million) in seven-year bonds. In light of these successful issues, commercial banks appetite for medium-term bond financing has grown, with 16 banks so far issuing a total of EGP3.08 billion ($895 million) in bonds in the Egyptian market. The last few market issues were those of Orascom Construction Industries (OCI), raising EGP280 million ($81 million) in February 1999, LAKAH Group, raising EGP400 million ($116 million) also in February 1999, the Commercial International Bank, raising EGP300 million ($87 million) in May 1999, Egyptian Company for Mobile Services, raising EGP340 million ($99 million) in October 1999, and Orascom Projects & Tourism Development, raising EGP100 million ($29 million)in January 2000.

The Jordanian corporate sector tapped the local fixed-income market in May 1998 with a JD3.5 million ($4.93 million) issue by the International Tobacco and Cigarettes Company. This was followed by Jordan Cement Factories Company with a JD10 million ($14.1 million) five-year bond in June 1998, while the International Industrial, Commercial and Tourist Investment Company issued a JD7 million ($9.9 million) bond in October 1999. Furthermore, Union Chemicals for Vegetables and Oil Industries issued a small JD3.5 million ($4.9 million) convertible bond in March 1999. The banking sector made a debut in the JD corporate bond market with a JD10 million ($14.1 million) move by Cairo Amman Bank in September 1999. Zara Investment Company came to the market in December 1999, with a JD10 million ($14.1 million) bond that has a five-year maturity and a ten per cent coupon rate.

Four corporate bonds were issued in 2000. The Jordan Hotels and Tourism Company issued a seven-year bond worth JD10 million ($14.1 million) in June 2000. In July 2000, a five-year bond for the Middle East Complex for Engineering Electronics and Heavy Industry worth JD5 million ($3.54 million) was issued, followed by Citibank Amman, which issued in September 2000 a JD5 million ($7.05 million) bond with a three-year maturity and a coupon rate of 7.5 per cent, the lowest so far in the JD corporate bond market. Several corporate bonds were in the pipeline in 2001.

Kuwait's corporate bond market is among the most advanced in the region. The primary market started in 1968 with the first issue placed in favour of the World Bank. Secondary market activities emerged in 1977, and in September 1985 KD bonds were allowed to be traded on the Kuwait Stock Exchange and were open to both Kuwaiti and other nationals, resident and non-resident. The KD bonds were also listed and traded for some time on the London and Luxembourg stock exchanges. During the period 1968–79, more than 60 bonds worth a total of KD400 million ($1.34 billion) were issued. Since then market activities have been slow, mostly involving local borrowers.

In the two years following the Gulf War, Kuwait's bond market became dormant because of lack of buyer interest. Activity revived gradually after December 1992 with a small bond issue by the Commercial Facilities Company. The company made a second draw on the bond market with a larger issue in December 1997, and Kuwait Real Estate Bank subsequently raised over KD55 million ($181 million) from bonds issued in 1993, 1994 and 1999. Moreover, the Kuwait Investment Projects Company and the National Investment Company both offered smaller-sized issues for KD12 million ($39 million) and KD8.25 million ($27.2 million) respectively in 1994 and 1996. The National Industries group issued bonds worth KD35 million ($115 million) in February 1999, followed in September 1999 by a KD20 million ($65 million) three-year bond issued by the Kuwait Real Estate Bank.

Lebanon's experience with the corporate bond market has been limited to foreign-currency issues, with the banking sector accounting for over 92 per cent of the total. Banque Audi made a debut in November 1996 with a $100 million Eurodollar note offer, and other commercial banks followed suit with subsequent issues worth $840 million. The $85 million issue by Societé des Ciments Libanais is the only non-banking outstanding bond in the market.

The Moroccan market started to develop in August 1996, following the government's decision to revoke its guarantee from former state-owned entities. Credit Immobilier Hotel (CIH) issued three dinar-denominated bonds in 1997 and 1998, followed by Credor, Taslif, Banque Nationale de Developement Economique, Sofac, Wafasalaf, Union Bail, Banque Marocainc du Commerce Internationale, Maroc Leasing and Credor among others for a total of MD3627 million ($373 million).

Bahrain made its debut local-currency issue in July 1994, with Bahrain Commercial Facilities Company selling bonds worth BD7 million ($18.5 million) to the public, followed by Aluminum Bahrain with bonds worth BD100 million ($260 million) and Bahrain International Bank, which issued bonds worth BD120 million ($312 million). Qatar broke new ground in December 1996 with a $1.2 billion eurobond issue by Ras Laffan Liquefied Natural Gas Company (Rasgas), in order to finance a large-scale liquefied natural gas project.

The UAE was the latest to start a corporate bond market in the region, with a AED350 million ($95 million) three-year bond issued by the National Bank of Abu Dhabi (NBAD) in favour of BMW US Capital Corporation, and became listed on the UAE stock market. NBAD launched its second AED-denomination bond for an international company on 5 June 2000 for Britain's Abbey National bank. The AED400 million ($108.9 million), five-year bond carries an interest rate of 45bps over three-month Libor, and was available in tranches of AED25,000 ($6806). The offer was open to both UAE nationals and expatriates with residence permits.

## THE SOVEREIGN ARAB EUROBONDS

Only six Arab governments have so far resorted to borrowing in the international bond market: the total amount of issues outstanding by end of 2001 was close to $11 billion, with Lebanon accounting for approximately half of that. Besides Lebanon, Tunisia has been a regular issuer in the international bond market and has been the only Arab country to issue bonds denominated in Yen in the Samurai bond market. Only Lebanon and Egypt tapped the eurobond market in 2001, with issues exceeding $4.3 billion, and Morocco is expected to come to the market in early 2002.

The Lebanese government issued $2.17 billion in international bonds in 2001, including a $1150 million bond in April and a $750 million bond in August. These were largely taken up by domestic banks, who also participated in a 300-million-euro reopening in October. These bonds were issued at a relatively low spread over US treasuries, despite growing concerns about the sustainability of the country's fiscal position. Egypt made its first eurobond issue in the international market on 29 June 2001. The issue raised a total $1500 million, in two tranches, and was three times higher than was initially forecast. The larger portion was a $1000 million facility with a maturity of 10 years, priced at 335 basis points over US treasuries. The coupon is 8.75 per cent. The other tranche was for $500 million with a maturity of five years, priced at 275 basis points and carrying a coupon of 7.625%.

Table 4.4
Sovereign Arab eurobonds (selected outstanding issues)

| Issuer | Issue Date | Amount | Maturity | Coupon (percentage) |
|---|---|---|---|---|
| Lebanon | Apr.. 2001 | $1,150 million | 5 years | 9.875 |
| Lebanon | Aug. 2001 | $750 million | 5 years | 10.125 |
| Lebanon | Oct. 2001 | eur300 million | 5 years | 8.875 |
| Egypt | Jul. 2001 | $500 million | 5 years | 7.625 |
| Egypt | Jul. 2001 | $1500 million | 10 years | 8.750 |
| Qatar | June 2000 | $1400 million | 30 years | 9.500 |
| Lebanon | June 2000 | $500 million | 5 years | 9.375 |
| Tunisia | Jul. 99 | eur225 million | 10 years | 7.500 |
| Qatar | May 99 | $1000 million | 10 years | 9.500 |
| Morocco | Mar. 99 | eur138.7 million | 5 years | 3.950 |
| Lebanon | Feb. 99 | eur300 million | 5 years | 7.250 |
| Lebanon | Sep. 99 | $450 million | 7 years | 8.750 |
| Lebanon | Mar. 98 | $500 million | 5 years | 8.625 |
| Lebanon | Mar. 98 | $500 million | 3 years | 8.125 |
| Lebanon | Oct. 97 | $400 million | 10 years | 8.625 |
| Oman | Mar. 97 | $225 million | 5 years | 7.125 |
| Tunisia | Sep. 96 | ¥15,000 million | 15 years | 4.950 |

Spreads on Arab sovereign bonds widened markedly in the wake of the attack in the US on 11 September 2001. For example spreads on Egyptian bonds rose by almost 1.5 per cent, to trade at about 500 basis points over treasuries. Higher spreads were also seen on sovereign bonds in Qatar, Oman and Morocco. The events of 11 September, which have significantly increased risk aversion, have resulted in a period where there have been little or no bond issuance. At least two bond issues from the Arab region that had been queuing up to come to market were put on hold following the attacks on the US, Morocco's 400–500-million-euro ($367–458 million) sovereign issue, and the $300 million debut corporate eurobond to be issued out of the GCC by the National Bank of Kuwait.

Bond issuance from the Arab region will undoubtedly resume in 2002. With interest rates falling in the US and Europe, managers of bond portfolios and mutual funds will be looking for higher yields, mainly in the emerging bond markets. Bonds issued by credit worthy sovereign Arab borrowers, such as Egypt, Qatar, Tunisia, Oman, and Morocco, will be in demand. Investors in these bonds will be rewarded with higher prices (capital gain), on top of the high interest coupon that these bonds pay. Existing eurobonds issues from the Arab region (with the exception of Lebanon) are considered to be an asset class that merits an added exposure in 2002.

## DEVELOPING THE REGION'S BOND MARKETS

The viability of domestic borrowing through the issuance of public-debt instruments in various Arab countries has already been tested; developing the markets for these instruments will follow in the future. It should therefore be possible to increase the volume of various government bonds and bills issued, fine-tune their flow into the primary and secondary markets, and refine their prices. Governments in the region should be able to sell their debt issues not only within their own domestic markets but also in other Arab countries. A developed government bond market would eventually give birth to a corporate bond market, interest futures market and, when large enough, to an interest rate options market.

As the region's financial markets gain depth, national and regional development institutions which require long-term funding (Arab Fund, Kuwait Fund, Arab Monetary Fund, agricultural and industrial development banks) as well as corporations and commercial banks, may be encouraged to issue their own debt instruments, now that a benchmark on pricing has been established by government bonds. However, governments and institutions need to be rated to become part of the global standard.

There are few Arab financial institutions with sufficient expertise to price, underwrite and sell a corporate bond issue, while the legal mechanism whereby bonds can be listed on the local stock exchanges is sometimes unclear. The secondary bond market also needs to be supported by an institutional infrastructure that includes efficient clearing and settlement arrangements and the presence of active market-makers. Without clear-cut arrangements, traders run many risks, such as those created by the unreliability of counterparties, fraud and multiple trades of the same securities.

The region needs creative financial institutions which can meet the changing financial requirements of the Arab countries, be it project finance, build, operate and transfer (BOT), floating-rate notes or any other form of fixed-rate financing. Investment-banking services are also needed, including strong financial analysis, underwriting of bond issues, floating of these bonds to the public-at-large and making markets of these issues.

Institutional investors hold the bulk of the bonds outstanding in the Arab region, especially those issued by governments. Bond-holdings by individuals are negligible. Institutional holders are 'buy and hold' investors whose main objective is to avoid or minimize mismatches in the maturities of their assets and liabilities. This suggests that there will be little incentive for secondary-market trading in bonds. Other factors – such as the lack of market-makers with access to liquidity support – also restrict bond-market development. Bond dealers run highly leveraged operations, and their inventories usually represent a certain multiple of their capital bases. Dealers can be market-makers only if they are able to obtain liquidity through the repurchase market.

In view of the globalization of markets and the liberalization of rules regarding financial transactions, the legal regulatory framework of the Arab countries should be in line with the rest of the world, and standards of accounting and disclosure should be raised to international levels. This is an important issue, because Arab financial markets and institutions will now have to compete more intensively with the more advanced international financial markets. The primary responsibility for regulating bond markets still lies with the central banks. Shifting this responsibility to newly created securities and exchange commissions (as is the case in Jordan and Egypt) will also contribute to the process of financial deepening in the region.

A key element for the development of Arab bond markets is to ensure that bonds are issued and traded at market rates and are not discriminated against by government policies or the legal system. To accomplish this, a number of steps need to be taken. There must be a requirement that all bonds be listed on the stock exchange to assure transparency of the debt markets. Listing on the stock exchange is often seen as a requirement for widening the investors' base and enhancing the accessibility of bonds, particularly when institutional investors are prohibited from holding unlisted securities. There must be a reconsideration of bankruptcy laws that discourage creditors and make bonds costlier than equity. By assuring bondholders that they will get some of their money back if the issuing company goes bankrupt, governments can contribute to the deepening of the region's debt markets. Taxes should not distort companies' choice between debt and equity. For example, in certain countries companies pay a lower corporate tax rate if enough of their shares are publicly traded, and there is an informal ceiling imposed on debt to equity ratios. Regulations that put in place elaborate and long-drawn-out issuing procedures for bonds should be abolished.

## CONCLUSION

The projected rapid growth of the region's bond markets is contingent upon the continuation of sound macroeconomic management and institutional reform. Most of the Arab countries have undertaken comprehensive policy reforms during the past decade that have laid the infrastructure for deepening financial markets, introducing new financial instruments, and establishing a modern legal framework. However, more reforms need to be carried out, particularly concerning regulatory authorities and institution-building, as well as upgrading the level of disclosure and financial transparency.

There is a growing trading culture in the region, illustrated by the rising number of individual investors in selective equities. The challenge is to transfer the same processes to the bond market, where trading bonds rather than holding them to maturity becomes commonplace. Putting in place the right infrastructure is equally important. Bond markets rely even more than equity markets on strong corporate governance, transparency and full disclosure, a viable legal system, contract enforcement, international accounting standards and active market participants. Bond markets will both promote the general development of the countries of the region and reflect this development.

# 5

# ARAB STOCK MARKETS: FACING UP TO NEW CHALLENGES

## INTRODUCTION

All over the world, investors want to buy new economy shares in technology, Internet, communications, media and information-related companies, since they have high growth prospects. There are few technology and telecommunications companies listed in the Arab stock markets. Old economy shares, such as those in financial institutions, utilities and property, constitute the bulk of the region's total stock-market capitalization. As has happened elsewhere, these markets have suffered from the rush to buy new economy shares; the few large increases in 1999 and 2000 were recorded by telecommunications companies such as Mobinil in Egypt and the Palestinian Telecommunication Company (Paltel).

The region lacks venture capital and IPO markets that are instrumental in the creation of innovative companies. A major obstacle facing start-up companies in the region is shortage of venture capital. According to Harvard Business School, a dollar of venture capital produces three to five times more patents than a dollar of R&D. The number of start-up companies in Korea doubled in 1999 to 4700, and the market capitalization for Korea's Kosdaq market increased 13 times to $100 billion by the end of 2000. It is very difficult for innovative companies in the Arab region to bypass traditionally cautious commercial bankers and go straight to investors through IPOs. Without an exit mechanism, investors will not put their money in venture-capital funds targeting new economy companies.

The start-up culture of tireless, low-paid work for a vague promise of future riches is still alien to today's Arab youth. The incentives for entrepreneurs to create innovative companies are not there. Invariably the laws governing joint-stock companies in the region do not allow the distribution of share options, nor do they recognize the significance of 'sweat capital' to young entrepreneurs.

Individual investors worldwide hooked on the thrill of online trading through the Internet have led the charge into technology shares in most countries. Arab stock markets have so far attracted a tiny fraction of this flow, and these markets are in general passed over by international investors. Factors explaining this include stock-market information unavailable online, barriers to foreign ownership, weak performance, lack of liquidity, poor reporting standards, absence of big firms, the shares of which tend to be more liquid, and underdeveloped corporate governance.

While Arab stock markets have come a long way in the past few years, the rest of the world has moved at a much faster rate. The positive steps taken in 1999–2001 to enhance accessibility and transparency, modernize and up-grade trading facilities and improve reporting and disclosure standards, will greatly enhance the status of Arab stock markets among the global investment community.

Any advances in the Middle East peace process would go a long way towards improving investors' confidence in the region's stock markets. Furthermore, these markets are trading on attractive valuation, with continued low correlation to other emerging stock markets, as well as to developed markets. The inclusion in 2001 of Egypt in the MSCI Emerging Markets Index should help boost international capital flow to that market. The burst of the technology 'bubble' and a more subdued performance of the US stock market in 2000 and 2001 have encouraged international portfolios to look elsewhere for growth and value. Being exposed to the Middle East stock markets – which are not correlated to other major stock markets – is an important part of that process.

## STRUCTURE OF ARAB STOCK MARKETS

By emerging market standards, Arab stock markets are small, accounting for 6.5 per cent of the total market capitalization of the 38 emerging markets in Asia, Latin America, Africa and Eastern Europe and for 0.6 per cent of the world's total stock-market capitalization of $32,000 billion in 2000. This is despite the fact that the region contains some of the developing countries' largest investors in international financial markets. Total capitalization of the 12 Arab stock markets stood at $154 billion at the end of 2000, with the Saudi stock market, the largest in the region, accounting for around 40 per cent of the total (figure 5.1). By comparison, in the US at the end of 2000 total capitalization of Citigroup was $187 billion, AOL was $168 billion and Microsoft was $600 billion. The Israeli stock market, with 670 companies listed, had a total capitalization of $75 billion. There are also 78 Israeli companies listed on NASDAQ, collectively valued at $70 billion.

Some 60 per cent of the capitalization of the Arab stock markets are accounted for by banking, investment, insurance and property firms, compared to 24 per cent in the 38 emerging markets. Less than 15 per cent of market capitalization is in manufacturing, compared to an average of 36 per cent in the other emerging markets. Governments are still among the largest shareholders in the region's stock markets, estimated at around 40 per cent of total capitalization. If this is taken out, the free float left would be around $110 billion. Of this, more than 30 per cent is held by families and strategic investors seeking control and board representation who are unlikely to trade their holdings. If those Arab stock markets that do not allow foreign shareholding are also removed, this would leave only a fraction of Middle East stock-market capitalization that could be considered by global investors. While Arab stock markets have become increasingly liquid in the past ten years, the value of shares traded as a percentage of total market capitalization still remains low, indicating good growth potential. Turnover ratio – value of shares traded as a percentage of market capitalization – did not exceed an average of 20 per cent for Arab stock markets in 2000, compared to an average of 88 per cent for all emerging markets (figure 5.2, table 5.2).

Figure 5.1
Arab countries' share of total stock market capitalization, 2000

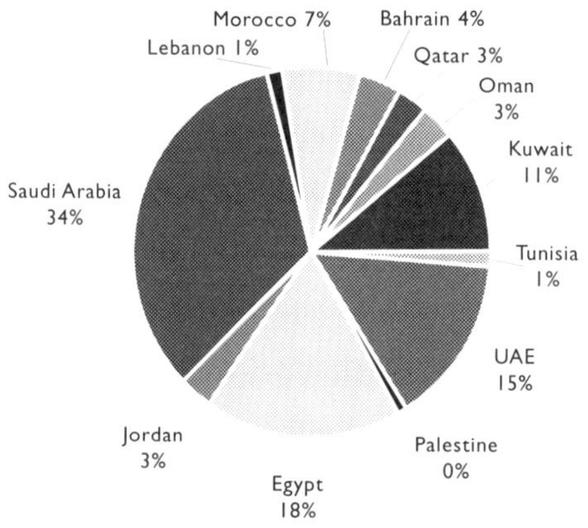


Table 5.1
Market capitalization of Arab stock markets

| Arab stock market | Market capitalization 1999 ($ million) | Market capitalization 2000 ($ million) | Market capitalization as percentage of GDP (1999) |
|---|---|---|---|
| Saudi Arabia | 60,853 | 63,434 | 43.6 |
| Egypt | 32,838 | 9178 | 37.0 |
| UAE | 27,000 | 24,950 | 52.2 |
| Kuwait | 20,320 | 17,035 | 63.1 |
| Morocco | 13,695 | 13,077 | 36.0 |
| Bahrain | 7155 | 6537 | 107.2 |
| Oman | 5897 | 3504 | 37.8 |
| Jordan | 5833 | 4343 | 76.7 |
| Qatar | 5488 | 4994 | 53.2 |
| Tunisia | 2710 | 3161 | 12.1 |
| Lebanon | 1920 | 2451 | 11.3 |
| Palestine | 849 | 943 | 19.9 |
| **Total** | **184,558** | **153,607** | **45.8** |

Figure 5.2
Arab stock-market liquidity

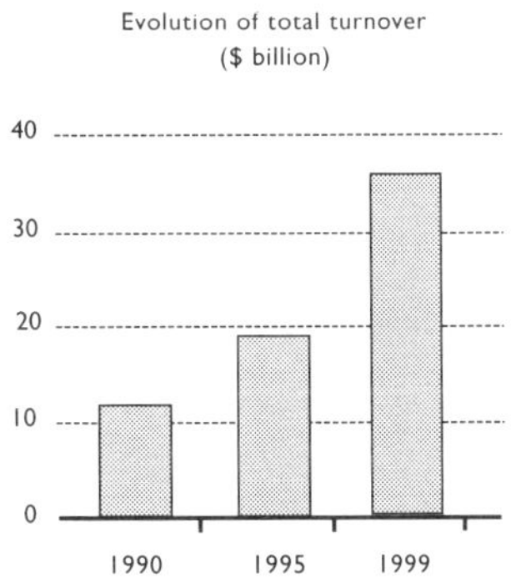


Table 5.2
Arab stock-market liquidity

| Arab stock markets | Value traded 2000 ($ million) | Turnover as percentage of market capitalization |
|---|---|---|
| Saudi Arabia | 15,100 | 24.8 |
| Egypt | 9702 | 29.6 |
| Kuwait | 6037 | 29.7 |
| Morocco | 4173 | 30.5 |
| Oman | 1201 | 20.4 |
| Jordan | 549 | 9.4 |
| Bahrain | 443 | 6.2 |
| Tunisia | 436 | 16.1 |
| Palestine | 150 | 17.7 |
| Lebanon | 91 | 4.7 |
| **Total** | **37,882** | **20.1** |
| Greece | 188,722 | 131.0 |
| Korea | 733,950 | 356.0 |
| Turkey | 81,277 | 103.0 |
| **Emerging markets** | **1,041,831** | **88.0** |

Growth potential of Arab stock markets can also be assessed by looking at market capitalization as a percentage of GDP. With the exception of the Bahrain stock market, where some Kuwaiti companies and the large regional offshore banks are listed (Arab Banking Corporation, Gulf International Bank, Investcorp, Arig etc) stock-market capitalization as a percentage of GDP is low, at an average of 46 per cent in 2000, compared to an average of 60 per cent for the emerging markets as a whole and as high as 166 per cent for Greece, 96 per cent for Korea and 95 per cent for Chile.

Middle East stock markets were found to be properly valued by the end of 2000, with an average price-to-earning (P/E) ratio of 17.4, price-to-book-value

(P/BV) of 2.4 and dividend-yield of 3 per cent. This compares favourably with Latin America, Eastern Europe and all emerging markets (table 5.1).

Table 5.3
Valuation of Middle East stock markets in comparison with other regional stock markets: 2000

| | P/E | P/BV | Dividend yield (percentage) |
|---|---|---|---|
| **Middle East** | **17.4** | **2.4** | 3.0 |
| Latin America | 19.7 | 1.7 | 2.5 |
| Eastern Europe | 44.1 | 5.1 | 1.2 |
| China | 54.0 | 2.5 | 0.7 |
| **All emerging markets** | **56.3** | **2.4** | **1.3** |

*Source: Standard & Poor's,* Emerging Stock Market Review *January 2001, other national sources*

## PERFORMANCE OF ARAB STOCK MARKETS

The performance of Arab stock markets between 1999 and 2001 was mixed: some markets benefited from higher oil prices and return of investors' confidence to emerging markets, while others were held back by low levels of economic growth and delays in reform and privatization.

Most of the 12 Arab stock markets performed poorly in 2000, with only Tunisian and Saudi shares ending the year with gains. Egypt recorded the worst performance with a 38 per cent decline, followed by Jordan, which was down 20.5 per cent. In 2001, Qatar, Jordan, the UAE and Kuwait recorded the best performances, while most of the rest ended the year in negative territories.

Despite higher oil prices, the Gulf stock markets, with the exception of Saudi Arabia, turned in a disappointing performance in 1999 and 2000. The majority of governments in the Gulf kept a tight rein on spending, which limited the impact of higher oil revenues on the private sector. This kept confidence in the stock markets low. Moreover, the Palestinian *Intifada* and escalating regional tension over the last three months of 2000 and throughout 2001 cast a shadow on stock markets in the region. In general, lack of transparency, poor information flow, the absence of large capitalized companies, and the slow uptake of privatization all added to the negative performance of the region's stock markets in 2000.

The best performance among the Arab stock markets in 1999 and 2000 was in Tunisia, where stocks rose by an impressive 30 per cent (Tunindex) in 1999 and 21 per cent in 2000. This followed a meagre 1 per cent increase in 1998 and a 21.6 per cent decline in 1997. Robust economic growth, declining interest rates, good corporate earnings, tax incentives for enlistment of firms and buoyancy in the industrial sector all contributed to the strong performance of Tunisian stocks. A correction was recorded in 2001, with the market index closing the year down 11 per cent.

Figure 5.3
Performance of Arab stock markets, 1999–2001

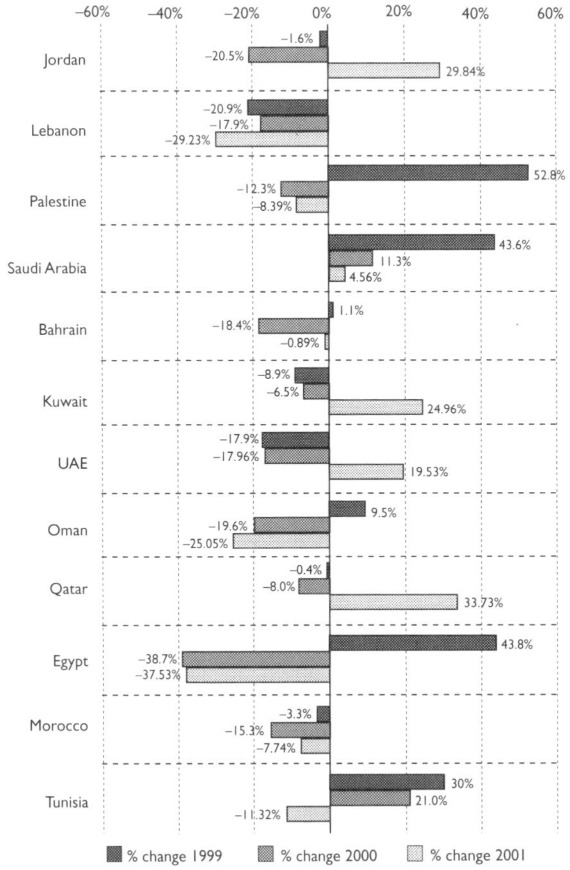


The Palestine Stock Exchange, which recorded the best performance among Arab stock markets in 1999 (the Jerusalem index was up 52.8 per cent), lost ground in 2000 and 2001, with the index down 12.3 per cent and 8.4 per cent respectively. This followed increases of 11.5 per cent and 39 per cent in 1998 and 1997 respectively.

The Cairo and Alexandria Stock Exchanges (CASE) put on almost 44 per cent in 1999 – an impressive performance. This helped the market recover the ground it had lost in 1998 (when it fell by 25 per cent) and ranked it among the region's best performances. The blue-chip stock, the Egyptian Company for Mobile Service (Mobinil), had risen by 679 per cent by the end of the year, giving a big boost to the market index. Egyptian stocks failed to maintain their strong performance in 2000, with equity prices down 38 per cent, recording the worst performance among Arab stock markets. Disenchanted investors have remained wary of the tight liquidity conditions prevailing in Egypt, and signs of improving domestic conditions in the last few months of the year failed to lift the stock exchange. In 2001, the market continued its downward trend, recording a 38 per cent loss. Bad performance of the telecom companies, macroeconomic concerns, instability in the Egyptian pound exchange rate, Moody's decision to lower its outlook on the Baa1 rating of local currency bonds from stable to negative and the impact of the attacks of 11 September on the US have all been dampening factors.

The Saudi stock market, the largest in the Arab world, recorded gains of 43.6 per cent in 1999, following a 28 per cent decline in 1998 and a 28 per cent rise in 1997. This was Saudi Stock Exchange's second-best annual performance since it was founded in 1985, following the 83 per cent rise recorded in 1991. Most of the increase was in the third and fourth quarters (13.7 per cent and 21 per cent respectively), as the upward trend in oil prices boosted the potential of the economy. Furthermore, stocks were driven higher following the announcement by the Saudi government to allow foreign investors to own shares in the Saudi market through mutual funds. The Saudi Stock Exchange posted the best performance among GCC stock markets in 2000, rising 11.3 per cent, spurred on by higher oil prices and government expenditure, the new foreign-investment law and much-improved budget and external balances. The market rose to 14.4 per cent in August 2001, but ended the year up only 4.6 per cent, due to the 11 September attack on the US and the subsequent drop in oil prices.

Oman's economy rose 9.5 per cent in 1999, after showing the worst performance in the region in the previous year, having fallen by 54 per cent. Most of the increase in 1999 was recorded in the second and third quarters, but share prices slipped lower in the months of October and November due to concerns over poor liquidity in the banking sector and weak corporate results. The Muscat Securities Market maintained its strong downward trend in 2000, losing 19.6 per cent on the year. Tight liquidity conditions and a bearish view among investors on the earning potential of listed firms kept the market index hovering near four-year lows, despite several measures by the market authorities aimed at improving transparency and confining insider trading. In 2001, the market continued its strong downward trend losing another 25.1 per cent, as disappointing bank results due to bad restrictions dragged the market down. In addition, the impact of the attack on the US left the market suffering from a severe liquidity crunch.

The Bahrain Stock Exchange ended 1999 up by a modest 1.1 per cent, as investors' confidence was depressed by tight fiscal policy and the rapid decline of the Kuwait Stock Exchange, where some key Bahraini stocks are dually listed. To attract foreign capital, the government relaxed ownership structure within the stock exchange as of March 1999. The new legislation allowed Arab GCC investors to own up to 100 per cent of listed Bahraini companies, and Arab non-GCC investors to own up to 49 per cent. Previously, GCC investors had been permitted to hold up to 49 per cent in most listed companies, and non-GCC investors had been limited to just 24 per cent. Despite the recent liberalization, foreign investment (non-GCC) in Bahraini equities remained low, accounting for only 7.95 per cent of total turnover in 1999. The Bahrain Stock Exchange remained hostage to the liquidity crunch in the market, with the index ending down 18.4 per cent in 2000. The market was doing well in 2001, rising by 3 per cent up to 11 September due to good corporate results and low share prices and low interest rates, but ended the year down 1 per cent.

Kuwait's stock market dropped by 8.9 per cent in 1999, after recording a 41 per cent decline in 1998 and a 40 per cent rise in 1997. The market reached a 42-month low in November 1999, instigated by the decision to liquidate the Kuwait International Investment Company and hampered by political worries and poor corporate results. In 2000, Kuwait's stock-market index dropped 6.5 per cent, due to political unrest and the government's failure to implement much-promised economic and market reforms. In the first eight months of 2001, the market surged by 34 per cent, mainly due to high oil prices and low interest rates. It slipped lower after 11 September to close the year up 25 per cent.

The over-the-counter UAE stock market remained feeble in 1999, falling 17.9 per cent, its worst performance ever, following increases of 9 per cent in 1998 and 32 per cent in 1997. The establishment of both official stock exchanges in Dubai and Abu Dhabi during 2000 failed to improve investors' confidence, with the National Bank of Abu Dhabi (NBAD) index registering losses of 18.7 per cent. The UAE's second trading floor, the Abu Dhabi Securities Market (ADSM) started formal trading in November 2000. Trading commenced with 12 firms listed on the market, none of which were listed on the Dubai Financial Market, and with a total market capitalization of AED12.7 billion ($3.45 billion). The listed companies include three banks, three insurance firms and six from the services sector. In 2001, the market rose 20 per cent. Good performance was mainly due to interest rates cuts, linkage between the UAE's two stock markets and the high demand for banking and telecom sector shares.

Qatar, the best performer amongst the Arab markets in 1998, recording gains of 34.4 per cent, ended 1999 with a marginal loss of 0.4 per cent, restricted by the lack of liquidity and depth in the market. The Doha Securities Market continued its lack-lustre performance into 2000, ending the year down 8 per cent. Better-than-expected results for the partly-privatized Qatar Telecom, and the opening of the stock market to non-Qatari investors through mutual funds, reflected positively on the market in 2001, with the index ending the year up 34 per cent, the best performing market among the Arab stock markets for that year.

The Beirut Stock Exchange recorded the worst performance among the Arab markets in 1999, dropping by 20.9 per cent, after a 32 per cent decline in 1998. The market was hampered by low trading turnover, amounting to $90.5 million in 1999, only 27 per cent of its level the year before. The BLOM index fell by a further 17.9 per cent in 2000, with weak economic performance, political uncertainty and continuing market illiquidity dampening investors' confidence. Solidere's 'A' shares fell 22 per cent to close at $6.625, while the company's 'B' shares lost 12 per cent to close at $7.375. The change of government in November 2000 failed to boost share prices, as investors preferred to wait and see how the new government would tackle the country's widening deficit and large public debt. In 2001, the market continued its downward trend, falling 29.2 per cent and recording the second worst performance among Arab markets after Egypt. Investor confidence was low due to the huge public debt exceeding 155 per cent of GDP, the slow progress on privatization, and Solidere's woes of postponed reconstruction activities.

The Casablanca Stock Exchange declined by 3.3 per cent in 1999, after climbing 20 per cent in 1998 and 48 per cent in 1997. The fall was attributed mainly to retail selling-spree pressure and institutional investors switching their holdings to fixed-income instruments, since the market continued to lack the ingredients to reverse the ongoing sluggish trend and attract dwindling local and foreign institutional investors. The market was further undermined by weak economic growth of 0.2 per cent in 1999, due to the drought and disappointing corporate results. In 2000, Moroccan stocks fell 15.3 per cent after another bad year of rain and a falling euro, leading to slow economic growth. In 2001, the drop in share prices was around 8 per cent. The stagnant market was waiting for the implementation of promised economic reforms in early 2002.

The Amman Stock Exchange also had a weak year in 1999, recording a fall of 1.6 per cent following a 0.5 per cent rise in 1998, due to economic stagnation and a dearth of foreign and institutional interest. Foreign investment in the Amman stock market in 1999 was approximately 44 per cent of total market capitalization, unchanged from 1998. Jordanian equities continued to slide throughout 2000, recording losses of 20.5 per cent. The market suffered from weak corporate results, lack of interest on the part of foreign and institutional investors, and the market's proximity to the violence in the Palestinian territories in the last quarter of the year. In 2001, the market rose 30 per cent, recording the second-best performance in the Arab region after Qatar. Profits were mainly due to the interest rate cuts, the heavy demand on industrial blue-chip companies stocks and the heavy weight Arab bank stocks, all of which helped the index to break 175-point mark for the first time in three years.

## RETURN OF CONFIDENCE TO EMERGING MARKETS

According to the IIF, private capital flows rose by almost $45 billion to about $188 billion in 2000 and to reach $212 billion in 2001, an increase of over 30 per cent in 2000 and 13 per cent in 2001, following modest growth of 1.2 per cent in 1999 and the sharp 47 per cent drop in 1998 (figure 5.4). Private flows have improved across all regions, with the most impressive improvement witnessed in the Asia–Pacific region, where net private flows doubled to $61.9 billion in 2000 and grew further to $76.1 billion in 2001, exceeding their pre-crisis level.

Figure 5.4
Net private capital flows to emerging markets

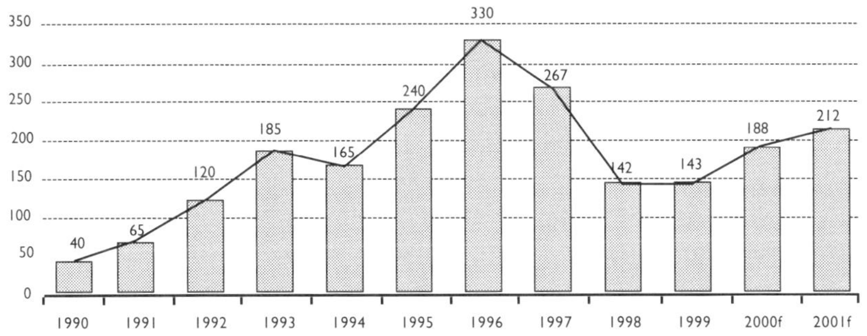


*Source: IIF*

The main improvement in emerging market capital flows is derived from the significant turnaround in net flows from private creditors (commercial banks and issuance of bonds), which rose to $26 billion in 2000, after a deficit of $17 billion in 1999. While overall non-bank private lending (bonds) remained stable at $29.4 billion, the major change in the private creditor sector relates to flows from commercial banks. Net withdrawals were substantial in 1998 (–$54.7 billion) and 1999 (–$46.7 billion), but only a slight deficit was recorded in 2000 (–$3.4 billion) and a net positive volume of over $16 billion is expected in 2001. Net commercial bank lending to emerging markets is likely to account for 8 per cent of total private capital flows in 2001, compared to 67 per cent in the early 1980s.

With regard to equity investments, the substantial increase in portfolio investment to $37.6 billion in 2000 from $17.8 billion in 1999 was almost entirely offset by a decline in direct investment to $124.2 billion, leaving net equity investment in 2000 only marginally higher on its 1999 level of $161.8 billion. In 2001, net equity investment is projected to moderate to $159.3 billion, due to an expected decline in portfolio equity flows as a result of lower international listings.

The Arab countries attracted around $11.6 billion in private capital flows in 2000, a rise of 22 per cent on the previous year's level, and further to $13.1 billion in 2001 (table 5.4). However, the share of the Arab world in total emerging-market capital inflows declined to 6 per cent in 2000, down from 6.4 per cent in 1999 and a high of 7.63 per cent in 1998.

In 2000, net equity investment in the Arab region (including direct and portfolio investment) rose to $9.5 billion, an increase of 13 per cent, from $8.4 billion in 1999. FDI in the Arab countries increased by 5 per cent in 2000 to $9 billion, with $5 billion going to Saudi Arabia and $1 billion to Egypt. However, FDI flows to the Arab world still constitute a small share of the global total at 7.2 per cent. Recent initiatives by several Gulf countries to open up their energy sectors to foreign participation, economic reform and liberalization policies across the region, and a stronger privatization drive in some Arab countries will help boost the Arab world's share of global FDI flows over the coming few years. FDI flows to the Arab region rose by a further 11 per cent to $10 billion in 2001.

Table 5.4
Private financial flows to Arab countries ($ billion)

| | 1997 | 1998 | 1999 | 2000 | 2001 |
|---|---|---|---|---|---|
| Total private flows to emerging economies (net) | 267.3 | 141.6 | 143.3 | 187.9 | 212.1 |
| Arab countries (net) | 9.7 | 10.8 | 9.2 | 11.6 | 13.1 |
| Equity investment (net) | 7.6 | 8.1 | 8.4 | 9.5 | 10.8 |
| Direct equity | 6.2 | 7.3 | 8.6 | 9.0 | 10.0 |
| Portfolio equity | 1.4 | 0.8 | –0.2 | 0.5 | 0.8 |
| Private creditors (net) | 2.1 | 2.7 | 0.8 | 2.1 | 2.3 |
| Banks (net) | 0.3 | 0.5 | –0.7 | 0.3 | 0.4 |
| Bonds (net) | 1.8 | 2.2 | 1.5 | 1.8 | 1.9 |

*Source: IIF and World Bank*

In line with global trends, net private credit flows (including bank loans and bond issuance) to the Arab countries improved from $800 million in 1999 to about $2.1 billion in 2000. Bank credits to the region in 2000 reached $300 million, after a net credit outflow of $0.7 billion in 1999. On the other hand, bond issuance in the international market by Arab governments and corporates increased to $1.8 billion in 2000, up from $1.5 billion in 1999 and $2.2 billion in 1998. Most of the bonds issued in 2000 came from Lebanon at a net increase of $1 billion, Qatar at $400 million and Tunisia, which raised ¥50 billion ($450 million) in the Japanese market.

## BARRIERS AND CONSTRAINTS HINDERING GROWTH OF THE ARAB STOCK MARKETS

The region's stock markets are in most cases still underdeveloped, and as such are not able to offer companies good alternative financing possibilities or to channel foreign portfolio capital into the private sector. The closed, family-owned nature of many companies in the region and the dominant role that the public sector continues to play in several countries has reduced the number of effectively quoted companies, and the markets have in general remained thin and illiquid.

The number of active investors in the region constitutes a small percentage of the total adult population, on average less than 2 per cent, compared to 50 per cent in the US. Yet experience elsewhere shows how stock markets can easily come to life within a relatively short period of time (e.g. Turkey, Indonesia and Argentina) if the economic conditions are right and the necessary legislation is put in place.

Unlike capital markets elsewhere, issuers of shares in the region tend to be the older companies, established in key sectors of the economy (e.g. banking, property, consumer goods, utilities), rather than start-ups in untested or high risk or growth industries (e.g. IT, biotech). This may be explained by the shallowness of the region's capital markets and the absence of financial resources dedicated for newly formed companies. Start-ups also lack the required track record and credibility with the financial community. Besides, the initial owners, including governments, are usually reluctant to give away large stakes in their entities to the investing public. The reduced 'free float' that results from an initial public offering (IPO) inflates prices of the offered shares to the benefit of the seller, and adds to the illiquidity of the offering. If at the time of the IPO the price reflects all the future proceeds discounted to present value, then there will be no room left for capital appreciation in the post-IPO market, which could lead to the subsequent tumbling of prices of newly listed stocks.

The decline in the shares of Qatar Telecom (Q-Tel) and of Bahrain's Arab Reinsurance Group (Arig) after their IPOs are two examples. Q-Tel went public in December 1998 when the government sold 45 per cent of it. Shares were nominally priced at 10 riyals, but were sold to the public at a premium of 60 riyals, and since then, they have largely traded below this level. By the end of 2001, Arig shares were also trading below their 1998 IPO level. The weakness of the Q-Tel and Arig share prices – among others – has delayed the privatization of other public-sector companies and discouraged investment in newly privatized issues.

The lack of liquidity is the most potent factor dissuading foreign fund managers from investing their assets in many of the MENA (Middle East North Africa) markets. While the inflow of foreign investment is failing to grow significantly, high interest rates in Lebanon, Egypt, Jordan and Morocco have contributed towards diverting domestic funds away from the equity markets. However, with dollar-rates edging lower in 2002, the region's central banks will be in a position to reduce further domestic interest rates, adding liquidity to the system, and this will help support the region's stock markets.

A lack of discrimination by domestic retail investors has also contributed to the tight liquidity conditions in certain Arab stock markets, as investors have been focusing on one or two stocks at the expense of the rest of the market. This has been particularly evident in Egypt and Jordan, where trading in Mobinil and Arab Bank has dominated these two markets, regularly accounting for more than half of daily turnover and driving prices of these companies up while the rest of the market has remained weak. Furthermore, retail investors have in general been active for speculative rather than investment reasons. The authorities should review ways of encouraging retail investors to invest in mutual funds, which are normally managed in a more professional way.

Insufficient transparency and insider trading is another vulnerability. In most countries, the companies listed on the region's stock exchanges do not issue quarterly financial figures, and many of them do not release their audited annual results in a timely manner. In several Arab countries there exist weaknesses in prudential regulation and supervision of financial systems, and in the enforcement of legal actions against insider trading. A stock market which is not properly regulated becomes a speculative paradise. Insider trading still goes unchecked in certain Arab stock markets, leading to price manipulation and market inefficiencies. Furthermore, clearing and settlement arrangements are not up to the standards found elsewhere in other emerging markets.

Major international investors are able to bypass the region's markets with a relatively clear conscience, as none of them is included in the Morgan Stanley Capital International (MSCI) index, the benchmark for emerging markets. But this is changing, as Egypt was added to the index in 2001, and there is no reason why other Arab countries (such as Morocco, Oman, Jordan, Tunisia) could not legitimately be included. As more Arab stock markets are included in the MSCI index, this will help open the door to serious portfolio capital flows from abroad.

## THE RISING POTENTIAL OF ARAB STOCK MARKETS

Middle Eastern markets have emerged at a time of low investor interest and are trading on attractive valuations with continued low correlations to other emerging markets and to the developed stock markets. While this is likely to change as they become better established, investing in these markets will undoubtedly provide immediate risk diversification benefits.

There is a vicious circle that has limited the growth of the region's stock markets. International and regional investors alike are deterred by the lack of depth and liquidity of these markets, but until more money flows into the region such problems will continue. Equally, the number of funds covering the region, a crucial ingredient for attracting foreign portfolios to the stock markets, will not increase rapidly until there is more appetite for exposure to the region.

**Figure 5.5**
**Correlation of Arab stock markets with major indices, 2000**

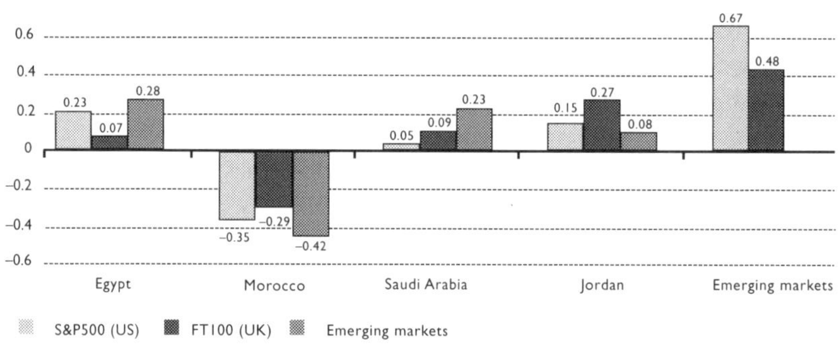

The inflow of international money will be determined by the ability of Arab markets to locate a position for themselves in the context of emerging markets. Only the most sophisticated international institutions currently see the merits of full-risk diversification. Those which do, recognize that exposure to the Middle East, which is correlated neither to other emerging markets nor to the advanced stock markets – as demonstrated in figure 5.5 – is a necessary part of that process. While the concept of full diversification is growing, it still has a long way to go before the major pension funds of the world will start looking for some investment in the Middle East. But for this to happen, returns will have to be commensurate with the risks associated with greater market immaturity.

International fund managers judge the attraction of a stock first of all on its own merits and then on the basis of both size (i.e. market capitalization) and liquidity (i.e. daily trading volume). A stock has to have more than a $50 million market capitalization and a minimum daily turnover of $1 million for it to be considered liquid and for fund managers to be able to get in and out of it quickly enough. If this rule is applied to those Arab stock markets open to foreign investors, international fund managers will withdraw completely from these markets for the time being, apart from two stocks in the Cairo Stock Exchange (Mobinil and Commercial International Bank), and one or two in the other Arab markets.

Many family-owned companies in the region are facing issues of succession and how to boost capital resources. As in other parts of the world, over time these businesses will become public companies with the founding family retaining perhaps some stake, while management is passed on to professional managers. This trend will create more companies that could be listed on the stock exchange, and will present more opportunities for investors, increase the size and liquidity of the market, as well as allowing the original family shareholders to liquidate some of their holdings.

Recent years have seen significant steps to enhance the status of Middle East markets among the global investment community. Many made substantial investments to modernize and up-grade their trading facilities. The Bahrain Stock Exchange, the Cairo and Alexandria Stock Exchanges and the Doha Securities Market have all installed additional technology to automate trading and back office operations, albeit to differing degrees. In late 2001, the Saudi authorities introduced an electronic trading system called 'tadawal', while the Amman Stock Exchange and Muscat Securities Market have already introduced electronic trading. Many stock exchanges are investing in new infrastructure, such as wide area networks, enabling brokers to trade from locations outside the exchange. Substantial investments in technology have also been made to enhance data-dissemination as the importance of online information for investors is recognized. The Internet is providing a further avenue for data-dissemination.

Such investments have been accompanied by improvements in disclosure and reporting standards, and efforts to curb insider trading. The Muscat Securities Market was restructured in 1999 and divided into three separate entities, the stock exchange, depository and regulatory bodies. The Saudi government is in the final stages of preparing a new set of capital-market regulations, including the setting up of an independent regulator. In Tunisia, new tax incentives have been announced to encourage investment in equities.

Foreign-ownership restrictions are being lifted. Bahrain threw its doors open to foreign investors in March 2000, with the passing of new legislation. Nationals of other GCC states are now permitted to own stakes of up to 100 per cent in local companies while non-GCC investors may own up to 49 per cent. The Commerce Ministry says that it may decide to extend this to 100 per cent at a later date if such a move is considered to be in the interest of the national economy.

There is a considerable rationale for investing in Arab stock markets. Arab stock markets offer good investment opportunities: attractive valuations; lower correlation and risk diversification; foreign ownership restrictions are being lifted (e.g. in Saudi Arabia); privatization programmes are being implemented; many markets are still absent from global investment portfolios; the recovery in emerging markets is looking more sustainable.

Legislation permitting non-GCC investors to participate in equity investment was also ratified in Kuwait. Foreigners are now allowed to acquire shares in companies listed on the Kuwait Stock Exchange, and to participate in the establishment of publicly listed companies through mutual funds managed by Kuwaiti financial institutions. In Saudi Arabia, the government now permits investment by non-Saudis in local shares through established mutual funds. The move could be the first step towards full market liberalization. Qatar has done the same thing and the long-awaited formal UAE share market was finally established in March 2000.

## CONCLUSION

The Arab countries' ability to enhance the role of equity markets depends on six key factors: first, perceptions of country risk should be reduced through the sustained implementation of adjustment and reform policies and improvements on the micro- and macroeconomic fundamentals. Second, more stringent reporting practices should be introduced and an efficient regulatory environment put in place to attract capital, which always goes to where the rules of the game are clearest. Third, governments should sell their holdings in telecommunications and other technology-related companies in order to add something of a 'higher tech' flavour to their stock markets. Fourth, venture-capital funds to provide capital for start-up businesses in new economy shares should be promoted. Fifth, a regional Arab NASDAQ needs to be established that would provide a friendlier atmosphere for IT-related companies and allow an exit mechanism for venture-capital funds investing in start-up businesses in the region and help attract part of the capital that has been invested in new economy shares abroad. Sixth, utilities, banks and other major industrial companies should soon be privatized in order to create large liquid stocks that would be of interest to international investors.

# 6

# DRIVERS OF CHANGE AFFECTING ARAB BANKS

## INTRODUCTION

Arab banks' traditional business of taking deposits and lending the proceeds is being redefined. What was once viewed as a conservative industry is having to adapt to dramatic financial, economic and social changes at both the local and international levels.

Banks worldwide are currently undergoing their third disintermediation. The first involved the growth of mutual funds at the expense of bank deposits; the second saw the bond market taking on some of the banks' traditional role as providers of credit. Now, in the third stage, the distribution of banking products is being disintermediated. This process has been going on for some years with the spread of automated teller machines (ATMs), telephone banking (over the past decade) and, more recently, online banking.

One driver of change affecting Arab banks is demographic and social trends. People are leading longer and busier lives, and as a result the balance of financial services is shifting from granting credit and processing transactions to the management of wealth and provision of diversified financial services. A good portion of banks' business should come from selling services rather than extending loans. People's tastes and habits are also changing, and increasingly more customers prefer direct-delivery channels to conduct their banking business. This will undoubtedly reduce the importance of branches and necessitate a cultural change in the way these branches are managed.

Another driver of change is the liberalization of trade in financial services under the auspices of WTO, which is expected to accelerate the scope of competition in Arab domestic markets and exert pressure on Arab banks' market share and profitability, while giving them the advantage of non-discriminatory treatment in all WTO member countries. A third driver of change is the revolution in IT and the delivery channels and products created. Online banking gives customers the ability to choose themselves, rather than have products chosen for them. This represents a critical shift in the relationship between customer and bank. Furthermore, banks would be able to use their online operations to expand into other markets.

Another driver of change is consolidation. This reduces operational cost, minimizes duplication, boosts efficiency, spreads the huge technology costs over a bigger base and cross-markets products on a larger scale. However, consolidation has to be planned for carefully and motivated strategically in order for it to be effective. Despite the few consolidation deals carried out in the region between 1998 and 2002, merger and acquisition activity remains sporadic. It seems that Arab banks are unlikely to pursue serious consolidation activity unless they are forced to do so by their respective monetary authorities.

After reviewing the recent performance of Arab banks and the structure of the regional banking scene, the challenges that these banks are likely to face in light of the changes affecting the global financial sector and how Arab banks should position themselves to benefit from these changes will be analyzed.

## THE REGIONAL BANKING SCENE

Aggregate financial results for Arab banks for the years 1999 and 2000 suggest that the region's financial institutions have ample room to grow. Most of them are now well positioned to benefit from better economic conditions expected in the years ahead. There is less concern over asset quality following the sharp rise in the levels of provisioning reported in 1999 and 2000. The problems faced by Arab banks are an inevitable part of the growing process of emerging-market financial sectors. Indeed, many of the same problems have been faced at some point by international banks in developed economies, be it in the field of overexposure to the construction sector, high-risk growth in consumer lending, non-strategic international expansion, internal managerial systems controlled by governments, or the interests of key shareholders.

To understand the kind of challenge facing Arab banks, one needs to look at what is happening in the US financial market, because where the US leads the rest of the world is likely to follow – especially in finance and technology. US banks now control only 28 per cent of the domestic financial-services market, one-third of their share 25 years ago, while Arab banks still control 95 per cent. Approximately 40 per cent of banks' revenues in the US come from fees, that is from selling services rather than extending loans or financing projects. These include commissions from trading currencies and securities, issuing credit cards, managing mutual funds, providing custody and investment banking services. Arab banks continue to derive most of their revenues from taking deposits and extending credit.

There has been a large drop in the use of branches in the US from 70 per cent of total banking services in the 1980s to 40 per cent in 2001. In the meantime, ATM use rose to 30 per cent, telephone banking to 28 per cent and online banking to 2 per cent. Customers utilize the convenience of 'direct-delivery channels' instead of going to the branch. In the Arab region, on average, more than 90 per cent of customers use branches. The banking ratio in the Arab countries measured by the number of residents per branch averaged 8800 in 2001, compared to 4000 in developed countries.

The banking sectors' concentration ratios, as measured by the market share of the top five banks in the region, are relatively high. In Saudi Arabia two banks – the Saudi American Bank (SAMBA) and the National Commercial Bank – hold almost 50 per cent of the sector's assets. The National Bank of Kuwait and the National Bank of Bahrain each holds 30 per cent of their country's respective banking assets. Egypt's four state banks have 50 per cent of total assets and control most of the retail network, while in Jordan the top five banks control 80 per cent of the assets.

Table 6.1
Major indicators of the Arab banking sector, 1998–2000

| | 1998 | | 1999 | | 2000 | |
|---|---|---|---|---|---|---|
| | Amount ($ billion) | Change (percentage) | Amount ($ billion) | Change (percentage) | Amount ($ billion) | Change (percentage) |
| Total assets | 460.6 | 10.2 | 500.8 | 8.7 | 526.3 | 4.2 |
| Foreign assets | 69.9 | 5.3 | 63.9 | –8.6 | 64.5 | 0.6 |
| Loans and advances | 267.3 | 13.1 | 302.4 | 13.1 | 321.3 | 9.6 |
| Total deposits | 303.2 | 9.6 | 328.6 | 8.4 | 322.5 | 5.6 |
| Shareholders equity | 46.7 | 9.3 | 53.5 | 14.6 | 59.7 | 8.3 |
| Net profits | 6.8 | 13.4 | 7.5 | 10.3 | 8.3 | 10.2 |

*Source: Union of Arab Banks, Beirut, August 2001*

Total assets of Arab banks rose by 4.2 per cent in 2000, reaching $526.3 billion, compared with an increase of 8.7 per cent in 1999 (table 6.1). Assets of Arab banks grew faster than the economies in which they operate, where average GDP growth did not exceed 3.5 per cent in 2000. Loans and advances were up by 9.6 per cent to $321.3 billion, compared with an increase of 13.1 per cent in the year before. Shareholders equity of Arab banks rose by 8.3 per cent in 2000 – following an increase of 14.6 per cent in 1999 – to $59.7 billion. Foreign assets remained generally flat at around $64.5 billion in 2000, following the 8.6 per cent decline recorded in 1999.

The 54 leading Arab banks which were among *The Banker* magazine's top 1000 banks in the world in 2000 (only those top Arab banks that had released their 2000 results by June 2001 were included in the report) accounted for approximately 2 per cent of the 1000 banks' aggregate assets, 2.4 per cent of their tier-one capital and around 2 per cent of their pre-tax profits (figure 6.1).

Domestic Arab banks remain quite small in comparison to their peers in Europe and the US. By the end of 2000, only four Arab banks (SAMBA, the National Commercial Bank [NCB], Riyad Bank of Saudi Arabia and Bahrain's Arab Banking Corporation) had assets exceeding $20 billion, which compares poorly to other leading international banks. The combined assets of all Arab banks in 2000, approximately $575 billion, remain smaller than the assets of any of the largest ten banks in the world. For example, the assets of HSBC Group alone were $600 billion in 2000 (figure 6.2).

Figure 6.1
Distribution of top 1000 banks' tier-one capital by region, 2000

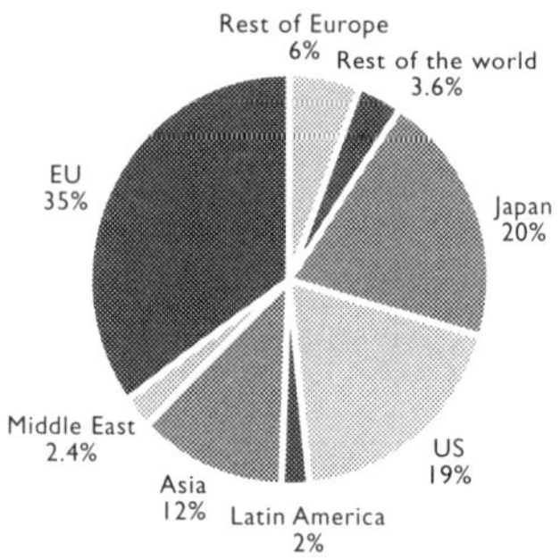


*Source:* The Banker, *July 2001*

Figure 6.2
Arab banks compared to the largest banks of the world by total assets, 2000
($ billion)

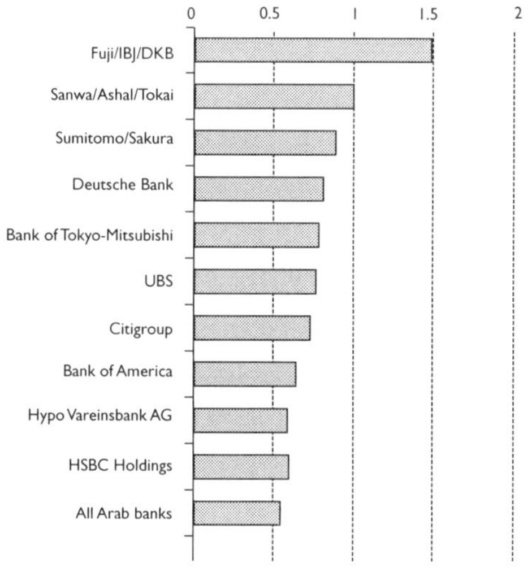


*Source: Fitch IBCA, IMF staff estimates*

*IBJ: Industrial Bank of Japan; DKB: Dia-Ichi Kangyo Bank; UBS: Union Bank of Switzerland*

The top Arab bank in the region in terms of equity, SAMBA, ranked as number 471 among the world's top 1000 banks in 2000 (table 6.2), followed by Riyadh Bank, which ranked 155, and Saudi Arabia's National Commercial Bank, with a rank of 162 in 2000.

## THE PERFORMANCE OF THE LARGEST ARAB BANKS IN 2000

Although the number of Arab banks in the top 1000 banks worldwide has increased from 77 in 1999 to 84 in 2000, the region's banks represent only 3 per cent of the top 1000 aggregate tier-one capital, and just 2 per cent of aggregate assets. Unlike in many other regions, mergers among Arab banks are not a preoccupation. This is largely because politics rules ahead of economics, while family ties and the fact that many banks still have strong public-sector ownership, hold back consolidation. In 2000, as in 1999, Saudi banks accounted for six of the top 15; the UAE was next with three. The most significant change is that the Commercial Bank of Syria has entered the top 25 for the first time, having almost doubled its tier-one capital to $738m in 1999 and 2000.

For most of the Middle East, 2000 was a reasonable year, with high oil prices contributing to improved returns on capital. In the Gulf, Saudi banks led the way with aggregate returns on average capital of 18.3 per cent, well up on the 15 per cent returns of 1999. As in 1999, Al Rajhi Banking and Investment Corporation was the top performer, with a strong 31.2 per cent return, followed by SAMBA, with 23.8 per cent. In Kuwait the banks averaged a 16.2 per cent return on capital, with the National Bank of Kuwait maintaining its leading position at 25.4 per cent. The UAE banks averaged 13.7 per cent, led by the National Bank of Abu Dhabi, with an 18.9 per cent return on equity.

Table 6.2
Top 15 Arab banks, 2000

| Region | World | Ranking | Tier-one capital ($ million) | Assets ($ million) | Pre-tax profits ($ million) | Return on equity (percentage) | Return on assets (percentage) |
|---|---|---|---|---|---|---|---|
| 1 | 147 | SAMBA | 2297 | 21,546 | 535 | 23.8 | 2.48 |
| 2 | 155 | Riyad Bank | 2139 | 17,496 | 324 | 15.2 | 1.85 |
| 3 | 162 | National Commercial Bank | 2069 | 26,676 | 395 | 21.1 | 1.48 |
| 4 | 164 | Arab Banking Corporation | 2065 | 26,675 | 196 | 9.5 | 0.73 |
| 5 | 188 | Al-Rajhi Banking and Investment Corporation | 1729 | 12,999 | 507 | 31.2 | 3.90 |
| 6 | 193 | Arab Bank | 1701 | 21,313 | 309 | 18.9 | 1.45 |
| 7 | 196 | Gulf Investment Corporation | 1657 | 19,603 | 155 | 9.5 | 0.79 |
| 8 | 236 | National Bank of Kuwait | 1353 | 13,394 | 338 | 25.4 | 2.52 |
| 9 | 277 | National Bank of Dubai | 1118 | 7664 | 111 | 10.0 | 1.45 |
| 10 | 282 | Qatar National Bank | 1091 | 6764 | 135 | 12.6 | 1.99 |
| 11 | 283 | National Bank of Egypt | 1089 | 22,491 | 154 | 14.5 | 0.68 |
| 12 | 299 | Emirates Bank International | 987 | 5335 | 149 | 16.0 | 2.79 |
| 13 | 305 | Saudi British Bank | 962 | 11,522 | 198 | 21.5 | 1.72 |
| 14 | 307 | Abu Dhabi Commercial Bank | 958 | 6889 | 168 | 18.5 | 2.44 |
| 15 | 311 | Al Bank Al Saudi Al Fransi | 943 | 10,148 | 174 | 18.5 | 1.72 |

*Source:* The Banker, *July 2001*

The combined net income of the largest 15 Arab banks reached $3848 million in 2000, 12 per cent higher than in 1999. The highest pre-tax profits were recorded by SAMBA at $535 million, followed the Al-Rajhi Banking and Investment Corporation, at $507 million, the National Commercial Bank, at $395 million, and the National Bank of Kuwait, at $338 million. Among the non-GCC banks, the Arab Bank recorded the highest profits, at $309 million.

The largest Arab bank in terms of equity was SAMBA with tier-one capital of $2297 million. SAMBA had a world ranking of 147 in 2000, and only seven Arab banks were ranked among the top 200 world banks by equity. The combined tier-one capital of the top 15 Arab banks ($22.2 billion) represented less than 40 per cent of the $54.5 billion of Citigroup, the world's largest bank in terms of capital.

A regional comparison of the cost-to-income ratio, a standard benchmark of banking efficiency, reveals that the Middle East enjoyed the lowest ratio at 47.1 per cent in 2000, compared to 79.5 per cent in Japan, 65.4 per cent in Latin America, 59.8 per cent in the EU, 57.6 per cent in Asia and 63.1 per cent in the US. The lowest cost-to-income ratio is that of the National Bank of Kuwait, at 33 per cent.

The disclosed non-performing loans of some Arab banks are among the highest in the world, with the Al-Ahli Bank of Kuwait recording 42.2 per cent of its total loan book as non-performing in 2000 , the highest ratio recorded among world banks. The second-highest ratio was recorded by the Bank Al-Jazira of Saudi Arabia, at 33 per cent, only slightly down from the 1999 level of 35.8 per cent, Fransabank of Lebanon ranked 18, followed by Mashreq Bank of UAE, which ranked 22. The lowest proportion of non-performing loans to total loans in the region were those of the National Bank of Kuwait, the Qatar National Bank, the National Bank of Dubai, and the Arab Bank, at 2.6 per cent, 4.3 per cent, 5.5 per cent and 5.6 per cent respectively.

Across the Middle East region, the capital-to-assets ratio is substantially higher than elsewhere, reflecting capital strength and conservative management. The average capital-to-asset ratio in the region was 19.6 per cent in 2000, the highest in the world, compared to 10 per cent in Japan, 14.3 per cent in the US, 14 per cent in Latin America, 14.9 per cent in the EU and 12.4 per cent in Asia. The Qatar National Bank exhibited the highest average capital–asset ratio of 50 per cent in 2000, followed by the National Bank of Dubai at 42.6 per cent, the Taib Bank of Bahrain at 36.6 per cent, and the Housing Bank for Trade and Development at 31.7 per cent. Return-on-assets ratios for the top banks across the Arab countries ranged from a low of 0.68 per cent for the National Bank of Egypt to a high of 3.9 per cent for the Al-Rajhi Banking and Investment Corporation of Saudi Arabia. The other top four Arab banks in terms of return on assets were the Emirates Bank International at 2.79 per cent, the National Bank of Kuwait at 2.52 per cent, SAMBA at 2.48 per cent and the Abu Dhabi Commercial Bank at 2.44 per cent.

## DRIVERS OF CHANGE AFFECTING ARAB BANKS

There are several drivers of change likely to have an impact on Arab banks, the most important of which are liberalization and globalization of banking services, transformation of management philosophy, the spread of Internet banking in the region, and the rising need for more consolidation of banking institutions.

### *LIBERALIZATION AND GLOBALIZATION OF BANKING SERVICES*

Accession to WTO means that sooner or later Arab countries will have to offer banks domiciled abroad the same treatment as local banks. Foreign institutions will be able to enter the domestic markets and will have the opportunity to attract the more profitable top-tier customers, offering a more comprehensive range of services than is currently available from the local banks. This process of globalization has been dominated so far by banking groups in the industrial countries exploiting the growth potential of emerging markets, as witnessed by the expansion of Spanish banks in Latin America, German banks in Eastern Europe, and North American banks in East Asia.

While there are considerable benefits to the Arab region from financial liberalization, it must be recognized that there are going to be adjustment costs, at least in the short term. Less efficient banks in the region, with high operating costs or providing inferior services, are likely to suffer from international competition. Companies and sectors that previously benefited from preferential access to credit may also suffer.

Nevertheless, the WTO agreement on financial services should be looked upon as an opportunity rather then a threat for those banks that are willing to take on the challenge. Arab banks are called upon to up-grade and modernize their competitive edge in order to meet the increased competition from abroad. Eventually, with continued liberalization of financial markets, significant benefits are likely to arise in domestic banking sectors. Enhanced competition in local financial markets, induced by open and liberal markets, will improve sectoral efficiency, leading to lower costs, better quality and a wider choice of financial services for the customer. Domestic banks are more likely to be attentive to the needs of their clients and would benefit more from the transfer of knowledge and technology than banks from abroad. Arab banks will also enjoy the advantage of non-discriminatory treatment in all WTO member countries if they have competitive services and products to offer in these markets.

The main worry associated with financial liberalization is the claim that foreign financial institutions are more efficient and will end up dominating the Arab banking industry. However, it is not always true that foreign banks are more efficient in the domestic market than local banks. They may be ahead in certain investment-banking products, technology and private banking, but the knowledge of the domestic market and the strong relationship that Arab banks have with their local clients will give them strong advantages over foreign competition. Besides, if domestic banks need more time to adjust to new competition, financial liberalization can be phased in over time.

Liberalization of the financial sector is also leading to the universalization of banking, which is increasingly blurring the boundary between bank and non-bank financial services. This trend is already well developed in certain European countries, as exemplified by the widespread distribution of insurance products through bank branches, a phenomenon known as 'bancassurance', and encourages the formation of conglomerates that provide all types of financial services. To some extent, this irreversible trend was confirmed in the US by the merger of Citicorp and the Travelers Group and the subsequent repeal in 1999 of the Glass–Steagall Act (which restricted banks' involvement in equity financing and artificially separated investment banks from commercial banks).

## *TRANSFORMATION OF MANAGEMENT PHILOSOPHY*

Power cultures have dominated management of Arab banks for a long time. The common features of these cultures include a centralized decision-making process, with tasks assigned downward by the chief executive; dedicated staff with extensive experience, a strict hierarchy tempered by heavy doses of paternalism, a stable environment in which competition is regulated, and banks providing clients with the kinds of service that they choose to make available rather than customized products. Management emphasis has been mainly on asset size and market share, in the belief that the large balance sheet would guarantee competitive advantage in the long term.

In the new structure, banks must be willing to accept constant change rather than stability, be organized around networks instead of rigid hierarchies, and depend more on partnerships and alliances rather than being self-sufficient. Banks will be outsourcing skills (back office operations, research, technology, financial products etc) to those who can perform these functions with greater efficiency. Outsourcing and partnering are well known by now, but in the new structure they will become more crucial. Managing this intricate network of partners and external relationships will be as important as managing internal operations.

The most profitable bank will manage information on markets and clients instead of focusing solely on physical assets. Balance-sheet size will no longer be the criterion for success. Markets will reward efficient businesses that add value.

Banks will constantly be looking for value-creating opportunities, and allocating more capital for them to grow. If the business return on equity does not cover its cost of capital, it will either be downsized or sold off, unless there is a compelling business strategy to keep the business. However, there should be no business in the organization that will constantly destroy value over time. This approach necessitates that the business be divided into discrete lines in which executives in charge would have a great deal of accountability for their decisions.

Instead of mass-production and providing clients with identical services, banks will be tailoring their products to each individual, giving their customers the technology to demand the kind of service they want. Mass-customization will produce individualized products and services. Banks will enjoy huge savings because they will no longer have to guess what and how much customers want. Competition from non-bank institutions (brokers, managers, insurers etc) will eventually force most banks to offer supermarket-style services within which clients have access to rivals' products as well. Competition will be more between brands and products rather than between banks.

To keep ahead of the competition, banks should attract and retain high calibre employees and freelance workers. Such talent would require more than good salaries. Banks need to have in place the kind of reward system (e.g. profit-sharing and stock options) that keeps the best minds engaged. Instead of having civil-service-like employees, mindful of rank and title and rewarded by seniority, the emphasis would be on empowerment: employees will be looking for personal growth rather than security, and the best will be given the chance to create and run new businesses.

In the new structure, banks will recognize that technology not only provides the means to make a business more efficient, but also has the potential to bring forth revolutionary improvements. It is not just about clever application of the latest software, it is about culture and mindset. The Internet should help banks to consolidate information on their clients and customize products and services suited to their specific needs. Top management should be inspirational rather than dogmatic, encouraging all employees to come up with new ideas and new businesses.

## *THE SPREAD OF INTERNET BANKING IN THE REGION*

The most fundamental development in Arab banking in the next few years will be the large-scale utilization of online-banking services. The *Financial Times* estimates that by 2005, 2 billion people will have access to the Internet, representing 90 per cent of global buying-power. These may have access to the Internet not only via a PC, but also through other channels, such as mobile telephones, personal digital assistants (e.g. Palm Pilot) and interactive TV.

While the Internet is perceived to represent a new distribution channel for existing products, it also provides efficiency in transaction cost and offers a way of reaching a broader range of new clients. It relieves the customer from the need to visit the branch to undertake simple banking transactions, instead offering him or her 'anytime, anyplace, anywhere' banking services. Sophisticated customers – who are usually the more profitable clients – value this service most. The crucial issue here is that if a product is not offered or priced competitively online, then customers will go elsewhere at the click of a mouse button. There are search-engines on the Internet that will find you the best price for a specific transaction or service.

Self-service or direct banking channels have now become the preferred method for customers to conduct their banking business. This is well recognized by banks across the world. Arab banks have invested millions to develop their ATMs, point-of-sale schemes and telephone banking, and most of them are now moving to Internet banking. This is happening at a time when the utilization rate of the branch has been gradually dropping. It is estimated that the cost of an ATM transaction is 10 per cent of a branch transaction, and if the same transaction is conducted on the telephone the cost drops to 1 per cent that of the branch cost and to a fraction of that if the same transaction is carried out on the Internet. With only 10 branches in India, Citibank was able to use ATMs and telephone banking to become the largest credit-card issuer in the country.

Arab banks have been slower to embrace the Internet than those in the US, mainly due to cultural differences and a low degree of access. Less than 1 per cent of the total Arab population had access to the Internet in June 2001, compared to 50 per cent in the US. All American banks have Internet sites, and many of them provide banking services on the Internet, such as: current-account management including payment of bills; issuance of credit cards; mortgages and personal loans; brokerage service; mutual funds.

The Bank of America already had two million account holders on the Internet by the end of 2001, and the number is expected to triple over the next two years. Wells Fargo has nearly as many, and Citigroup has around 500,000 online customers. Elsewhere, Merita Nordbanken (MNB) of Finland had 1.2 million customers, while SEB of Sweden said that by June 2001, a quarter of its total customer-base was using its Internet Bank. The basic online activity of these banks is paying bills, which lends itself naturally to integration with e-shopping. MNB, for example, has online links with more than 900 shops which accept its 'solo' payment system.

As the branches become less utilized, they should be turned into marketing outlets that sell products and provide direct-delivery channels to customers. In the west, 80 per cent of the branch space is allocated to 'customers', 20 per cent to 'staff'. Branch employees will change from being clerks doing routine work to becoming customer service employees selling funds and other banking services.

Banks can use e-banking to improve customer service. They could use the data they have on their customers to predict the behaviour of those customers throughout changes in their lifestyle, and thus provide them with the right product at the right price.

There are two main Internet-banking business models: the integrated approach and the stand-alone Internet bank. Most of the big banks in the world have opted for the integrated approach, whereby they keep their existing brand name for their Internet banking services, which they offer as an extension to branch, ATM and telephone based services. The stand-alone Internet bank has been adopted mainly by small-to-medium-sized institutions or by major banks that do not have a large market share in a particular market or product.

A stand-alone Internet bank can be used to pick and choose competitors' customer-bases via selective pricing and/or greater use of customer-segmentation information. Such banks have the advantage of flexibility and innovation, and they benefit from low cost-bases because they avoid staff costs and branch expenses of traditional banks. The overwhelming weight of opinion today is that the stand-alone Internet model has a limited appeal, unless it can exploit an established brand (e.g. Charles Schwab) or offer a product specifically suited to the Internet (equity trading).

Lack of brand recognition and significant marketing costs are likely to be the main barriers to Arab banks planning to offer banking services on the Internet. The technology and know-how could be bought practically off the shelf, even though start-up costs have proved to be large. The fundamental element of success on the Internet is the number of hits the site obtains. This volume is essential in order to leverage the large marketing and technology costs. Arab banks should have both the brand recognition that attracts customer visits and the broad product ranges for their sites to invite repeat custom. A thorough and well-executed Internet strategy is therefore a must if the traditional banks are to maintain their inherent advantage over the new competition.

One unique aspect of Internet banking is the potential for online bill-presentation and payment associated with e-commerce and the business-to-business market. Bill-presentation is a challenge, in that it requires the formation of networks of banks and merchants, much in the same way that the credit-card network system operates. The cost savings for banks and merchants would be huge, and it would be very convenient for customers. A consortium of Arab banks that include the National Bank of Kuwait, the National Bank of Dubai, the Commercial International Bank of Egypt, the Arab Bank of Jordan and SAMBA, is developing a regional business-to-business electronic market-place with integrated financial services targeting the Middle East.

Financial institutions from the region have more credibility in the provision of Islamic banking and Arab-related banking and investment services than institutions from abroad, but they need good marketing and brand recognition to carve out a market share for themselves online.

## *THE RISING NEED FOR MORE CONSOLIDATION OF BANKING INSTITUTIONS*

The banking sectors in the Arab countries are expected to witness greater merger and acquisition (M&A) activities in the years ahead, either between domestic banks wishing to capture larger market share in their respective markets or through cross-border acquisition to facilitate intraregional expansion of Arab banks. The last few years had seen a handful of deals closed (table 6.3), but for most banks, talk about

M&A activities remains more lip-service than policy. Even the merger of two government-owned UAE banks (the Emirates Bank International and the National Bank of Dubai) has gone nowhere. It seems that any significant consolidation activity in the region will not take place unless the monetary authorities force banks to do so.

Table 6.3
**Mergers and acquisitions among banks in the Middle East**

| Acquirer | Country | Merged, acquired or took strategic interest |
|---|---|---|
| United Saudi Bank | Saudi Arabia | Saudi Cairo Bank (1997) |
| Wafabank | Morocco | Unibank (1997) |
| Bank Audi | Lebanon | Credit Commercial de Moyen Orient (1997) |
| Byblos Bank | Lebanon | Banque Beyrouth pour le Commerce (1997) |
| Jordan National Bank | Jordan | Business Bank (1997) |
| KIPCO | Kuwait | Burgan Bank (56%) (1998) |
| Bank of Beirut | Lebanon | Transorient Bank (1998) |
| Bank Audi | Lebanon | Orient Credit Bank (1998) |
| Fransabank | Lebanon | Universal Bank (1998) |
| Emirates Bank International | UAE | Bank of Beirut (10%) (1998) |
| Gulf Bank | Kuwait | United Bank of Kuwait (27%) (1999) |
| SAMBA | Saudi Arabia | United Saudi Bank (1999) |
| Gulf International Bank | Bahrain | Saudi International Bank, UK (1999) |
| Arab Banking Corp. | Bahrain | Arab African Bank of Egypt (1999) |
| Societé Générale Libano-Européenne de Banque | Lebanon | Middle East Investment Bank of Jordan (35%) (1999) |
| United Bank of Lebanon | Lebanon | Banque Libanais pour le Commerce (2000) |
| Faisal Islamic Bank | Bahrain | Islamic Investment Company of the Gulf (2000) |
| United Bank of Kuwait | Kuwait | Al-Ahli Commercial Bank of Bahrain (2000) |
| Commercial Bank of Oman | Oman | Bank of Muscat (2000) |
| EFG Hermes | Egypt | Fleming CIIC (2001) |
| Bank Audi | Lebanon | Lebanon Invest (2001) |

Increasingly, we are likely to see banks in one Arab country taking minority shareholding interest in banks elsewhere in the region, while others may opt for a strategic alliance. This would help participating banks to concentrate on their core competence while outsourcing needed services from their partners. Cross-border alliances between Arab banks will make it possible for them to work jointly on specific projects, share products and risks, reduce costs and broaden their customer-base. Small Arab banks that are unable to invest in up-to-date technology will find it very difficult to survive. Even at retail level, domestic banks will be facing competition from the international banking giants providing online banking services to prime customers. Online banks do not need a local presence, and the accommodation of different languages on the Internet allows banks to operate across borders.

Given the constraints of the local markets, a number of institutions are beginning to envisage their future growth depending more on regional, rather than national, platforms. The process has already started. NCB has applied for a licence to open a full commercial branch in Bahrain, and SAMBA is in the process of establishing representative offices in Egypt and the UAE, already having one in Lebanon. The National Bank of Kuwait, which has a strong presence in Lebanon, is finalizing its acquisition of a bank in Egypt. Lebanon is perceived as a good market for private and investment banking. Egypt provides good retail, corporate and trade finance opportunities, and the UAE is looked upon mainly as a trade-finance operation. While the establishment of representative offices could be the first step in gaining an understanding of a new market, bolder strides could follow.

In a liberalized global financial market, Arab banks have no choice but to consolidate. This would reduce operation costs, minimize duplication, spread huge technology expenses over a wider base and allow banks to benefit from economies of scale. Consolidation has been particularly strong in the Lebanese banking community, where six mergers between domestic banks have been concluded since 1998. Another big transaction has taken place in Saudi Arabia. The merger between SAMBA and the United Saudi Bank produced the second largest bank in the Kingdom after the National Commercial Bank asset terms.

The Bank of Muscat and the Commercial Bank of Oman completed their merger to create one of Oman's largest banks, with $3.38 billion in assets. The Dar al-Maal al-Islami, the Faysal Islamic Bank of Bahrain and the Islamic Investment Company of the Gulf merged to create the Shamil Bank. The Islamic Investment Company of the Gulf was the lead player in another deal when it acquired the Arab Islamic Bank in late 1998. The other major development is the move by the Dallah Albaraka group to consolidate its own diverse Islamic banking and finance assets under a Bahrain-based holding company. When completed, the new institution will be one of the largest Islamic banks in the world.

The merger of the Bahrain-based Gulf International Bank and the London-based Saudi International Bank was the first major cross-border deal. The effective acquisition of Bahrain's Al-Ahli Commercial Bank by London-based United Bank of Kuwait is another good example of cross-border alliance. Products originated and developed in London can be sold through a strong retail franchise. The United Bank of Kuwait is likely to make similar moves in other regional markets as well.

In a region that is generally considered to be over-banked, prospects for banks to be licensed to branch regionally are slim. Besides, given the present speed of financial liberalization, successful horizontal expansion is better and faster achieved through acquisition. The large Arab banks are constrained less by the size of their capital than by the size of the markets in which they are operating. To attain growth, capture economies of scale and benefit from huge investments made in technology, Arab banks such as the National Commercial Bank, the National Bank of Kuwait, SAMBA, the Arab Banking Corporation, the National Bank of Qatar, Riyad Bank, now see the merits of going regional. This strategy could be implemented either by acquiring fully existing banks (e.g. the Arab Banking Corporation buying the Egypt Arab African Bank) or by taking a minority interest in other banks (e.g. the Emirates Bank International buying 10 per cent of the Bank of Beirut, or the Societé Générale Libano-Européenne de Banque acquiring 35 per cent of the Middle East Investment Bank of Jordan). There are also the prospects of establishing a strategic alliance with another bank to work closely on specific deals or share products and expenses and broaden customer-base (e.g. the National Commercial Bank and the National Bank of Kuwait). Increasingly more of these cross-border acquisitions and alliances will be seen in the Middle East region in the foreseeable future.

Arab banks are also confronted with the radical changes taking place in the banking and financial industry worldwide. The distinction between commercial banks, investment banks, brokers, insurers and bond managers will become less and less important. Instead of developing these services internally, banks with the ambition to provide comprehensive financial services will find it more advantageous to acquire institutions that have these services. The process has started: Bank Audi of Lebanon acquired Lebanon Invest (an investment bank), while Byblos Bank merged with an insurance company to provide bancassurance services.

The last few years saw a handful of successful M&A deals in the region. These were mostly between profitable and well-managed institutions, which saw a natural fit or complementarity with the counterpart with which they merged. Similarity of size was less important than similarity of outlook. Two weak institutions put together do not produce a strong institution; on the contrary, such a merger will add to the existing problems of the two institutions and could make things worse for management.

Banks should not merge simply to benefit from the incentives given by the monetary authorities to encourage consolidation among domestic financial institutions. A merge should be a well-studied business decision, based on the ability of the merged institutions to add value and increase return to their shareholders' equity. In the Western world, where most banks are listed companies, management which is completely separate from ownership is the one which leads the merger process. In the Arab world, banks are still predominantly owned by a family or group of families. This is particularly the case case in Lebanon and Jordan. In Egypt, Syria, Qatar and the UAE, governments still feature as major shareholders of large banks. In those cases, the management is not necessarily in control and decisions are not always made on the basis of maximizing shareholders' value. Prominent families whose ownership of banks reflects the social and political power and prestige would resist M&A deals in order not to lose their dominance.

Recent experiences indicate that the success or failure of mergers and acquisitions have less to do with faulty selection or paying too much for an acquired bank, and more with disagreement after the deal had been sealed. The clash of cultures in the two institutions, the self interests of two different boards and different CEOs, the demoralization of the staff of the acquired bank and the absence of a well-thought-out process on how to proceed were the main reasons for failure.

Merging companies should not rush: it is more important to make correct decisions than quick ones. The communication process should start as early and as far down as possible. Employees at all levels should be involved to make them feel more committed to the new entity. The board and management rivalry should be tackled from the start to come up with a well-defined and agreed-upon management structure and business plan. To limit rivalry between two CEOs, banks which merge could opt to have two co-CEOs – similar to Citigroup and Travelers, when they merged in 1998 – or have an executive chairman and a CEO, with the relationship between them well-defined from the beginning.

In most Arab countries, banks do not have the freedom to hire and fire easily, as is the case in the West – especially the US. Since an important benefit of M&A is to reduce duplication and cut down on staff expenses, the absence of such a benefit will discourage the M&A process in the region. The legal and monetary authorities should introduce laws that allow institutions that merge to reduce the number of employees, and banks should be compensated for the extra cost incurred if a huge redundancy package is required.

In M&A deals the emphasis should be on the marriage and not the wedding. The hardest questions should not be left till after the merger deal is done. Banks that agree on a clear strategy and management structure before merging stand a better chance of success.

There is an important role to be played by investment banks in the region which understand the local culture and the business structure of Arab banks and can help promote M&A activities. Other than identifying those banks which do complement each other and carrying out the leg-work of valuation of the assets of the two institutions, they could help banks agree on post-merger strategies and contribute to solving associated problems.

## CONCLUSION

Arab banks are confronted with radical changes as they enter the new millennium. The distinction between banks, brokers, insurers and fund managers will become less and less important as buying financial services online is increasingly becoming possible. Online banking and other direct-delivery channels will become the preferred method for customers to conduct their banking business.

Arab banks' governing management objective in the new millennium should be to maximize shareholder value. This necessitates selling businesses where the returns do not cover cost of capital, and allocating more resources to those activities that add value over time. Enhanced profitability could also be achieved by reducing operating expenses through the effective use of modern technology such as the Internet.

Internet banking places emphasis on two factors, customer awareness and accessibility to the Internet, neither of which the region has had success with so far. If business is only the click of a mouse away, Arab banks will have to understand their products and their customers' needs much better and invest more in technology if they are to survive the onslaught of new competition. And if they are too slow to adapt, the consequences could be detrimental. Look at what has happened in just four years to share-trading on the Internet. the stock market with the highest proportion of Internet trading is not in New York but in Seoul.

To cope with the new world of liberalized, deregulated and electronically linked financial markets, the role of the regulators will also have to develop. Strong systems of checks and balances need to be put in place and rigorously imposed. This process will be partly facilitated by the growing demand for transparency from the global market-place, where progress has already been made.

The power of monetary authorities to control money supply is likely to be hampered as 'electronic money' and online banking services become widely used. However, central banks can set monetary policy by controlling interest rates rather than by altering money supply. This is why it has become imperative for countries of the region to develop their domestic bond markets. The availability of government bonds would allow the central banks to use open market operations to set domestic interest rates even in a market where cash balances are disappearing.

The region needs as well to develop its corporate bond markets in order for these markets to be drawn upon when needed to substitute for the decline in bank financial intermediation and limit the effect of economic shocks if and when they occur. Had a functioning bond market existed in several East Asian countries, the crisis there may have been far less severe. Because Sweden has a corporate sector with a variety of non-banking funding sources, the crisis that hit banks in the early 1990s when property prices there collapsed did not impact the ability of corporates to borrow. In contrast, because the Japanese financial system has mainly banks as financial intermediaries, with the corporate bond market playing a much smaller role than elsewhere, the crisis there has taken much longer to be resolved, leading to a protracted credit crunch.

# 7

# ARAB CURRENCIES: FIX OR FLOAT?

## INTRODUCTION

Most of the Arab countries have chosen fixed exchange rate regimes, whereby their currencies are pegged to the US dollar, either officially (Jordan and Oman) or *de facto* (Egypt, Lebanon and the GCC states). Having a fixed exchange rate maintains investor confidence in the currency, encourages domestic savings and investments, and discourages capital outflows. If inflation rate in a country whose currency is pegged to the dollar is higher than that of the US, then interest rates on the local currencies will have to be higher than those on the dollar to preserve its attractiveness. The spread between domestic and dollar interest rates varies from one Arab country to another depending on the country's economic fundamentals, level of external and internal imbalances, inflation differential with that of the US, credibility and transparency of government policies, availability of foreign reserves and markets' assessment of the risks of devaluation.

Countries that are suited to having their currencies pegged to the dollar are normally small in size, mostly exporting agricultural, commodity and/or mineral products (oil, gas, phosphates, cotton etc) that are usually priced in dollars, where devaluation would not add to their price-competitiveness in the export market. A dollar peg will be the right choice for countries in which capital flows constitute a higher ratio of GDP than trade flows and where current-account deficits are normally financed by capital inflows rather than by foreign borrowing. Here the perceived stability of the exchange rate is very important to the maintenance of confidence of domestic and foreign investors.

No single currency regime is right for all countries or at all times. The choice of exchange rate arrangement should depend on the economic fundamentals of that country, its trade and capital flows and the ability and willingness of its government to implement credible and transparent policies. Currency crises usually occur when governments say one thing and end up doing another. It is, therefore, crucial for countries to stick to one exchange-rate regime, be it fixed or floating.

## MAJOR EXCHANGE-RATE REGIMES

There are floating and fixed exchange-rate regimes. The floating regime has three variants: free floating, defined as the absence of any intervention in the foreign-exchange market, allowing forces of supply and demand to dictate exchange rates; target zone or band, which allows the currency to fluctuate within a margin around some central parity; adjustable peg, whereby the exchange rate is fixed vis-à-vis an international currency but without commitment to resist devaluation or revaluation in the presence of large balance-of-payment disequilibrium. Other variants of flexible exchange-rate regimes include: basket peg, defined as fixing not to a single foreign currency but to a weighted average of other currencies, and crawling peg, defined as a pre-announced policy of devaluing a bit each week or each month.

The fixed exchange-rate regime has three variants. The first is the fixed peg, defined as maintaining a fixed exchange rate with respect to the dollar or any other major currency. Here there is a clear commitment on the part of the government to stick to the declared peg and to use monetary policy and direct intervention in the foreign exchange market to attain this. The second is the currency board, in which fixing the exchange rate is done not by policy but by law and any increase in monetary base is backed one-for-one with foreign reserves. Here a strong, stable and committed government is very important, supported by sound fiscal policy and a solvent banking sector. The third is monetary union, the adoption of a common currency as legal tender (e.g. the euro) or the use of a foreign currency as the official currency (full dollarization).

Figure 7.1
Countries with a fixed or floating exchange rate: 2001

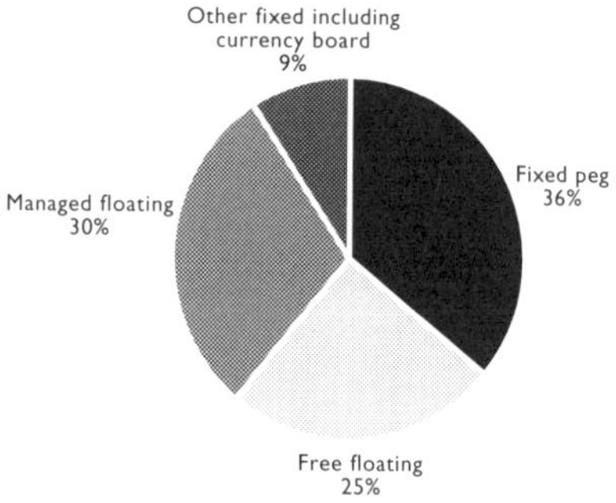


Over the past two decades, especially after the crisis that hit Southeast Asia in 1997, many developing countries have opted to shift from fixed exchange-rate regimes to more flexible arrangements. To date, 55 per cent of IMF members countries follow floating exchange-rate regimes, compared with 35.7 per cent who follow fixed peg regimes and 9.3 per cent who have opted for other regimes, including currency boards and full dollarization (figure 7.1). Among those following floating exchange-rate regimes, more than half have in place a managed float, allowing for some intervention in the exchange market to dampen huge fluctuations in the currency.

## CHOOSING BETWEEN FIXED OR FLOATING EXCHANGE RATE REGIMES

The choice of exchange-rate regimes involves trade-offs between the advantages of fixing the currency and those of floating it (table 7.1). The main advantage of fixing a country's exchange rate is that it maintains investors' confidence in the currency and reduces transaction costs and exchange-rate risks, thus encouraging domestic saving and investment, and discouraging capital outflow. A fixed exchange rate also reduces inflationary pressures associated with devaluation and provides a credible anchor for non-inflationary policy, restricting monetary expansion or arbitrary printing of the currency.

However, in a world of increasingly mobile capital, countries cannot fix their exchange rate and at the same time maintain an independent monetary policy. Domestic interest rates should follow those on the dollar (in case of dollar pegging), even if the country's economic cycle is not 'in sync' with that of the US. This undoubtedly puts more pressure on fiscal policy to be sound and in balance.

Another drawback of the fixed exchange-rate regime is the fact that such a system cannot be used to adjust for external shocks or imbalances. Countries following a fixed peg do not have the option of devaluing to make imports more expensive, thus reducing their impact on the country's balance of payments and/or giving a boost to their exports of goods and services.

A fixed peg is also a fixed target for speculators. A serious drawback, seen in Thailand and other Asia–Pacific countries affected by the 1997 crisis, is that by appearing to eliminate currency risk, firms and banks were encouraged to borrow heavily in foreign currency, usually at cheaper interest rates than on domestic funds. This money can then inflate speculative 'bubbles', especially in the property market. The result of all this is that the economy overheats and the financial sector is left dangerously exposed. In other words, without a well-supervised and regulated banking sector, the fixed peg is liable to convert a currency crisis into a banking crisis.

The basic argument in favour of the floating exchange rate is that the price mechanism embodied in it makes it easier for the economy to adjust to external imbalances. For example, lower export prices and higher import prices help the country regain external equilibrium. Another advantage of the floating exchange rate is that it allows pursuit of an independent monetary policy. When an economy suffers a downturn, the government can soften the impact via a monetary expansion and/or devaluation, irrespective of the trend in dollar interest rate (for currencies pegged to the dollar).

But floating exchange rates have their disadvantages as well. They can overshoot and become highly unstable, especially if a large amount of capital flows in and out of a country. That instability carries real economic costs, leading to speculation, volatility and high interest rates. Moreover, floating rates can reduce investors' faith in the currency, thus discouraging capital inflows and making it harder to finance current-account deficits.

The IMF and the economic gurus have been giving conflicting advice to developing countries on the exchange-rate regime to be followed. For example, following the 1997 crisis the Asian countries, which for years had their currencies pegged to the dollar, were advised to change to floating exchange-rate regimes. According to the IMF, Asian countries got into trouble partly 'because their exchange rates were pegged to a rising currency, the US dollar'. In 1998, the IMF reversed its position and lent billions of dollars to Brazil and Russia to try to help them maintain their dollar peg. The IMF has consistently praised Hong Kong for its super-strict currency board and China for resisting devaluation pressure on its currency vis-à-vis the dollar, while it has invariably called on Egypt and several other Arab countries to consider devaluation as a way to boost exports and tackle trade deficits.

Table 7.1
Advantages and disadvantages of fixed and floating exchange-rate regimes

| Advantages | Disadvantages |
|---|---|
| **Fixed exchange-rate regimes** | |
| ■ Maintains investors' confidence in the currency, thus encouraging domestic savings and investment and discouraging capital outflows.<br>■ Reduces inflationary pressures associated with devaluation and provides a credible anchor for non-inflationary policy, restricting monetary expansion or arbitrary printing of the currency. | ■ Does not allow the implementation of independent monetary policy; domestic interest rates should follow those of the dollar in case of dollar peg.<br>■ Exchange rates cannot be used to adjust for external shocks or imbalances.<br>■ A fixed peg is also a fixed target for speculators. |
| **Floating exchange-rate regimes** | |
| **Advantages** | **Disadvantages** |
| ■ Allows pursuit of an independent monetary policy, when an economy suffers a downturn, monetary expansion can soften the impact.<br>■ Allows a country to adjust to external shocks through exchange rates; that is lower export prices and higher import prices would help the country regain external equilibrium. | ■ Reduces investors' faith in the currency, thus discouraging capital inflows to avoid exchange risk.<br>■ Floating rates can overshoot and become highly unstable, leading to speculation, volatility and high interest rates. |

Deep divisions about exchange-rate regimes exist among the mainstream economists. Jeffery Sacks of Harvard University called on Brazil to float its currency, which it did on 15 January 1999. MIT's Rudi Dornbusch was adamant that a currency board similar to that of Argentina is the best solution for Brazil. Paul Volcker argues that floating exchange rates make no sense for developing countries with small financial sectors. A well publicized study by the World Bank in 1998 showed that over the past 30 years more crises have struck countries with flexible rates than with fixed rates, although the crises have been more severe for fixed-rate markets.

## WHICH CURRENCY REGIME SHOULD THE ARAB COUNTRIES CHOOSE?

Most of the Arab countries have put in place fixed exchange-rate regimes, whereby their currencies are either pegged to the US dollar, whether officially (Jordan and Oman) or *de facto* (Egypt, Lebanon, Saudi Arabia, the UAE, Qatar, and Bahrain), or pegged to a basket of currencies in which the dollar is dominant (Kuwait) or to a basket in which the French franc (euro) is dominant (Tunisia and Morocco) (table 7.2).

Table 7.2
Exchange-rate regimes for Arab countries

| Country | Exchange-rate regime | Degree of convertibility |
|---|---|---|
| Egypt | *De facto* dollar peg | Some capital-account restrictions |
| Morocco | Peg to basket/French franc (euro) | Some capital-account restrictions |
| Tunisia | Peg to basket/French franc (euro) | Some capital-account restrictions |
| Algeria | Managed float against French franc (euro) | Some capital-account restrictions |
| Jordan | Official dollar peg | Full convertibility |
| Lebanon | *De facto* dollar peg | Full convertibility |
| Saudi Arabia | *De facto* dollar peg | Full convertibility |
| Kuwait | Peg to basket/US dollar | Full convertibility |
| UAE | *De facto* dollar peg | Full convertibility |
| Oman | Official dollar peg | Full convertibility |
| Qatar | *De facto* dollar peg | Full convertibility |
| Bahrain | *De facto* dollar peg | Full convertibility |

There is no perfect exchange-rate system, and it all depends on the characteristics of the particular economy. As already mentioned, countries that should follow a fixed dollar peg are those that mostly export agricultural and mineral products. A fixed peg also suits those countries in which sales taxes or value added taxes are high enough to render expenditures on imports less responsive to price changes associated with devaluation. Countries with successive current-account deficits financed mainly by capital inflows withdrawn by individuals and national institutions are also better off with a fixed exchange-rate regime. Here, the perceived stability of the local currency is very important to the maintenance of investor confidence, both domestic and foreign.

It is clear that most – if not all – of these characteristics apply to the Gulf countries as well as to Jordan, Egypt and Lebanon. Since the early 1980s, the currencies of the Gulf countries have been pegged to the US dollar, yet these countries have not been much affected even when the US currency has greatly appreciated in value.

On the contrary, this has helped reduce inflationary pressure and has boosted the purchasing power of the average Gulf consumer. The argument that currency depreciation is stimulative, because it makes exports cheaper in international markets does not apply here. The Gulf countries' exports include oil, petrochemicals, aluminum, liquefied natural gas, steel and food products. Most of these products are denominated in dollars and will not benefit from devaluation of domestic currencies. On the import side, a rise in dollar and Gulf currency exchange rates lead mainly to a decline in prices of imports from Europe and the Far East, bringing a slight re-orientation of imports to countries whose currencies have depreciated.

By eliminating inflationary finance and creating a stable monetary environment, fixed exchange rates in the Gulf region have been instrumental in encouraging capital inflows. Successive current-account deficits recorded by the Gulf countries during the past decade have not been financed by foreign borrowing but rather by capital repatriated by Gulf nationals and institutions and foreign investors seeking joint-venture opportunities in the region. External debt outstanding in the Gulf countries is still at a relatively low level.

Maintaining a fixed dollar peg has in effect allowed interest rates on the dollar to determine domestic interest rates, even if the economic cycle of the region has not been moving in tandem with that of the US. This undoubtedly has put more pressure on fiscal policy to be more accommodative, leading to successive budget deficits and rising internal debt conditions. However, this is considered a reasonable price to to pay for the maintenance of financial stability and the preservation of the confidence of savers and investors.

It has also been advantageous for the other countries in the region (Jordan, Lebanon and Egypt) to follow a fixed dollar peg, because their economies are closely linked to those of the Gulf countries. Remittances of nationals working in the GCC states, together with FDI, tourism and exports of other services to the Gulf countries, constitute important sources of revenues to Arab countries of West Asia. As long as the Gulf currencies are dollar-based, it is advisable for countries like Egypt, Jordan and Lebanon to have their currencies also pegged to the dollar. Besides, the main exports of those countries are also priced in dollars (e.g. cotton, oil, Egypt's Suez Canal revenues, phosphate, potash and cement etc) and devaluation will not add to their price-competitiveness in export markets. Because these countries have had a history of currency devaluation, putting in place a fixed exchange rate will greatly mitigate any residual risk of devaluation that is still on the mind of savers and investors.

## INTEREST-RATE DIFFERENTIALS ON THE DOLLAR

Historically, there has been a spread between domestic interest rates in Arab countries whose currencies are pegged to the dollar and those on the US currency. The spreads have fluctuated over time and have varied from one country to another depending on the country's economic fundamentals, the size of the differential between its foreign reserves inflation and that of the US, and markets' assessment of the risks of devaluation of Arab currencies. The availability of such spreads helped preserve the attractiveness of local currency and provided support to its fixed dollar peg.

An improvement in a country's economic fundamentals invariably made it possible for the monetary authorities to steer domestic interest rates lower, closer to those on the dollar. However, there is a limit to how much interest-rate differentials could be reduced without threatening the fixed dollar peg. A spread is needed to compensate holders of the local currency for the higher risk incurred (both actual and perceived) when holding the local currency.

Interest rates on the Jordanian dinar have historically been maintained at relatively high levels to help bolster monetary stability and support the peg on the US dollar that was officially introduced in October 1995 at $1.41 to the Jordanian dinar. Uncertainty associated with the sickness of the late King Hussein in summer 1998 forced the Central Bank to tighten monetary policy, with the benchmark yield on three-month certificates of deposit (CDs) rising to 10.45 per cent in August 1998 and maintaining high levels until the end of the year. However, the smooth transition of power to King Abdullah and the slow-down of economic activity in the country, coupled with a strong build-up in foreign reserves and the decline in US dollar interest rates, allowed the Central Bank to shift to an expansionary monetary policy. Rates on three-month CDs assumed a declining trend in 2000 and 2001, dropping to a monthly average of 9.45 per cent in January 2000 and 4.25 per cent in December 2001.

Interest rates have also been trending lower in Lebanon amidst regained confidence in the Lebanese pound and a noticeable slow-down in economic activity. By December 1999, yields on the benchmark two-year treasury bills were down from 16.02 per cent in May to 14.14 per cent, narrowing the spread on US treasury bills of equal maturity to 8.14 per cent. Similarly, rates on three-month Lebanese treasury bills declined to 10 per cent by December 2001 from an average of 12.7 per cent in 1998, 13.4 per cent in 1997 and 15.2 per cent in 1996.

In Egypt, rates have also followed a downward curve over the past few years, albeit at a slower pace than in Lebanon and Jordan. The three-month treasury bill rate was lowered from 10.2 per cent in 1996 to 9.8 per cent in 1997, 9.4 per cent in 1998 and 8 per cent by June 2001. The pressure on the Egyptian pound in the foreign-exchange market, particularly in light of widening external imbalance, has seen domestic interest rates edging slightly higher in the last months of 2001. The country's foreign reserves dropped to $14 billion by the end of 2001 from more than $19.3 billion at the beginning of 2000.

Other countries in the region have also witnessed a decline in interest rates. In Morocco, deposit rates dropped from 12.3 per cent in 1994 to 7 per cent in June 2001. Tunisia's rates were down from 8.8 per cent to 5.9 per cent in the same period.

In the Gulf countries, domestic interest rates rose in the first quarter of 1999, even though dollar-rates have been stable. For example, Saudi riyal three-month deposit rates reached a high of 6.85 per cent in March 1999, from less than 6 per cent in November 1998, while corresponding dollar-rates dropped from 5.2 per cent to 4.9 per cent in the same period. Interest-rates differentials between Saudi riyal and dollar deposits rose from a low of 0.35 per cent in January 1998 to a high of 1.95 per cent in March 1999. The widening spreads were a reflection of heightened speculative pressure against the riyal at a time when oil prices were on the decline, dropping to their lowest average of $11.37 for Brent crude in the first quarter of 1999. With the rise in oil prices in 2000 and 2001, speculative pressure on the Saudi riyal subsided with riyal/dollar interest-rate differentials dropping to 0.3 per cent in December 2001. During periods in which there is little or no speculation against the Gulf currencies, interest rates on local currency deposits tend to move in tandem with corresponding dollar-rates.

## ASSESSING RISKS OF DEVALUATION FOR SELECTED ARAB CURRENCIES

To assess risk of devaluation for the Arab currencies vis-à-vis the US dollar there are four key questions: is the local currency overvalued against the US dollar? Is the current-account deficit rising? Are foreign reserves falling? Are interest-rate differentials between the domestic currency and the dollar rising? If the answer to these most or all of these questions is yes, then the risk of devaluation is high.

If consumer prices in a country whose currency is pegged to the dollar rise at a higher rate than those of the US, then over time this currency becomes overvalued. The exchange rate can sustain an overvalued level for a period of time, but sooner or later mispricing will show up in rising current-account deficits and in the depletion of foreign-exchange resources. Overvalued currencies also distort prices of domestic services and adversely affect domestic financial markets.

During the period 1995–8, inflation rates as measured by consumer prices in Egypt, Jordan, Lebanon, Morocco and Algeria exceeded those of the US, leading to the gradual appreciation of the exchange rate of the currencies of these countries versus the dollar (table 7.3). Since then, only Egypt and Algeria have reported higher inflation rates than those of the US, putting downward pressure on the Egyptian pound vis-à-vis the dollar.

The foreign reserves of Egypt, although still high at $12 billion, have been on the decline since 2000, and so have the foreign reserves of Lebanon, Tunisia, Morocco and Algeria. On the other hand, the foreign reserves of Jordan have risen, approaching an all-time high. The current-account deficits of Egypt, Morocco, Lebanon and Tunisia have been expanding, while that of Algeria has been declining. Jordan has recorded small current-account surpluses in the past four years (table 7.4).

Finally, interest-rate differentials between three-month local treasury bills or bank deposits and three-month US treasury bills have been trending lower for

Table 7.3
Inflation trends in selected Arab countries compared to that of the US

| | 1995 | 1996 | 1997 | 1998 | 1999 | 2000 |
|---|---|---|---|---|---|---|
| Egypt | 7.3 | 6.2 | 3.8 | 3.8 | 2.8 | 3.0 |
| Jordan | 2.4 | 6.5 | 3.0 | 3.1 | 0.6 | 0.9 |
| Lebanon | 10.6 | 8.9 | 7.8 | 5.0 | 1.4 | 0.5 |
| Morocco | 6.1 | 3.0 | 0.9 | 2.8 | 0.8 | 2.5 |
| Tunisia | 6.3 | 3.8 | 3.7 | 3.1 | 2.7 | 3.0 |
| Algeria | 29.8 | 20.7 | 5.8 | 5.6 | 2.7 | 3.1 |
| Bahrain | 2.8 | –0.2 | 0.2 | –0.4 | 0.5 | 1.7 |
| Kuwait | 2.7 | 3.6 | 0.7 | 1.2 | 3.7 | 2.0 |
| Oman | –1.1 | 0.3 | –0.4 | –0.5 | 1.2 | 1.2 |
| Qatar | 3.0 | 7.4 | 2.8 | 2.9 | 2.2 | 2.7 |
| Saudi Arabia | 5.0 | 0.9 | –0.4 | –0.2 | –1.2 | –0.9 |
| UAE | 4.4 | 3.2 | 3.3 | 2.1 | 2.1 | 2.5 |
| **US** | **2.8** | **2.9** | **2.3** | **1.6** | **1.9** | **2.8** |

*Source: IMF,* International Financial Statistics, *June 2001, IIF country reports (2000), and other sources*

Table 7.4
Exchange rates, current accounts and foreign reserves of selected Arab countries ($ million)

| | 1993 | 1994 | 1995 | 1996 | 1997 | 1998 | 1999 | 2000 |
|---|---|---|---|---|---|---|---|---|
| Egypt | | | | | | | | |
| EP/$ | 3.372 | 3.391 | 3.39 | 3.388 | 3.388 | 3.388 | 3.396 | 3.650 |
| Foreign reserves | 12,904 | 13,481 | 16,181 | 17,398 | 18,665 | 19,340 | 17,500 | 14,400 |
| Current account | 409 | 386 | –184 | 119 | –2479 | –1724 | –1171 | –2900 |
| Jordan | | | | | | | | |
| JD/$ | 0.693 | 0.699 | 0.701 | 0.709 | 0.709 | 0.709 | 0.709 | 0.709 |
| Foreign reserves | 1637 | 1692 | 1973 | 1759 | 2200 | 1750 | 2625 | 3000 |
| Current account | –630 | –399 | –256 | –157 | 21 | 16 | 287 | 94 |
| Lebanon | | | | | | | | |
| LP/$ | 1711 | 1647 | 1596 | 1552 | 1527 | 1508 | 1508 | 1515 |
| Foreign reserves | 2260 | 3884 | 4533 | 5932 | 5976 | 6556 | 7100 | 5500 |
| Current account | –3757 | –4172 | –4646 | –4616 | –4189 | –3409 | –3376 | –3350 |
| Morocco | | | | | | | | |
| MD/$ | 9.651 | 8.960 | 8.469 | 8.800 | 9.714 | 9.225 | 9.750 | 10.100 |
| Foreign reserves | 3655 | 4352 | 3601 | 3794 | 3993 | 4435 | 4103 | 4200 |
| Current account | –380 | –675 | –1186 | 35 | –87 | –245 | 19 | –209 |
| Tunisia | | | | | | | | |
| TD/$ | 1.046 | 0.991 | 0.951 | 0.998 | 1.147 | 1.101 | 1.25 | 1.460 |
| Foreign reserves | 854 | 1461 | 1605 | 1897 | 1978 | 1850 | 1604 | 1500 |
| Current account | –1300 | –512 | –822 | –479 | –593 | –675 | –450 | –766 |
| Algeria | | | | | | | | |
| AD/$ | 24.1 | 42.9 | 52.2 | 56.2 | 58.4 | 60.4 | 69.3 | 70.7 |
| Foreign reserves | 1475 | 2674 | 2005 | 4235 | 8047 | 6846 | 5166 | 5500 |
| Current account | 787 | –1805 | –2230 | 838 | 3453 | –880 | 57 | 2176 |

*Source: IMF,* International Financial Statistics, *November 1999 IIF, country reports, 1999, and Jordinvest estimates*

Jordan, Morocco and Tunisia, but rising for Egypt, Lebanon and Algeria. Based on this methodology, only Egypt, Algeria and Lebanon exhibit a high risk of devaluation, Tunisia and Morocco have medium risk of devaluation, and Jordan has a low risk (table 7.5).

Consumer prices in Saudi Arabia and Oman have been deflating over the past few years, and in Bahrain and Kuwait they have been trending below those of the US. This means that the real exchange rates of the Saudi riyal, the Omani riyal, the Bahraini dinar and the Kuwaiti dinar have been depreciating, suggesting that the four currencies are not overvalued and have been experiencing an improvement in their international competitiveness. Inflation rates in Qatar and the UAE have exceeded those of the US, representing a real exchange-rate appreciation and rendering the two currencies slightly overvalued.

The improvement in oil prices in 2000 and 2001 has helped to reduce current-account deficits of the six GCC states and added to their foreign-exchange reserves. The fact that there has been little or no speculation against the Gulf currencies since oil prices started to surge early in 2000 has led to the decline in differentials between interest rates on local currencies and those on the dollar. As such, risks of devaluation for Gulf currencies are believed to be minimal in the immediate future.

## CONCLUSION

Maintaining a fixed peg on the US dollar has served most of the Arab countries well so far, suggesting that the status quo should be maintained. However, to remove any residual risk of devaluation, this exchange-rate regime should be backed by sound economic fundamentals and government policies that are credible, transparent and market-friendly. Crisis occurs when governments say one thing and do another. Arab countries that continue to run large budget deficits and in which domestic inflation is higher than that of the US, should follow tight monetary policy that provides interest-rate support for their dollar-pegged currencies.

Having a fixed exchange-rate regime is like putting the economy in a strait-jacket. There is nothing wrong with that as long as there are no excesses. If governments overspend, or external deficits surge, the jacket will become tight and cracks will start to appear. Remedial measures would then have to be taken, putting the economy on a strict 'diet' of fiscal discipline, higher interest rates and additional liberalization and privatization deals to attract foreign capital. Imposing restrictions or introducing bureaucratic hurdles on foreign exchange transactions to preserve an overvalued exchange-rate peg can actually make things worse. Capital controls, like those applied by Malaysia recently, could limit currency speculation but have an economic cost, and could lead to inefficiency in the allocation of limited capital resources.

Drawing on foreign reserves to support the currency will only succeed if accompanied with corrective policies on the fiscal and monetary fronts. Since most Arab countries allow free current- and capital-account transactions, speculative pressure generated by adverse economic conditions and high turnover in the foreign-exchange market would quickly deplete the countries' foreign reserves. Intervention in the foreign exchange market will not necessarily preserve the fixed exchange-rate peg. Pushing down a currency's value may be easier, since the government can sell as much of its currency as it wants to print. Such an intervention can be 'sterilized' when the central bank offsets its effect on money supply by selling government securities.

Table 7.5
Assessing risks of devaluation vis-à-vis the dollar for selected Arab currencies

| | Is the currency overvalued? | Is the current-account deficit rising? | Are foreign reserves falling? | Are interest-rate differentials on the dollar rising? | Devaluation risk outlook |
|---|---|---|---|---|---|
| West Asia and North Africa | | | | | |
| Algeria | Yes | No | No | Yes | Medium |
| Egypt | Yes | Yes | Yes | Yes | High |
| Morocco | No | Yes | Yes | No | Medium |
| Tunisia | No | No | Yes | No | Low |
| Jordan | No | No | No | No | Low |
| Lebanon | No | Yes | Yes | Yes | High |
| GCC | | | | | |
| Saudi Arabia | No | No | No | No | Minimal |
| Kuwait | No | No | No | No | Minimal |
| UAE | No | No | No | No | Minimal |
| Oman | No | No | Yes | No | Minimal |
| Bahrain | No | No | No | No | Minimal |
| Qatar | No | No | Yes | No | Minimal |

# 8

# NORTH AFRICA

## EGYPT

Table 8.1
Egypt: main economic indicators

| | 1995/96 | 1996/97 | 1997/98 | 1998/99 | 1999/2000 | 2000/01F |
|---|---|---|---|---|---|---|
| Nominal GDP (EGP billion) | 229 | 256 | 280 | 302 | 315* | 335 |
| Nominal GDP ($ billion) | 67.5 | 75.5 | 82.7 | 89.1 | 92.4* | 91 |
| Nominal GDP growth | 12.3% | 11.8% | 9.4% | 7.9% | 4.3%* | 5.0% |
| Real GDP growth | 5.0% | 5.3% | 5.7% | 6.1% | 4.2%* | 3.3% |
| Average annual inflation | 7.3% | 6.2% | 3.8% | 3.8% | 2.8% | 3.0% |
| **Fiscal indicators (EGP million)** | | | | | | |
| Total revenues | 60,893 | 64,498 | 67,963 | 73,279 | 77,065 | – |
| Total expenditure | 63,889 | 66,826 | 70,783 | 86,009 | 89,116 | – |
| Overall balance | –2996 | –2328 | –2820 | –12,730 | –12,051 | – |
| (as percentage of GDP) | –1.3 | –0.9 | –1.0 | –4.2 | –3.8 | 3.4 |
| Total external debt | 31,043 | 28,774 | 28,076 | 28,224 | 27,783 | 23,500 |
| (as percentage of GDP) | 45.90 | 38.0 | 34.0 | 31.7 | 28.3 | 25.8 |
| **External Indicators ($ million)** | | | | | | |
| Exports | 4609 | 5345 | 5128 | 4445 | 6388 | 5495 |
| Imports | –14,107 | –15,565 | –16,899 | –17008 | –17,861 | –18,750 |
| Current account | –185 | 119 | –2479 | –1724 | –1171 | –2900 |
| (as percentage of GDP) | –0.30 | 0.20 | –3.00 | –1.90 | –1.20 | –3.10 |

**Jordinvest*
*F: Forecast*

*Source: Ministry of Economy, Ministry of Finance, Central Bank of Egypt*

### *ECONOMIC OVERVIEW*

Egypt today is one of the most significant markets in the Middle East, given the size of its economy, and its strategic importance as a power-broker in the region. At the start of the 1990s the government embarked on a fully-fledged economic recovery and structural adjustment programme (ERSAP) consisting of reforms and measures aimed at reducing internal and external imbalances, making the economy market-oriented, and placing it on a sustainable long-term growth path.

As a result of prudent economic policies, Egypt managed to maintain macro-economic stability while facing a series of local and external shocks. Between 1997 and 1999, a combination of factors – including the drop in oil price, the impact of the Asian crisis on investment patterns in emerging markets, and the heavy fall in tourism earnings following the Luxor massacre in November 1997 – had a negative impact on the economy. Nonetheless, real growth rates during the period 1996–9 averaged over 5 per cent annually.

Despite the country's impressive growth record, particularly in the second half of the 1990s, concerns over Egypt's macroeconomic health resurfaced in 2000 and 2001, mainly in relation to a widening balance of payments and dollar/liquidity shortages in the market. The tight money conditions in Egypt trace their origins back to late 1998 and early 1999, a period marked by a significant increase in domestic assets within the banking system and a shift in the balance of payments, from a comfortable surplus to a large deficit. Higher government expenditure on ambitious infrastructure and industrial-development-related projects was the key driver of this asset growth. Around 60 per cent of imports consisted of capital goods being used in huge public-sector projects, in which the government invested $3.7 billion in 1999, and which will cost $120 billion over 20 years.

The fall in oil and tourism receipts which started in late 1997 drove the current account into a deficit equal to 3.4 per cent of GDP in 1997/98 after having been near balance for several years in a row. This put substantial pressure on the exchange rate peg. The government's unwillingness to raise interest rates and curtail credit expansion at the time for fear of suppressing growth, or to shift to a more flexible exchange-rate regime, led to pent-up demand in the foreign-exchange market.

Despite a relative easing of restrictions on foreign-currency allocations in late 1999, liquidity shortages endured, with the government ordering the Central Bank to limit credit to the private sector. The change in government policy towards bank lending led to a marked deterioration in the financial position of small- and medium-sized investors, who found themselves unable to acquire financing. This instigated a higher rate of bankruptcies, with negative implications on economic growth. More seriously, the authorities' inconsistent response to the problems facing the economy has undermined their credibility and the negative impression on investors' confidence has lingered.

In June 2001, Standard & Poor's revised its rating of Egypt from stable to negative, while maintaining its rating at an investment grade of BBB–. The country's slow pace of structural reform, combined with widening fiscal deficits and inflexible monetary policy, has put pressure on Egypt's credit standing.

Both the government and the Central Bank's rather vague policy stance in 1999 have been a major source of uncertainty and instability in the market. It took until

April 2000 for the government to acknowledge overspending in the 1998/99 budget, which resulted in an actual deficit equal to 4.2 per cent of GDP, not the 1 per cent previously claimed. Moreover, in the face of mounting pressures on the exchange-rate peg it was only in the summer of 2000 that the government allowed the Egyptian pound to depreciate, after some $5 billion of foreign exchange reserves had been spent over 18 months to defend the overvalued rate of EGP3.42 to the dollar.

Following the failure of earlier efforts, the currency stabilized somewhat with the introduction in January 2001 of a new structured policy pegging the Egyptian pound against the dollar at $1=EGP3.85, with a 1 per cent fluctuation band. However, there have been concerns about the policy's influence on the local money market, given that the fluctuation policy was not limited to a specific time period, which effectively allows the currency to crawl. The Egyptian pound remained under pressure in the second half of 2001 and was devalued in December by 8.5 per cent to $1=EGP4.50.

Undoubtedly, the Egyptian economy has suffered in 2000 and 2001 from weak economic growth, monetary policy inconsistencies, slow structural reforms and a yawning trade-deficit gap. However, the external economic indicators released in early 2001 suggest a limited improvement in the economy's health. According to official figures, in 2000 real GDP growth remained robust at 5 per cent and the inflation rate was kept low at 2.8 per cent. Moreover, Egypt's tourist traffic has returned to pre-Luxor-attack levels before suffering a new setback following the attack on the US on 11 September 2001. Egypt's external balance is also on the mend, with the balance-of-payments deficit narrowing to $156 million in the fourth quarter of 2000, compared to over $1.4 billion over the same period in 1999.

Progress in liberalization and economic reform has been slow recently. However, the government's privatization programme is expected to expand significantly in 2002, building on several years of fluctuating results. Progress in the privatization of the banking sector has been particularly disappointing, with the planned sale of the first of the four fully state-owned banks postponed indefinitely. Egypt's privatization programme was started in 1995 when the sale of public companies raised EGP1.2 billion for the Egyptian government. 1996 saw an improvement in the volume of sales, with the total reaching EGP2.791 billion. In 1997, privatization revenues jumped to EGP3.396 billion. In 1998, however, the figure fell to EGP2.361 billion, rising only slightly in 1999 to EGP2.871 billion. In 2000 the overall figure for privatization stood at EGP2.467 billion.

The country's plan to privatize 49 companies in 2001 as part of the country's ongoing divestment of public-sector-affiliated companies under Law 203 did not come through. The Ministry of Economy and Foreign Trade has received approval to begin the privatization of 25 joint-venture companies and five joint-venture banks. The proceeds from privatization in 2001 are estimated at EGP1.3 billion ($338 million). Privatization in the communications sector has been delayed due to poor global market conditions. After much delay, the government has selected a team led by Merrill Lynch to advise on the strategic sale of a 20–34 per cent stake in Telecom Egypt. Moreover, the privatization of the electricity sector appears to be underway, and the authorities have already started separating the electricity-generating and distribution activities of the seven regional electricity companies as part of the pre-privatization restructuring process.

The government recently announced that it is now placing market-driven, export-led growth at the heart of its reform agenda. However, it first needs to restore market confidence if it is to resume its so-far impressive growth pattern. Without a forceful renewal of the reform agenda and a clear handling of market uncertainties surrounding the exchange-rate regime, the country may face a prolonged slow-down in growth.

## *GROWTH*

Real growth in the Egyptian economy slowed down in 1999/2000 after a strong growth record in the previous few years. Following real growth of 6.1 per cent and 5.7 per cent in 1998/99 and 1997/98 respectively, Jordinvest estimates that real GDP growth fell to 4.2 per cent in the fiscal year ending June 2000, as tight liquidity conditions constrained both consumption and investment spending. This is considerably below the rather optimistic government estimate of 6.5 per cent, a figure inconsistent with a slow-down in electricity, cement and steel output volume growth, broad money supply, domestic credit and government-expenditure expansion. Moreover, growth in Egypt is still largely public-sector led and funded, and while the government may believe in such policies to support growth, they are in effect crowding out the private sector and pushing back the process of privatization that the government is so keen to promote.

Despite signs of a slow recovery, lower interest rates and optimistic government projections of 5.5 per cent real GDP growth in the 2001 fiscal year, Jordinvest estimates that growth has moderated to 4 per cent as a result of subdued domestic demand. Heightened regional uncertainties and the impact of the 11 September attack are likely to also reflect negatively on the performance of the recovering tourism sector. Moreover, although the economy is largely driven by internal dynamics, with exports accounting for a modest 7 per cent of GDP, the country is not immune to slow-down in global economic growth. With the domestic industry still not fully recovered from the recent liquidity crisis, exports and FDI were expected to be the main drivers of growth, a now unlikely scenario in light of the global economic slow-down. Nonetheless, growth may resume at a stronger pace if interest rates drop further and the government follows through on its promise to settle arrears to the private sector, easing the liquidity crunch and stimulating the economy. In the longer term the government is targeting a growth rate of 7–8 per cent by 2004. However, this will be dependent on the pace at which the government is able to revitalize and deepen its economic reforms.

## *MONETARY POLICY*

The main features of monetary developments in Egypt over the past few years have been rapid credit expansion and a drawdown of foreign assets held by the banking sector and, more recently, by the Central Bank. Following growth rates of 13 per cent and 14.9 per cent in the fiscal years 1997/98 and 1996/97 respectively, domestic credit grew by 18.5 per cent in the fiscal year 1998/99 to reach EGP256.6 billion, and by a further 11.6 per cent to EGP286.1 billion in 1999/2000.

The strong expansion in domestic credit was primarily financed by a rationing of foreign assets held by commercial banks. The shocks to the Egyptian economy in 1997 and 1998 narrowed down foreign exchange inflows into the economy and put pressure on the exchange rate, a process which was aggravated further by increasing demand for foreign exchange to finance higher import consumption. The monetary authorities chose to maintain the peg, but did not want to jeopardize growth by raising interest rates and reigning in strong credit expansion. Instead, the Central Bank rationed the availability of foreign exchange and forced commercial banks to draw down their foreign assets in order to alleviate foreign currency pressures.

The resulting situation was unsustainable, and the Central Bank was eventually forced to satisfy excess demand from its own reserves. Foreign-exchange reserves fell from a high of $20 billion in early 1998 to $14 billion in June 2001.

## *INFLATION*

In line with its bold stabilization efforts aimed at containing inflation, the government was able to reduce inflation rates from 25.2 per cent in 1986/87 to 3.8 per cent in 1998 and 1999. According to official estimates, the inflation rate in 2000 was 2.8 per cent. Limited price pressures in 2000 and 2001 were mainly a result of subdued economic activity, along with tight monetary policy and a fall in food import prices. Inflationary pressures are likely to reassert themselves in 2002 and 2003 as world commodity prices pick up and the effect of the depreciation of the currency is felt. Inflation for 2001 is put at approximately 3 per cent, and is expected to rise further to 3.4 per cent in 2002.

## *EXCHANGE RATE*

The stability of the Egyptian pound continues to form the cornerstone of Egypt's monetary policy. Following devaluation in 1990 and the introduction of a unified exchange rate, the stability of the pound has been upheld by an overall surplus in the balance of payments, large and continuing capital inflows, and increasing foreign-exchange reserves. However, monetary policy decision-making over the period 2000–1 has been hasty and *ad hoc*, with the Central Bank divided between trying to slow the rate of depreciation of the pound against the dollar on the one hand, and being constrained by the tightening effect its actions has on domestic currency liquidity and interest rates on the other. Following over one year of steady deprecation of the pound against the dollar, the recent shift to a managed peg could bring order to what has been a rather chaotic foreign-exchange market, assuming the Central Bank of Egypt proves sensitive to market forces in managing the peg.

Pressure on the Egyptian pound resurfaced in 1999 and extended into most of 2001 and 2001, bringing about a decline in the country's foreign-exchange reserves. As a result, the Egyptian pound weakened against the dollar from EGP3.41 at the end of the fiscal year 1998/99 to EGP3.767 in December 2000. Foreign-exchange reserves stood at $15.031 billion in March 2000, compared to $20 billion in the first quarter of 1998, falling to $14.38 billion at the end of December 2000 and $14 billion by June 2001. The dwindling foreign-currency reserves were a direct result of the Central Bank's injections of dollars into the market to compensate for dollar shortages. To maintain the stability of the Egyptian pound and its *de facto* peg to the dollar at EGP3.40, the Central Bank continued releasing dollars into the market and draining liquidity in the local currency. This led to an Egyptian pound liquidity shortage, reflected in higher overnight inter-bank lending rates, which climbed to a high of 17 per cent at various points during 1999 and early 2000 before settling down in the 10–12 per cent range.

The Egyptian currency market stabilized in the first half of 2001, following the government's adoption of a structured policy in January 2001. Following months of inconsistency, the government pegged the pound against the dollar at EGP3.85 with a 1 per cent fluctuation band, and was devalued further by 8.5 per cent in December 2001 to $1=EGP4.50. The Central Bank will periodically review the new rate and possibly revise it according to market conditions. A series of measures will be taken to stop exchange bureaux from buying and selling above the central rate. Exchange bureaux will have to report prices to the Central Bank each hour, take steps to ensure transparency, sell foreign-exchange surpluses at the end of each day to banks, and must have a paid-up capital of EGP10 million, up from the previous minimum of EGP1 million.

## *INTEREST RATES*

The Central Bank lowered the discount rate four times in 2001, to close the year at 9 per cent. High market interest rates have undermined private-sector activity, dragging on growth and pushing up the risk premium further. The cumulative cut in domestic interest rates goes some way – but not far enough – towards keeping up with the decline in dollar-deposit rates since December 2000 . Nonetheless, Egypt continued to run an excessively tight monetary policy in which the real spread between Egyptian pound and dollar-rates remained excessively high, at over 700bps by the end of 2001. In light of the large fiscal deficit expected and weaker demand for Egyptian exports from a slowing global economy, the authorities need to cut rates more aggressively to achieve the targeted GDP growth rate.

Table 8.2
Egypt: summary of national budget operations (EGP million)

| | 1995/96 | 1996/97 | 1997/98 | 1998/99 | 1999/00 |
|---|---|---|---|---|---|
| **Total revenues** | **60,893** | **64,498** | **67,963** | **73,279** | **79,416** |
| Tax revenues | 38,249 | 40,518 | 43,962 | 48,096 | 52,200 |
| Transferred profits | 11,133 | 11,423 | 10,780 | 9501 | 10,229 |
| Other non-tax revenues | 5104 | 5238 | 5293 | 5161 | 4581 |
| Non-central government revenues | 6407 | 7319 | 7928 | 10,521 | 12,406 |
| **Total expenditure** | **63,889** | **66,826** | **70,783** | **86,009** | **91,689** |
| Current expenditure | 51,196 | 53,030 | 54,747 | 60,524 | 67,238 |
| Of which: interest payments | 12,231 | 12,337 | 12,219 | 14,081 | 16,000 |
| Foreign interest payments | 3796 | 3114 | 2724 | 2325 | 1797 |
| Investment expenditure | 12,581 | 14,070 | 15,635 | 25,321 | 24,074 |
| **Overall balance** | **–2996** | **–2328** | **–2820** | **–12,730** | **–12,273** |
| Overall balance as percentage of GDP | –1.3 | –0.9 | –1 | –4.2 | –3.8 |

*Source: Ministry of Finance*

## *FISCAL POLICY*

The 2000/01 budget deficit target is 3.4 per cent of GDP, down from actual levels of 3.8 per cent of GDP in 1999/2000. The deficit in the first quarter of 2000/01 (July to September), as a percentage of GDP, came out to 3.5 per cent, but fell to 0.2 per cent in the following quarter (October to December), compared to 1.8 per cent and 0.6 per cent in the first and second quarter of 1999/2000 respectively. In April 2001, the cabinet approved the 2001/02 budget with the deficit for the year projected at 3.3 per cent of GDP.

The Egyptian government revised the budget deficit for fiscal year 1998/99 from 1.3 per cent of GDP to 4.2 per cent. This came after a commendable fiscal performance, with the deficit having been slashed to around 1 per cent of GDP since the mid-1990s following budget deficits averaging 18–20 per cent of GDP in the 1980s. With a curb on spending, reduced subsidies, enhanced tax collection and increased revenue-generation, a budget deficit of 0.9 per cent of GDP was attained in 1997/98. The release of the revised figures immediately prompted Standard & Poor's to downgrade its outlook on Egypt from stable to negative.

The substantial widening of the deficit in 1998/99 was primarily due to a 21.5 per cent increase in public expenditure that overshadowed a healthy increase in revenues. The increase in expenditure was concentrated in capital spending, which rose by 62 per cent on the previous year, reinforcing the view that heavy government spending on infrastructural projects in 1999 was a major contribution to the liquidity crisis. The 1999/2000 budget results show some improvement on the previous year, with the deficit-to-GDP ratio down to 3.8 per cent. Revenues rose 5 per cent to EGP77.06 billion, while expenditure increased by 3.6 per cent on the year before to EGP89.12 billion, bringing the deficit down by 5 per cent to EGP12.05 billion.

Despite the most recent budget figures, fiscal achievements over the past decade cannot be overlooked. During the period 1992–2001, the government cut public spending by nearly 40 per cent, reducing food, electricity and fuel subsidies, slashed public employment and decreased defence spending. Government spending represented 32.2 per cent of GDP in 1993/94, 27.1 per cent of GDP in 1999/2000. Government investment cuts are being outweighed by broader private-sector participation in infrastructure projects through BOT contracts, especially in telecommunications and power sectors.

The government managed to boost revenues through a series of revenue-enhancement measures, which included a new sales tax, higher custom duties and increased Suez Canal fees (20 per cent of public revenues). As a result, the ratio of public receipts to GDP rose from 23.6 per cent of GDP in 1998/99 to 25 per cent in 1999/2000. While tax revenues accounted for 66.1 per cent of total public receipts over the period (64.6 per cent), proceeds from privatization represented a major source of revenues, reaching 1.4 per cent of GDP over the 1996/99 period. Privatization proceeds stood at approximately EGP2.7 billion in 1996/97, EGP3.5 billion in 1997/98, and considerably lower at EGP0.9 billion in 1998/99.

The government is aiming to reduce the budget deficit to 2 per cent of GDP in 2003, from 3.8 per cent in 2000. Concerning revenue, a major reform package is being prepared that will emphasize addressing tax evasion and collecting taxes in arrears. On the expenditure side, the government is planning to bring down overall spending by reducing the rate of growth of expenditure on huge infrastructure projects and by rationalizing current expenditures. However, cutting spending is unlikely to be an easy task, especially as the government will face ongoing pressure to increase social spending in the face of strong public grievances over poverty, unemployment and social inequality.

## *DOMESTIC DEBT*

As a percentage of GDP, domestic debt remains at comfortable levels, and compares favourably to other emerging or even developed economies. Total public debt rose from EGP132.3 billion in 1995/96 to EGP201.9 billion at the end of 1999/2000 and to EGP204.2 billion as of the end of 2000. As a percentage of GDP, public domestic debt has stood at less than 55 per cent since 1993/94, dropping to 49 per cent in 1999/2000 and 46 per cent at the end of 2000. Domestic debt is primarily fuelled by government borrowing from the National Investment Bank (NIB) as well as by the servicing of the budget deficit through the issuance of treasury bills and bonds. Since 1995, the Finance Ministry has issued several long-term bonds with maturities of five and seven years for a total amount of EGP5 billion ($1475 million).

Table 8.3
Egypt: structure of outstanding domestic debt (EGP million)

| | 1995/96 | 1996/7 | 1997/98 | 1998/99 | 1999/2000 | Dec. 2000 |
|---|---|---|---|---|---|---|
| **Total public debt*** | **132,257** | **148,470** | **159,919** | **182,071** | **201,927** | **204,164** |
| **1. Government** | **114,098** | **125,493** | **136,745** | **147,155** | **164,392** | **165,178** |
| Securities | 83,296 | 90,065 | 84,654 | 77,684 | 77,689 | 81,410 |
| Treasury bonds | 39,848 | 40,446 | 35,446 | 40,830 | 40,830 | 40,830 |
| Treasury bills | 27,282 | 33,131 | 38,000 | 25,558 | 25,393 | 28,869 |
| Social security | 3029 | 3029 | 3029 | 3029 | 3029 | 3029 |
| Energy bonds | 5118 | 5382 | 0 | 0 | 0 | 0 |
| Housing bonds | 153 | 151 | 144 | 143 | 142 | 142 |
| Banks recapitalization bonds | 7092 | 7083 | 7082 | 7098 | 7203 | 7318 |
| Government borrowing from NIB | 44,642 | 55,459 | 68,884 | 78,999 | 88,947 | 91,154 |
| Credit balances with banking sector | 13,840 | 20,031 | 16,793 | 9528 | 2244 | 7386 |
| **Public economic authorities memorandum items** | **18,159** | **22,977** | **23,174** | **34,916** | **37,535** | **38,986** |
| Public debt/GDP | 58% | 58% | 57% | 60% | 60% | 57% |
| Government claims/GDP | 50% | 49% | 49% | 49% | 49% | 46% |

* *Including net claims on central and local governments, public service authorities and public economic authorities*

*Source: Central Bank of Egypt.*

## *EXTERNAL DEBT*

The Egyptian government was able to bring down foreign debt from more than $46 billion in 1986 to about $27.78 billion in 2000, representing 28.3 per cent of GDP. The country's external debt fell by 24 per cent in the first half of the 2001 to $21.1 billion.

Following the Gulf War in 1990, all of Egypt's debt to Arab creditors was cancelled, as well as military debt owed to the US in recognition of the country's support for the UN coalition formed to liberate Kuwait. This was followed by the cancellation of half of the net present value of the long-term concessionary debt owed to Western governments, known as the Paris Club ($22 billion) and the rescheduling of the remaining balance. Debt structure is favourable and debt service and exports amounted to less than 10 per cent in 2000. Approximately 80 per cent of the debt is due to the Paris Club, of which 65 per cent is due to four creditors: the US, France, Germany and Japan. Short-term facilities represent less than 10 per cent of the total external debt, leaving Egypt in a good position on the financial markets and vis-à-vis its external creditors.

Table 8.4
Egypt: external debt by type and maturity ($ million)

| | 1996/97 | 1997/98 | 1998/99 | 1999/2000 | Dec. 2000 |
|---|---|---|---|---|---|
| Total external debt | 28,774 | 28,076 | 28,224 | 27,783 | 21,109 |
| Medium- and long-term public and publicly guaranteed debt | 27,226 | 26,226 | 26,010 | 25,774 | 25,004 |
| Bilateral loans | 22,263 | 21,102 | 21,027 | 20,518 | 19,871 |
| Loans from international organization | 3832 | 4302 | 4326 | 4275 | 4224 |
| Credit to suppliers and buyers | 1131 | 822 | 657 | 981 | 908 |
| Short-term debt | 1541 | 1719 | 1830 | 1628 | 1778 |
| Private-sector debt | 7 | 131 | 384 | 381 | 327 |
| Total external debt (percentage of GDP) | 38 | 34 | 31.7 | 28.3 | 27.1 |

*Source: Central Bank of Egypt*

## *EXTERNAL SECTOR*

The current account deficit widened to $2.48 billion, or 3.4 per cent of GDP, in the fiscal year 1997/98, following a modest surplus of $119 million the previous year. The deterioration in the current-account balance in the fiscal year 1997/98 was mainly a result of a widening trade balance, driven by higher imports and a drop in exports, and a 24 per cent decline in the services balance on the back of lower tourism receipts. Tourism revenues, which account for about a third of services receipts, fell to $2.9 billion in 1997/98 from $3.6 billion the previous year in the wake of the Luxor incident in November 1997.

The current-account deficit narrowed in the fiscal year 1998/99 to $1.7 billion, equivalent to 1.9 per cent of GDP, reflecting a 27 per cent improvement in the service balance, mainly as a result of recovering tourism receipts. On the other hand, the trade balance deteriorated further despite almost zero import growth that year. Imports increased by less that 0.5 per cent in in 1998/99, compared to average import growth of almost 10 per cent annually over the previous three years. However, exports fell by 13.3 per cent to $4.4 billion, largely due to a further decline in oil export receipts to $1 billion, down from $1.7 billion in 1997/98. Despite an overall improvement in the current account position, the capital account dropped sharply in 1998/99 to $919 billion, from $3.4 billion the previous year. Direct investments into Egypt slowed down in 1999, while portfolio investments have been in net deficit since the economic shocks of 1997.

The year 1999/2000 saw a further improvement in the current account to a $1.17 billion deficit (–1.2 per cent of GDP), from $1.71 billion (–1.9 per cent of GDP) the previous year. This was driven primarily by an 8.7 per cent improvement in the trade balance to a deficit of $11.47 billion, from a $12.56 billion deficit in 1998/99, which in turn was a result of a 43 per cent rise in exports to $6.39 billion. Imports rose at a more modest rate of 5 per cent to $17.86 billion. The services balance fell by 5.8 per cent, and similarly transfers declined by 3.9 per cent. The capital account deteriorated significantly in 1999/2000, showing a deficit equal to $1.28 billion, compared to a surplus of $919 million the year before. As a result, the balance of payments showed a deficit of $3.0 billion in 1999/2000, equivalent to –3.1 per cent of GDP, compared to a $2.1 billion deficit (–2.4 per cent of GDP) the previous year.

Table 8.5
Egypt: balance of payments ($ million)

| | 1996/97 | 1997/98 | 1998/99 | 1999/2000* | 1999/2000* Jul./Dec. | 2000/01* Jul./ Dec. |
|---|---|---|---|---|---|---|
| **Trade balance** | **–10,219** | **–11,771** | **–12,562** | **–11,474** | **–5889** | **–4814** |
| Export | 5345 | 5128 | 4445 | 6388 | 2759 | 3450 |
| Petroleum | 2578 | 1728 | 1000 | 2273 | 937 | 1272 |
| Other export | 2768 | 3400 | 3445 | 4115 | 1822 | 2178 |
| Import | –15,565 | –16,899 | –17,008 | –17,861 | –8648 | –8264 |
| **Services (net)** | **6193** | **4692** | **5969** | **5624** | **3012** | **2802** |
| Receipts | 11,241 | 10,455 | 11,025 | 11,420 | 5831 | 6080 |
| Suez Canal | 1849 | 1776 | 1771 | 1781 | 885 | 894 |
| Travel | 3646 | 2941 | 3235 | 4314 | 2219 | 2250 |
| Investment income | 2052 | 2081 | 1923 | 1833 | 896 | 934 |
| Other | 3693 | 3657 | 4086 | 3493 | 1831 | 2002 |
| Payments, of which | 5048 | 5764 | 5056 | 5796 | 2819 | 3278 |
| Interest | 995 | 716 | 789 | 770 | –391 | –367 |
| **Transfers (net)** | **4146** | **4601** | **4869** | **4680** | **2245** | **1743** |
| **Current account** | **119** | **–2479** | **–1724** | **–1171** | **–631** | **–269** |
| (as percentage of GDP) | 0.2 | –3.4 | –1.9 | –1.2 | – | – |
| **Capital account** | **2041** | **3387** | **919** | **–1281** | **–1205** | **–1121** |
| Errors and omissions | –247 | –1043 | –1312 | –573 | –594 | 678 |
| **Overall BOP** | **1913** | **–135** | **–2117** | **–3025** | **–2430** | **–712** |
| (as percentage of GDP) | 2.5 | –0.2 | –2.4 | –3.1 | – | – |

* *preliminary figures*

*Source: Central Bank of Egypt*

The first half of the fiscal year 2000/01 (July to December 2000) also vouches for the continued improvement in the country's external balance. Exports over the first six months of the year increased by an impressive 25 per cent to $3.45 billion, compared to $2.76 billion in the first half of 1999/2000. Petroleum exports increased by 35.8 per cent over the same period, while non-oil products also performed well, with an increase of 19.5 per cent. Imports, on the other hand, decreased by 4.4 per cent.

The services balance also fell by 7 per cent in the first half of 2000/01 compared to the same period a year previously. However, this was caused by a rise in payments rather than a decline in revenues, which actually rose by 4.3 per cent. As a result of the strong improvement in the country's trade balance, the current-account deficit at the end of the first half of 2000/01 narrowed significantly to

$269 million, compared to a deficit of $631 million over the same period in 1999/2000. For the entire fiscal year 2000/01 a worsening of the current account to approximately $2.9 billion is to be expected as a result of weakening exports on the back of lower oil prices in the second half of the year, and an increase in imports by approximately 5 per cent.

# MOROCCO

Table 8.6
Morocco: main economic indicators

| | 1996 | 1997 | 1998 | 1999 | 2000 | 2001 |
|---|---|---|---|---|---|---|
| Nominal GDP (MD billion) | 319 | 318 | 341 | 351 | 371 | 404 |
| Nominal GDP ($ billion) | 36.64 | 33.42 | 35.55 | 35.89 | 36.87 | 40.19 |
| Nominal GDP growth | 13.1% | -0.3% | 7.2% | 2.9% | 5.7% | 9.0% |
| Real GDP Growth | 12.2% | -2.3% | 6.5% | 0.2% | 1.2% | 6.0% |
| Consumer price percentage change | 3.0 | 0.9 | 2.8 | 0.8 | 1.9 | 2.5 |
| **Fiscal indicators (MD billion)** | | | | | | |
| Revenues | 37 | 70 | 78.7 | 87 | 88.2 | – |
| Expenditure | 41 | 81 | 90.3 | 95.4 | 102.6 | – |
| Deficit/surplus | –4 | –11 | –11.6 | –8.5 | –14.3 | – |
| (as percentage of GDP) | –1.3 | –3.5 | –3.4 | –2.4 | –3.9 | – |
| Total external debt ($ million) | 21,715 | 19,383 | 20,031 | 19,191 | 19,452 | – |
| (as percentage of GDP) | 59.3 | 58.0 | 56.3 | 53.5 | 52.8 | – |
| Total debt service ($ million) | 3343 | 3159 | 2056 | 2880 | 2919 | – |
| **External indicators ($ million)** | | | | | | |
| Exports | 6886 | 7039 | 7262 | 7890 | 8770 | – |
| Imports | –9079 | –8903 | –9599 | –10,300 | –11,670 | – |
| Current-account balance | 35 | –87 | –245 | 19 | –209 | – |
| (as percentage of GDP) | 0.1 | –0.3 | –0.7 | 0.1 | –0.6 | – |

*Source: Direction de la Statistique (Morocco) and IIF*

## *ECONOMIC OVERVIEW*

Morocco's commitment to sound economic policy during the 1990s has given the country an admirable record of internal and external stability. Morocco's adjustment process, implemented initially with IMF support in response to the debt crisis of the late 1970s and early 1980s, has achieved much on the economic front. During the period 1996–2000, inflation has been contained under 3 per cent, the current-account deficit remained below 1 per cent of GDP, the external debt burden has been brought under control and official reserves have built up. On the political front, the transition of power to the new king, Mohammed VI, went smoothly, indicating widespread support for the country's political institutions and continued political liberalization.

A recent development that could significantly alter the country's economic prospects is the discovery of oil reserves in the Talsinnt region in eastern Morocco, just 125 miles from the Algerian border. In August 2000, King Mohammed VI announced the discovery of an oil deposit with reserves estimated at 1500–2000 million barrels of oil equivalent, representing between 25 and 30 years of Morocco's energy consumption. If the new finds prove to be substantial, Morocco stands to make major savings on oil import costs, estimated at $1300 million in 1999. The development of the field and further oil exploration in the region will also attract major foreign investments, another boost for the Moroccan economy. According to the country's energy minister, investment in developing the area is likely to leap to $1000 million from an initial $160 million.

The main challenge facing the authorities today is to achieve higher, sustainable economic growth. Persistent reliance on drought-sensitive crops in the context of large climate fluctuations has produced significant volatility in output. As a result of increasingly frequent drought conditions in the 1990s and disappointing growth in the non-agricultural sector, GDP growth has exhibited a cyclical pattern, with a yearly average of less than 3 per cent.

Such growth levels have been insufficient to tackle the worsening unemployment situation in the country – estimated at 19 per cent in urban areas – or to reverse the deterioration in social conditions and affluence, particularly in rural areas. Labourforce growth is outpacing not only job creation but also the overall population growth rate due to the demographic structure of the population, with a high percentage in the 15–24 age bracket, and increased female participation in the labourforce.

Growth in the non-agricultural private sector must be supported by complementary reforms. In this respect, Morocco recently initiated a corporate upgrading programme to assist local industrial firms in meeting the challenge posed by further trade liberalization in the context of the EU Association Agreement. The trade agreement will expose the so-far highly protected local industries to tough competition, as a result of which many firms will be forced to leave the market. However, in the longer term it should lead to higher efficiency, improved resource-allocation and greater access to export markets.

Morocco's medium-to-long-term prospects will to a large extent reflect the pace of implementation and the effectiveness of structural reforms. Substantial progress has already been achieved on market-oriented reforms, albeit at a gradual pace. Reform on the fiscal front has been particularly slow, with several persistent weaknesses, including a high wage bill, an ineffective system of subsidies and low capital expenditure – especially in light of the country's serious need for a physical and social infrastructure. In addition, the tariff dismantling required under the EU accord will diminish a major revenue source for the government.

The privatization programme, which started in 1993, has recently witnessed renewed momentum with the sale of the second GSM mobile telephone licence in

1999 to the international consortium Medi Telecom for approximately $1.1 billion. Morocco's plans to privatize the highly lucrative state-owned Maroc Telecom and Royal Air Maroc are also well underway.

A real commitment to reform and privatization will guarantee the country a continued flow of FDI. Direct-equity investment topped $1.3 billion in 1999, boosted by the GSM deal. This is particularly needed given the constraints on external borrowing. Despite sound debt-management that has resulted in substantial reductions in debt ratios over the past decade, the economy continues to be weighed down by a heavy debt burden.

## *GROWTH*

The main weakness of the Moroccan economy lies in its reliance on the volatile agricultural sector, resulting in pronounced swings in GDP growth rates. The agricultural sector accounts for around one-fifth of the country's GDP and employs 40 per cent of the labourforce. Erratic growth has severely hampered the country's efforts to take advantage of low inflation and accelerate the level of domestic investment.

Table 8.7
Morocco: GDP growth, 1997–2000

| | 1997 | 1998 | 1999 | 2000 |
|---|---|---|---|---|
| Nominal GDP (MD billion) | 318.0 | 341.0 | 351.0 | 365.0 |
| Nominal GDP ($ billion) | 33.4 | 35.6 | 35.9 | 37.7 |
| Nominal GDP growth | -0.3% | 7.2% | 2.9% | 4.0% |
| Real GDP growth | -2.3% | 6.5% | 0.2% | 1.2% |

*Sources: IIF*

The shift in growth levels has been dramatic, particularly in the 1990s. The economy contracted by 6.6 per cent in 1995, recovered with an impressive 12.2 per cent growth in 1996, declined by 2.3 per cent in 1997, surged by 6.5 per cent in 1998, then once again fell into recession in 1999 with growth stagnant at 0.2 per cent, caused by a 12.3 per cent contraction in the agricultural sector due to drought early in the season.

Real GDP rose by a modest 1.2 per cent in 2000, less than an initial forecast of 6.5 per cent, again due to negative drought effects on the agricultural sector. However, weak growth in agricultural output was partially offset by rising investment levels as the revenues from privatization were used for infrastructure projects, and more government divestiture attracts fresh flows of foreign investment. Moreover, Morocco, as is the case with Tunisia, stands to benefit from higher economic growth forecasts in the EU, its main export destination. According to official figures, real GDP growth in 2001 is expected to be 6 per cent.

In the longer term, and in order to achieve high and sustainable economic growth, one of the main priorities in Morocco is to modernize farming methods and expand irrigation so as to introduce an element of predictability to the volatile agricultural sector. In parallel, economic diversification and plans to develop the non-agricultural economy must be at the top of the government's reform agenda. Non-agricultural growth has been mediocre recently, hovering around 3 per cent in the 1990s, a rate that does not provide sufficient jobs to reduce the prevalent high unemployment level.

## *MONETARY POLICY*

Money-supply targets are the central bank's key policy tools, alongside the maintenance of a strong domestic currency. Monetary growth, which is monitored on the basis of M3, expanded by 10 per cent in 1999 compared to 6 per cent and 9.2 per cent in 1998 and 1997 respectively. However, broader measures of liquidity and quasi-liquidity reveal steeper growth in liquid investments over the past two years than that indicated by M3. In order to tighten monetary control, the central bank is working on introducing additional monetary instruments and developing the secondary market.

## *INFLATION*

Monetary policy in Morocco since 1996 has been successful in containing inflation below 3 per cent. Inflation averaged 0.7 per cent in 1999, compared with 2.7 per cent in 1998, due mainly to slowing domestic demand. However, inflation rose to 1.9 per cent in 2000 reflecting higher oil prices and rising food costs as a result of a poor harvest for two years in a row. The inflation rate for 2001 is forecast at 2.5 per cent.

## *INTEREST RATES*

Interest rates in Morocco have been on the decline, averaging approximately 5 per cent over the period 1993–2001. The central bank has sought to stimulate the economy via lower interest rates, cutting rates on its treasury bill by more than 3 per cent in 1999–2001. Morocco's banking institutions have been reluctant to pass on the full benefits of lower interests rate to their customers, and lending rates have been slow to adjust as a result of low competition among domestic banks. However, the recent opening up of the sector to foreign institutions should result in greater competition.

## *EXCHANGE RATES*

The local currency is pegged against a basket of currencies of its principal trading partners, and the peg served Morocco well in providing a firm nominal anchor during the disinflation process.

However, the dirham has appreciated by around 15 per cent in real terms since 1992 against its major trading partners, a fact which has adversely affected the competitiveness of Moroccan exports, in conjunction with the absence of noticeable improvements in productivity and quality. The planned dismantling of tariffs in the context of the EU accord will aggravate the problem, possibly requiring that the authorities re-examine their exchange-rate policy in the medium term.

In April 2000, Morocco devalued its national currency by 5 per cent against the dollar to an average MD11.5 in an attempt to strengthen the country's exports and reduce the trade deficit. The unexpected devaluation, the first in 11 years, put the exchange rate of the dirham at an average 10.25 against the euro. The EU is Morocco's main trading partner, accounting for two-thirds of its foreign trade. Exporters' associations in recent years repeatedly urged the government to devalue the dirham in order to boost exports. Morocco's trade deficit stood at 45.2 billion dirhams in 2000, up 40 per cent from 1999. The move was also motivated by expected low inflation, healthy foreign reserves estimated at six months' imports and a relatively good 2000/01 cereals harvest. The inflation rate is put at 2.5 per cent in 2001, against 1.9 per cent in 2000, and the cereals harvest is expected to reach between 5 and 5.5 million tonnes, sharply up from 1.8 million tonnes in the previous season.

## *FISCAL POLICY*

The Moroccan government has made a concerted effort to reduce its budget deficit in recent years. The 1998/99 deficit reached MD8.1 billion ($820 million), equivalent to 2.3 per cent of GDP, down from the MD11 billion (3 per cent of GDP) projected in the budget proposal presented in June 1998. The better-than-projected fiscal results in 1999 reflected a substantial improvement in revenues, which more than offset a further increase in expenditures. The strong revenue performance was a result of exceptional fiscal measures, mainly the special levy on state monopolies and the fiscal amnesty. This was supported by successful efforts to cut domestic and foreign debt.

While the government has been successful in reducing the large fiscal deficits recorded in the 1980s (averaging 8.3 per cent of GDP), several fiscal challenges persist. For one, new revenue measures will be needed to compensate for the gradual reduction in tariffs in accordance with the EU Association Agreement. Tariffs account for around 19 per cent of fiscal revenue and, given that more than 50 per cent of the country's imports are from the EU, Morocco faces the prospect of substantial revenue losses.

On the expenditure side, a strong approach to civil service reform, alongside direct steps to curb additional recruitment, will be necessary to lighten the burden of the wage bill. Likewise, a gradual removal of the current inefficient food-subsidy system would free resources for a better-targeted assistance programme. Continued active debt-management should also assist the government in reducing debt-servicing requirements, with interest on total public debt amounting to MD17.7 billion in the 1999 budget, just under 20 per cent of total expenditure. On the revenue side, the authorities need to broaden and harmonize VAT and excise taxes and to extend tax coverage to untaxed or undertaxed sectors.

## *PUBLIC DEBT*

Prudent external borrowing and an active debt-management policy has substantially reduced Morocco's external debt burden. External debt reached a peak of 130 per cent of GDP and 400 per cent of exports in 1985 and was rescheduled nine times between 1983 and 1992. By the end of 2000, Morocco's total external debt is estimated to have fallen to less than $19.2 billion, or 54 per cent of GDP.

The bulk of Moroccan debt is owed to the governments of France, Spain, and Italy. Over the past few years, several measures have been taken to reduce foreign debt by speeding up the transfer of debts owed to France into investments, early repayment of expensive loans, and reducing the country's indebtedness to international banks, known as the London Club. High cost debt has also been refinanced with cheaper loans. The government plans to reduce the country's external debt by $1 billion per annum over the coming years.

## *EXTERNAL SECTOR*

Following a modest deficit of $0.2 billion (0.7 per cent of GDP) in 1998, the current account is estimated to have recorded a small surplus in 1999. Morocco has gradually reduced barriers to trade over the last decade, although the level of protection remains high. The maximum tariff rate is 35 per cent, except for a few agricultural products for which quantitative restrictions were replaced by tariffs of up to 290 per cent, in line with Morocco's WTO commitments. In addition to tariffs, there is an import surtax of up to 15 per cent on most goods.

Morocco runs a chronic merchandise trade deficit, which is generally offset by receipts from tourism, workers' remittances and foreign investment. In 1999 exports grew by 8 per cent and imports by 7 per cent. While foreign investment increased dramatically in the last few years, tourism receipts and workers' remittances have generally been weak.

Export performance has been lacking in recent years, and the real appreciation of the dirham over the past few years has adversely affected the competitiveness of the export sector. Morocco is hoping that the EU accord will encourage the participation of foreign investors in the restructuring of the industrial sector.

Table 8.8
Morocco: current-account balance ($ billion)

| | 1997 | 1998 | 1999 |
|---|---|---|---|
| Trade balance | –1.9 | –2.3 | –2.4 |
| Exports | 7.0 | 7.3 | 7.9 |
| Imports | -8.9 | -9.6 | -10.3 |
| Services balance | –0.4 | –0.2 | 0.0 |
| Net transfers | 2.2 | 2.3 | 2.4 |
| Current-account balance | –0.1 | –0.2 | 0.0 |
| (as percentage of GDP) | –0.3 | –0.7 | 0.0 |

*Source, IIF*

# TUNISIA

Table 8.9
Tunisia: main economic indicators

| | 1996 | 1997 | 1998 | 1999 | 2000 | 2001 |
|---|---|---|---|---|---|---|
| Nominal GDP (dinar million) | 19,066 | 20,898 | 22,600 | 24,844 | 26,819 | 29,307 |
| Nominal GDP ($ billion) | 19.59 | 18.9 | 19.85 | 20.93 | 19.6 | 21.06 |
| Nominal GDP growth | 11.8% | 9.6% | 8.1% | 9.9% | 8.4% | 9.5% |
| Real GDP growth | 7.1% | 5.4% | 4.8% | 6.2% | 5.0% | 5.2% |
| Consumer price index, average | 3.8% | 3.7% | 3.1% | 2.7% | 3.0% | 2.9% |
| Exchange Rate, end period (TD/$) | 1.00 | 1.15 | 1.10 | 1.25 | 1.46 | 1.37 |
| **Fiscal indicators (TD million)** | | | | | | |
| Revenues | 4787 | 5191 | 5707 | 6123 | 6833 | 6940 |
| Expenditure | 5611 | 6081 | 6415 | 7005 | 7655 | 7790 |
| Deficit/surplus | –824 | –890 | –708 | –882 | –822 | –850 |
| (as percentage of GDP) | –4.3 | –4.3 | –3.1 | –3.6 | –3.1 | –2.9 |
| Total external debt ($ million) | 11,408 | 11,087 | 11,585 | 11,841 | 11,610 | 12,098 |
| (percentage of GDP) | 58.2% | 58.7% | 58.4% | 56.6% | 59.2% | 57.4% |
| **External indicators ($ million)** | | | | | | |
| Trade balance | –1761 | –1955 | –2151 | –2149 | –2280 | –2410 |
| Exports | 5519 | 5559 | 5724 | 5870 | 6120 | 6550 |
| Imports | 7280 | 7514 | 7875 | 8019 | 8400 | 8960 |
| Current-account balance | –479 | –593 | –675 | –450 | –766 | –785 |
| (as percentage of GDP) | –2.4 | –3.1 | –3.4 | –2.2 | –3.9 | –3.7 |

*Source: Central Bank of Tunisia and IIF*

## *ECONOMIC OVERVIEW*

The process of reform and gradual liberalization of the Tunisian economy has contributed to a strengthening economy. Encouraged by more liberal exchange, trade and regulatory regimes, the private sector has expanded rapidly in the export and tourism sectors, while domestic demand has been sustained by the rising real incomes of a large middle class. This economic success is also the result of coherent and prudent macroeconomic policies, pursued in a medium-term perspective. Combined with progressive social policies, this approach has produced remarkable growth rates and significant advances in social indicators.

Tunisia has taken important steps towards achieving its development targets. Real growth has averaged around 5.7 per cent over the 1996–2000 period and inflation has been reduced to around 3 per cent, the current account deficit stood at 2.2 per cent of GDP in 1999, down from over 4 per cent in 1995, thanks to steady export growth and rising tourism receipts, and the government has, to a large extent, been successful in restructuring revenues away from oil income and import tariffs and towards VAT and income taxes.

Nonetheless, several challenges still persist. In particular, fiscal consolidation remains a top priority as dismantling tariffs under the EU Association Agreement is expected to significantly erode the revenue base. Unemployment remains high, at approximately 16 per cent, and planned structural adjustments such as privatization could aggravate the situation further. Moreover, although the government has eased its grip on the economy, it is still seen to be in control.

Tunisia has made significant strides towards an open economy. The Association Agreement with the EU will eliminate all protection on industrial goods by 2007/08. The agreement further calls for a comprehensive harmonization of standards and norms of the regulatory structure. This will present a number of policy challenges during the transitional period, particularly in the fiscal area.

Structural reforms have proceeded on several fronts, including in the banking sector, enterprise restructuring, and in private-sector development. The country's industrial modernization programme has contributed to a more dynamic private sector with a greater attractiveness to foreign investors. Tunisia began reducing tariffs against EU manufactured goods in 1996, but overall trade protection remains high, and significant restructuring is still needed to meet the challenges of free trade with the EU.

The privatization programme was boosted by the sale of three major cement factories in 1998 and 2000, and a new privatization drive involving 41 public enterprises has been announced for 2001 and 2002. Meanwhile, the state retains extensive control over the economy through a large public-enterprise sector and controls on prices and market access. Privatization needs to be extended to the Tunisian banking system, which remains heavily dominated by the public sector. Notable progress has been made towards restoring bank stability in the country and in restructuring public-sector banks and reinforcing prudential regulations in the banking sector. The capital–asset ratio for the banking sector as a whole rose from 8.9 per cent in 1998 to 10.1 per cent in 1999 (only one bank failed to reach the minimum 8 per cent ratio). Furthermore, the level of unprovisioned bad loans was reduced to 14.1 per cent of total liabilities in 1999 from over 20 per cent in 1997. However, the burden of non-performing loans is still high (20 per cent of GDP in 1999), and will continue to affect the cost of financing.

Tunisia's macroeconomic policies remain fundamentally sound, and the outlook for the economy is favourable. To increase private-sector initiative, the government needs to complete its withdrawal from direct intervention in productive activities such as banking, communications and transport. The pace of structural reform must be accelerated, especially in the privatization area, if the government is to achieve its ambitious growth targets.

Figure 8.1
Tunisia: growth in fixed-capital formation outpaces real GDP growth

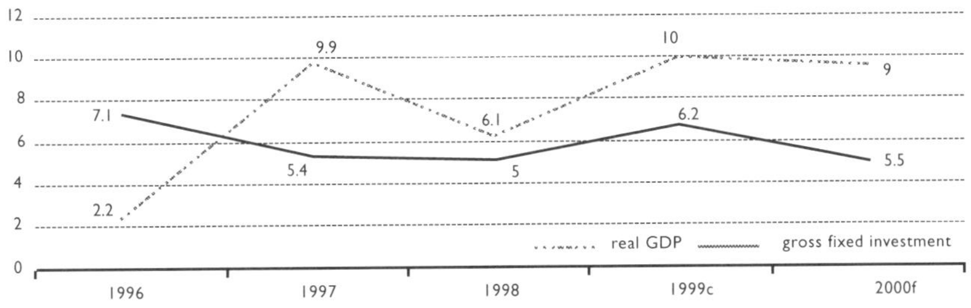


*Source: IIF*

## *GROWTH*

Real growth strengthened to an average rate of 5.7 per cent between 1996 and 2000, as gradual economic liberalization and prudent macroeconomic policies allowed Tunisia to reap the benefits offered by stronger integration into the world economy. GDP growth has been robust in all sectors, particularly services and manufacturing, while domestic demand growth has been buoyed by rising real incomes and strong investment, particularly in the services and export-oriented manufacturing sectors.

The growth performance in 2000 confirms recent favourable trends. Despite the negative impact of drought conditions, overall GDP growth reached 5 per cent in 2000. The rebound of agricultural production, as well as sustained growth in foreign and domestic demand, pushed GDP growth to 5.2 per cent in 2001. According to government figures, the agricultural sector grew by 6.5 per cent in 2001 following a 1 per cent decline in 2000. Cereal output is put at 1.8 million tons in 2001 compared with 1.09 million tonnes in 2000 as a result of severe drought conditions. Growth in the services sector is estimated to reach 6 per cent in 2001, up from an estimated 6 per cent in 2000. Investment is forecast to rise 10 per cent to TD7.755 billion ($5.407 billion) in 2001, accounting for 26.4 per cent of the economy's projected gross output.

Gross fixed investment has been the most dynamic component of aggregate demand over the past couple of years. The industrial modernization programme and the associated efforts by the export sector to up-grade and modernize production capacity has resulted in an accelerated growth in gross fixed capital formation to an estimated 10 per cent in 1999, boosting the investment rate to 29 per cent of GDP, up from 25 per cent in 1996. Meanwhile growth in private consumption is estimated to have decelerated slightly in 1999 to 4 per cent, following a 5 per cent expansion in 1998.

## *MONETARY POLICY*

Monetary policy is largely on target, insofar as credit and monetary aggregates have grown roughly in line with GDP. The monetary authorities have largely been successful in both controlling inflation and maintaining a stable real effective exchange rate. A slight easing in monetary policy was noted in 1999, following a tight stance the year before aimed at maintaining the low inflation environment. Following growth in money supply (M2) of 13.6 per cent and 16.5 per cent in 1996 and 1997 respectively, expansion declined to 5.6 per cent in 1998 but picked up in 1999, to 19.5 per cent. Money-supply growth slowed down in 2000 to an estimated 10.8 per cent, and is expected to be approximately 10 per cent in 2001.

Figure 8.2
Tunisia: consumer pricing index, annual average

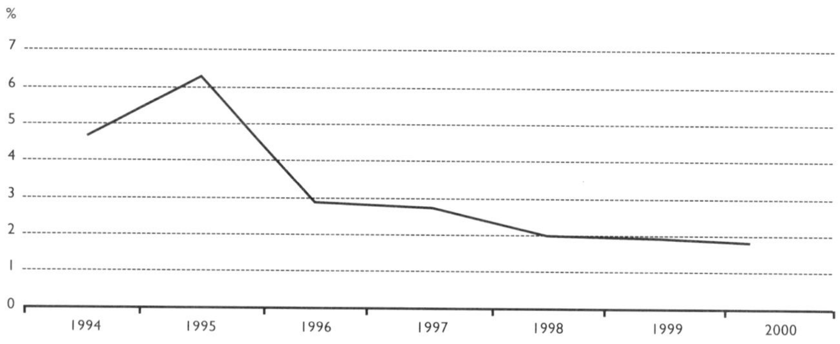


*Source: IMF and Jordinvest estimates*

## *INFLATION*

As a result of prudent monetary policy, inflation has tracked a steady downward trend since 1995, when it equalled 6.4 per cent. The consumer price index fell to a low of 3.1 per cent in 1998, despite the increase in VAT rates and substantial increases in administered prices and in the prices of public transportation and other utilities. Inflation moderated further in 1999, to around 2.7 per cent, its lowest level in three decades, as a result of weaker food-price inflation. The inflation rate rose moderately to 3 per cent in 2000, with inflationary pressures generated from the moderate private-sector wage increase negotiated around mid-1999 for the period 1999–2001 being offset by gains in productivity and declines in import prices. Inflation is expected to remain roughly unchanged at around 2.9 per cent in 2001.

## *EXCHANGE RATE*

The exchange-rate policy in Tunisia plays a critical role in preserving external price-competitiveness, particularly in light of the ongoing tariff dismantling with the EU. The central bank aims at maintaining the stability of the real effective exchange rate against a basket of currencies of main trading partners. Nonetheless, the dinar/dollar-rate has been appreciating persistently in real terms since early 1997. In the face of a weakening euro, the central bank departed from its fixed real exchange rate rule during 2000, allowing the dinar to depreciate slightly in real effective terms. The anticipated recovery of the euro against the dollar is expected to lead to a reversal of the depreciation trend of the dinar against the dollar.

**Table 8.10**
**Tunisia: central government budget, 1997–2001 (TD million)**

| | 1997 | 1998 | 1999 | 2000B | 2000E | 2001B |
|---|---|---|---|---|---|---|
| Total revenue | 5933 | 6579 | 7180 | 7625 | 7837 | 8208 |
| Tax revenue | 4231 | 4770 | 5207 | 5624 | 5832 | 6105 |
| Social security contributions | 993 | 1114 | 1220 | 1220 | 1361 | 1368 |
| Non-tax revenue | 709 | 695 | 753 | 753 | 644 | 735 |
| Total expenditure and net lending | 6804 | 7223 | 7828 | 8572 | 8623 | 9033 |
| Deficit (excluding grants, privatization) | −871 | −644 | −648 | −947 | −786 | −825 |
| (as percentage of GDP) | −4.2 | −2.8 | −2.6 | −3.5 | −2.9 | −2.8 |
| Deficit (including grants, privatization) | −803 | −136 | −564 | −686 | −445 | 296 |
| (as percentage of GDP) | −3.8 | −0.6 | −2.3 | −2.6 | −1.7 | 1.0 |

*B: Budget*
*E: Estimate*

*Source: IMF*

## *FISCAL POLICY*

The budget deficit target set for 2000 (3.5 per cent of GDP) appears to have been comfortably met, as supplementary spending on petroleum price supports and continued tariff reductions were more than offset by higher tax revenues. The consolidated deficit is estimated at 2.9 per cent of GDP in 2000, slightly up on its level of 2.6 per cent the year before but well below much higher levels of 5.1 per cent and 4.2 per cent in 1996 and 1997 respectively. Including grants and privatization proceeds, this brings the deficit down to 1.7 per cent of GDP in 2000, compared to 2.3 per cent in 1999.

The Tunisian government's commitment to deficit reduction is reflected in the draft budget law for 2001. The budget plan for the year 2001 puts expenditures at TD9.0 billion, and total revenues at TD8.2 billion, resulting in a deficit of TD825 million (before grants and privatization proceeds), equivalent to 2.8 per cent of GDP. Privatization proceeds are expected to reach TD10.2 billion in 2001, its highest level in years. As a result, the budget, after grants and privatization proceeds, is expected to show a modest surplus of TD296 million, or 1 per cent of GDP.

The pursuit of deficit reduction over the medium term in a context of declining trade tariff revenues will require that existing fiscal rigidities be addressed, especially as the government will need to maintain or even increase spending to modernize public administrations. The main budget rigidity lies in the wage bill, which is high by international standards. Pay rises and wage-drift alone produce annual increases of about 5 per cent in the wage bill. The government's intention of limiting recruitment to the higher education and health sectors and to meet the demands in other sectors as far as possible through redeployment of staff, is a step in the right direction. However, a lasting reduction in the public payroll will require a comprehensive civil-service reform, therefore, downsizing the public sector and rationalizing current expenditure should remain high on the government's agenda. Savings are also possible on foodstuff subsidies (approximately 0.7 per cent of GDP), as the social targeting of this spending is particularly inefficient.

To offset the revenue effect of the trade-tariff reductions, compensatory tax measures will have to be introduced, mainly through a broadening of the tax base and more efficient tax collection. Major steps in this direction were already taken in 1999, in particular by raising the minimum tax to 20 per cent. The adoption of a new tax procedure code, to be introduced in early 2002, should also improve tax collection in a context of greater transparency.

## *EXTERNAL SECTOR*

Despite a widening trade balance, the current account deficit showed a notable improvement in 1999, down by 33 per cent to TD516 million. This follows two years of worsening current-account deficits. The current deficit as a percentage of GDP fell to 2.1 per cent in 1999, compared to 3.4 per cent and 3.1 per cent in 1998 and 1997 respectively.

Much of the credit for the improvement in the current-account balance in 1999 is due to a healthy rise in the services surplus to TD2 billion, driven by a 14 per cent increase in tourism receipts, compared to a more modest increase of 9.4 per cent in 1998. Workers' remittances also rose by 12.5 per cent, reflecting the favourable economic environment in Europe, where the majority of Tunisian expatriates reside.

Strong export growth, alongside a more moderate increase in imports, also helped keep the trade deficit in line. Merchandise exports grew by 6.9 per cent in 1999, while imports rose by 6 per cent, following more robust growth of 8 per cent and 17 per cent in the previous two years respectively. As a result, the trade deficit widened by a modest TD91 million, or 3.7 per cent, to TD2540 million.

Despite its strong fundamentals, international financial-market conditions in 1998 prevented Tunisia from financing its current-account deficit through borrowing on international capital markets, forcing it to draw on its reserves. However, better borrowing conditions and calmer international markets in 1999 allowed Tunisia to strengthen its external financial position.

The capital account in 1999 showed a healthy surplus of TD1336 million compared to a deficit of TD558 million in 1998. Foreign participation in domestic investments fell from TD778 million in 1998 to TD481 million in 1999, mainly because of lower privatization receipts. On the other hand, loans and capital inflows from both international bodies (namely the World Bank, the African Development Bank and the IDB) and international capital markets (namely the European bond market) increased to TD787 million in 1999, up from a net outflow of TD290 million in 1998. As a result of the improvements in both the current and the capital account, the balance of payments showed a surplus of TD820 million, or 3.3 per cent of GDP, in 1999, up from a deficit of TD213 million in 1998 (–0.9 per cent of GDP).

Table 8.11
**Tunisia: main balance-of-payments indicators**

| | 1997 | 1998 | 1999 | 2000 |
|---|---|---|---|---|
| Current account | –655 | –769 | –516 | – |
| (as percentage of GDP) | –3.1 | –3.4 | –2.1 | – |
| Trade balance | –2646 | –2971 | –3104 | –3723 |
| Exports | 6148 | 6518 | 6967 | 8004 |
| Imports | 8794 | 9490 | 10,061 | 11,728 |
| Capital account | 1054 | 558 | 1336 | – |
| Overall balance | 373 | –213 | 820 | – |
| (as percentage of GDP) | 1.8 | –0.9 | 3.3 | – |

*Source: Central Bank of Tunisia*

Tunisia's trade deficit reached TD3.723 billion ($2.786 billion) in 2000, up almost 20 per cent on the 1999 level. Imports increased 16.5 per cent to TD11.728 billion compared to 1999, while exports rose 14.9 per cent to TD8.004 billion. The trade cover ratio (the percentage of imports covered by the value of exports) for 2000 was 68.2 per cent, down from 69.1 per cent in 1999. Europe is Tunisia's main export outlet, mainly for clothing and leather products. The trade deficit with the EU has widened since 1998, when a trade association accord with the European bloc came into force. The accord provides for a phasing-out of tariffs and gradual opening of the Tunisian market to European goods and services. The current account deficit is expected to widen slightly as a result of the expected recovery in import growth over the coming few years, particularly imports of capital goods and equipment associated with the industrial modernization programme. The lower tariff structure in light of the EU Association Agreement will also encourage higher imports that will not be totally offset by export growth in the short term.

### *EXTERNAL PUBLIC DEBT*

According to the IIF, total external debt in Tunisia stood at $13 billion in 1999, equivalent to 64 per cent of GDP. Around 30 per cent of the country's external debt is owed to international financial institutions, 29 per cent to official bilateral creditors, 25 per cent to private creditors – through international bonds – and the remaining 15 per cent to commercial banks. The country's external indebtedness is manageable in light of Tunisia's easy access to external borrowing and international bond markets, and the limited share of short-term debt (at approximately 15 per cent of total debt in 1998).

Table 8.12
Tunisia: structure of external debt ($ million)

| | 1997 | 1998 | 1999E |
|---|---|---|---|
| **Total external debt** | 12,238 | 12,718 | 12,991 |
| Medium–long-term | 10,854 | 10,870 | 10,671 |
| Short-term | 1384 | 1847 | 2320 |
| International financial institutions | 3841 | 3823 | 2834 |
| Official bilateral creditors | 3675 | 3739 | 3582 |
| Commercial banks | 1757 | 1972 | 2021 |
| Other private creditors | 2964 | 3184 | 3554 |

*E: Estimate*

*Source: IIF*

## ALGERIA

### *ECONOMIC OVERVIEW*

Since the early 1990s, Algeria has achieved successful financial stabilization by addressing its fiscal problems through sound yet aggressive macroeconomic policies, under the auspices of international financial institutions. Most importantly, inflation was pruned to single digit levels, and large account deficits have been converted into surpluses during the 1992–97 period. Meanwhile, the stabilization effort was also supported by substantial external debt reduction, an exchange-rate devaluation and liberalization, and current account restrictions were removed.

Table 8.13
Algeria: main economic indicators

| | 1995 | 1996 | 1997 | 1998 | 1999 | 2000 |
|---|---|---|---|---|---|---|
| Nominal GDP (AD billion) | 1967 | 2495 | 2716 | 2782 | 3182 | 3533 |
| Nominal GDP ($ billion) | 41.3 | 45.6 | 47.1 | 47.4 | 47.8 | 51.1 |
| Nominal GDP growth | 33.6% | 26.9% | 8.9% | 2.4% | 14.4% | 11.0% |
| Real GDP growth | 3.8% | 3.8% | 1.3% | 5.1% | 3.6% | 4.2% |
| Inflation | 29.8% | 20.7% | 5.8% | 5.6% | 2.7% | 3.1% |
| Exchange rate, end of period (AD/$) | 52.2 | 56.2 | 58.4 | 60.4 | 69.3 | 70.7 |
| **Fiscal Indicators (AD billion)** | | | | | | |
| Government revenue | 600.9 | 824.8 | 926.6 | 774.5 | 963.8 | 1009.2* |
| Government expenditure | 629.1 | 749.9 | 860.5 | 882.8 | 996 | 1085.7* |
| Fiscal deficit | −28.2 | 74.9 | 66.1 | −108.3 | −32.2 | −76.4 |
| (as percentage of GDP) | −1.4% | 3.0% | 2.4% | −3.9% | −1.0% | −2.2% |
| Total external debt ($ million) | 35,690 | 34,381 | 32,680 | 32,117 | 29,701 | 28,688 |
| (as percentage of GDP) | 86.5 | 75.4 | 69.4 | 67.8 | 62.1 | 56.2 |
| **External Indicators ($ million)** | | | | | | |
| Trade Balance | 160 | 4120 | 5690 | 1510 | 3346 | 5700 |
| Exports | 10,260 | 13,210 | 13,820 | 10,140 | 12,446 | 15,450 |
| Imports | 10,100 | 9090 | 8130 | 8630 | 9100 | 9750 |
| Current-account balance | −2530 | 838 | 3453 | −880 | 57 | 2176 |
| (as percentage of GDP) | −6.1 | 1.8 | 7.3 | −1.9 | 0.1 | 4.3 |

** 2000 budget*

*Source: IIF*

President Bouteflika, elected in April 1999, has launched several initiatives aimed at restoring political stability to the country, and a new government was appointed. Although there has been little progress, if any, on the structural reform front over the past few years, the new government has promised to reinvigorate the process, particularly in the banking sector. The privatization drive in the country is also picking up speed: the Algerian government has recently introduced a new privatization law that will facilitate the sale of 250 state entities through a phased privatization programme.

Algeria's financial sector is largely controlled by five major public-sector financial institutions: Banque Nationale d'Algerie, Banque Exterieure d'Algerie, Credit Populaire d'Algerie, Banque Algerienne de Développment, and Caisse Nationale d'Epargne et de Prevoyance – which hold approximately 95 per cent of total assets and deposits. Specialized banks have also contributed to the inefficient allocation of banking resources to government projects. Despite the introduction of market based reforms to the banking sector in the 1990s, the sector remains inefficient and suffers from a legacy of non-performing loans, weak financial credibility and inefficient and costly operations.

The government has taken several tangible steps towards improving the efficiency and performance of the financial sector, with the implementation of a new strategy targeting the promotion of the private sector and encouraging the establishment of new private banks. The initiative has also opened the door for private minority participation in state-owned banks' capital and allowed for the gradual entry of foreign banks into the domestic market, the establishment of a securities market and the pursuit of organizational restructuring at state-owned banks.

The Algerian economy remains heavily reliant on the performance of the hydrocarbon sector, which represents approximately 25 per cent of GDP, about half of the government's revenues and almost all of the country's export revenue. The contribution of the hydrocarbons sector renders the economy extremely sensitive to fluctuations in world commodity prices. Although Algeria managed the oil-price crash of 1998 relatively well, it did come not out unscathed. The current account fell into a deficit of almost $1 billion that year, compared to a surplus of $3.5 billion in 1997, and the budget deficit widened to 3.6 per cent of GDP.

Although higher oil prices bode well for Algeria's economic development, they do not contribute greatly to dealing with the wider economic and social problems. The country is rich in natural resources and well placed to take advantage of any future agreements with the EU. However, only by re-accelerating the reform process and convincing the world that the civil war, which has lasted more than seven years, is coming to an end will Algeria be able to take its place among the emerging tigers of the Mediterranean.

## *GROWTH*

Algeria's economy grew at an annual average of 6 per cent during the period between the late 1970s and 1987, aided by rising oil prices. However, weakened oil prices in the mid-1980s forced a slow-down of economic growth which lingered throughout the end of the decade amid rising political unrest, thus further contracting economic output, by a 2.5 per cent average annual rate until 1994. The stabilization reform programme, which was enacted in 1992, bore fruit in 1995, with the economy expanding by an average annual rate of approximately 3 per cent in real terms.

Table 8.14
Algeria: GDP growth

| | 1997 | 1998 | 1999 | 2000 |
|---|---|---|---|---|
| Nominal GDP (AD billion) | 2716 | 2782 | 3182 | 3533 |
| Nominal GDP ($ billion) | 47.1 | 47.4 | 47.8 | 51.1 |
| Nominal GDP growth | 8.9% | 2.4% | 14.4% | 11.0% |
| Real GDP growth | 1.3% | 5.1% | 3.6% | 5% |

*Source: IIF*

In 1998, the external environment worsened with the drop in oil prices. Nevertheless, thanks to a recovery in agricultural output and a turnaround in industrial activity, real GDP grew by an impressive 5.1 per cent, compared with 1.3 per cent in 1997. Growth declined to 3.6 per cent in 1999 in light of the slow-down in the major non-hydrocarbon sectors. The strong upturn in the oil markets provided the impetus for accelerating economic growth, with real GDP growth of 4.2 per cent in 2000. Real growth in 2001 is put at 3.5 per cent, supported by government plans to accelerate economic reforms.

## *INFLATION*

Inflation has been on a declining trend since the mid-1990s, falling from approximately 32 per cent in 1995 to approximately 5.6 per cent in 1998 and a low of 2.7 per cent in 1999. This reflects conservative monetary policies, which focus on controlling monetary growth and curbing inflation by employing interest rates control mechanisms. As a result, the bank of Algeria bid up the Interbank overnight rate to 20 per cent in 1995, before gradually reducing it to 10 per cent in 1999. Inflationary pressure is expected to remain subdued, as the government will be keen to maintain hard-won macroeconomic stability, especially by keeping wage rises under control.

## *EXCHANGE RATE AND FOREIGN RESERVES*

Under the reform programme of the IMF, the central bank has resorted to consecutive exchange rate devaluation since 1993 as a means of promoting non-hydrocarbon exports. Officially, the Algerian dinar is linked to a trade-weighted basket of hard currencies. The depreciation of the dinar against the dollar of nearly 13 per cent up in 1999 reflected both the strength of the dollar and the fact that the central bank followed the advice of the IMF to counter the effects of falling oil prices in 1998. In the future, the monetary authorities are likely to take the opportunity afforded now by the ongoing oil price rise to contain further depreciation of the dinar.

Foreign reserves continued their decline in 1999, mainly due to lower disbursements from official creditors that resulted in the widening of the capital account deficit. At the end of 1999, foreign reserves reached $4.5 billion, compared to $6.8 billion at the end of 1998.

## *FISCAL POLICY*

Although Algeria has achieved some improvement in public-finance management, fiscal conditions deteriorated in 1998 amid lower oil prices, moving to a deficit of 3.6 per cent of GDP in 1998, from a surplus of 2.4 per cent of GDP in 1997. With a relatively high wage bill and an elevated interest-payment burden (40 per cent of expenditure), the government had limited room for manoeuvre on current spending. In the meantime, the state was faced with serious challenges in dealing with such social issues as housing, education and health, which put some upward pressures on capital spending.

Table 8.15
Algeria: government budget (AD billion)

| | 1998 | 1999 | 2000B |
|---|---|---|---|
| **Total revenue** | **774.5** | **963.8** | **1009.2** |
| Hydrocarbon revenue | 378.6 | 560.1 | 526.0 |
| Tax revenue | 329.8 | 334.0 | 406.2 |
| Non-tax revenue | 661.0 | 69.7 | 77.0 |
| **Total expenditure** | **875.8** | **996.0** | **1085.7** |
| Current | 663.9 | 766.0 | 795.4 |
| Capital | 211.9 | 230.0 | 290.2 |
| **Budget balance** | **–101.3** | **–32.2** | **–76.4** |
| (as percentage of GDP) | –3.6% | –1.0% | –2.2% |

*B: Budget*

*Source: IIF*

Through prudent fiscal management, and supported by higher oil prices, the Algerian authorities were able to contain the 1999 budget deficit to an estimated 1 per cent of GDP. This compares favourably with an initial target of 2.3 per cent of GDP. Similarly, the year 2000 budget targets a fiscal deficit of 2.3 per cent of GDP. However, this is based on a conservative average oil price assumption of $15 a barrel for the year. With oil prices averaging $29 in 2000, the Algerian budget showed a surplus in 2000, equivalent to at least 1.5 per cent of GDP. Fiscal performance in the medium term will, however, depend on the ability of the government to bring spending under control and find ways to diversify the revenue base by reforming the tax structure and diversifying the economic structure away from the oil sector.

## *EXTERNAL SECTOR*

After recording a deficit of almost $1 billion in 1998, the current account recovered in 1999 on the back of higher oil prices, moving into a modest surplus of $0.1 billion. The recovery in earnings of hydrocarbon exports in 1999 more than doubled the trade balance to $3.3 billion, compared to $1.5 billion in 1998, and a high of $5.7 billion the year before. In the meantime, the deficit in the balance of services and income widened to $4.1 billion while net transfers declined to $0.8 billion.

A further strengthening of the current-account position took place in 2000, due to yet higher hydrocarbon exports, given the continued strength of oil prices and higher gas-export volumes and prices. In 2000 the trade balance reached almost $10 billion, with hydrocarbon export revenues for the year at $19 billion. As a result the current account showed a surplus exceeding $6 billion.

Table 8.16
Algeria: current-account balance ($ billion)

| | 1997 | 1998 | 1999 | 2000 |
|---|---|---|---|---|
| Trade balance | 5.7 | 1.5 | 3.3 | 9.9 |
| Exports | 13.8 | 10.1 | 12.4 | 19.6 |
| Hydrocarbons | 13.8 | 10.1 | 12.4 | 19.0 |
| Others | 0.6 | 0.5 | 0.4 | 0.6 |
| Imports | –8.1 | –8.6 | –9.1 | –9.7 |
| Services and income balance | –3.3 | –3.5 | –4.1 | –4.4 |
| Transfers (net) | 1.1 | 1.1 | 0.8 | 0.9 |
| Current account | 3.5 | –0.9 | 0.1 | 6.4 |

*Source: IIF*

Table 8.17
Algeria: external debt ($ billion)

| | 1997 | 1998 | 1999 | 2000 |
|---|---|---|---|---|
| Total external debt | 32.7 | 32.1 | 29.7 | 28.7 |
| By maturity: | | | | |
| Medium–long-term | 30.9 | 30.8 | 28.4 | 27.4 |
| Short-term | 1.8 | 1.4 | 1.3 | 1.3 |
| By creditor: | | | | |
| International financial institutions | 5.9 | 5.8 | 5.3 | 5.1 |
| Official bilateral creditors | 21.1 | 21.1 | 19.6 | 19.1 |
| Commercial banks | 5.5 | 5.0 | 4.6 | 4.2 |
| Other private creditors | 0.2 | 0.2 | 0.2 | 0.2 |

*Source: IIF*

## *EXTERNAL DEBT*

Algeria's total external debt was estimated at almost $30 million at the end of 1999, equivalent to around 62 per cent of GDP that year. External debt declined by around $2.4 billion in 1999 as a result of net amortization and, to a limited extent, the exchange rate valuation effect. It had dropped further to $28.7 billion by the end of 2000. Approximately two-thirds of this debt is owed to official bilateral creditors with the remaining due to multilateral institutions and commercial banks. Short term debt accounts for less than 5 per cent of the total.

# 9

# LEVANT

## JORDAN

Table 9.1
Jordan: main economic indicators

| | 1996 | 1997 | 1998 | 1999 | 2000 | 2001F |
|---|---|---|---|---|---|---|
| Nominal GDP (JD million) | 4983 | 5193 | 5646 | 5724 | 5895 | 6142 |
| Nominal GDP ($ million) | 7028 | 7324 | 7963 | 8073 | 8315 | 8664 |
| Nominal GDP growth | 4.4% | 4.2% | 8.7% | 1.4% | 3.0% | 4.2% |
| Real GDP growth | 2.1% | 3.1% | 2.9% | 3.1% | 3.9% | 4.0% |
| Inflation | 6.5% | 3.0% | 3.1% | 0.6% | 0.9% | 1.5% |
| **Fiscal Indicators (JD million)** | | | | | | |
| Total revenues | 1650.5 | 1620.0 | 1699.5 | 1815.9 | 1850.0 | 2142.0 |
| Total expenditure and net lending | 1799.0 | 1775.0 | 2055.1 | 2039.4 | 2015.0 | 2300.0 |
| Deficit/surplus (excluding grants) | −368.4 | −380.0 | −558.6 | −422.0 | −410.0 | 400* |
| (as percentage of GDP) | −7.4 | −7.3 | −9.9 | −7.4 | −7.0 | −6.0 |
| External Debt | 4722.8 | 4580.6 | 5009.8 | 5186.2 | 4794.7 | – |
| (as percentage of GDP) | 94.8 | 88.2 | 88.7 | 90.6 | 81.1 | – |
| Internal Debt | 1006.4 | 914.2 | 1119 | 1024 | 1203 | – |
| (as percentage of GDP) | 20.2 | 17.6 | 19.8 | 17.9 | 20.4 | – |
| **External Indicators (JD million)** | | | | | | |
| Exports | 1288 | 1301 | 1278 | 1299 | 1345.3 | – |
| Imports | 3042 | 2907 | 2712 | 2623 | 3204 | – |
| Current-account balance | −157 | 21 | 16 | 287 | 94.3 | – |
| (as percentage of GDP) | −3.2 | 0.4 | 0.3 | 5.0 | 1.6 | – |

**Actual deficit before grants is expected to fall to JD380 million*
*F: Jordinvest forecasts*

*Sources: Central Bank of Jordan, Ministry of Finance and Jordinvest estimates*

## *ECONOMIC OVERVIEW*

The Jordanian economy has assumed a higher growth path in 2000 and 2001 than the one that prevailed in the previous four years. The government, headed by Prime Minister Ali Abu Al-Rageb, has announced its commitment to strengthening the economy, and is forging ahead with economic reforms. Real GDP growth slowed to an annual average of about 2.8 per cent in 1996–9 (the average was equal to 1.4 per cent prior to the revision of GDP figures in November 2000), due mainly to weakness in domestic demand, constraints on exports to neighbouring countries and the end of the post-Gulf-War construction boom. By 1998, the fiscal deficit had widened to about 10 per cent of GDP, largely reflecting the slow-down in economic activity. Domestic and regional political uncertainties combined with the large fiscal deficit and high domestic interest rates also put downward pressure on growth in 1997–9.

Some improvement in economic conditions and confidence has been noted in the course of 1999, as indicated for example by the rebound in international reserves and a lower fiscal deficit. In April 1999, Jordan agreed with the IMF on a new external fund facility (EFF) for the period 1999–2001. The programme is designed to address the major challenges facing the economy, including higher GDP growth rates, a reduction of the substantial fiscal deficit and the acceleration of structural reforms.

Both King Abdullah and the Jordanian government have exhibited a renewed commitment to macroeconomic stabilization and structural reforms. The previous government had made some progress in implementing tax and financial-sector reforms, improvements in tax administration and expenditure control, and trade liberalization. Although there have been delays, the privatization programme is actively being pursued. The sale of a 40 per cent stake in the Jordan Telecommunication Company was completed in early 2000 after a lengthy postponement, and the privatization of the national airline, Royal Jordanian, the electricity company and the phosphate mines, among others, are underway.

Jordan has joined the worldwide trend towards full trade liberalization, as attested by its recent membership to the WTO and its free-trade agreement with the US. In the short term, trade liberalization will strengthen foreign competition in the market, while the competitiveness of local production in the domestic market will be hard-hit as custom duties decline. This will result in unfavourable shifts in Jordan's external trade patterns and a widening of the industrial trade deficit in the short to medium term.

On the positive side, foreign competition will provide an incentive to improve the quality of Jordanian production and increase competitiveness, thereby guaranteeing better quality products that are better able to penetrate sophisticated markets. Trade liberalization and the accompanying intellectual property legislation will also create a more hospitable climate for foreign investment in the country.

In October 2001, Jordan and the US completed a free trade agreement – taking effect in December 2001 – that eliminates trade barriers between the two countries over a phased 10-year period. This makes Jordan the fourth country worldwide – after Canada, Israel and Mexico – to enjoy free access to the US market. Jordan hopes it will attract an influx of foreign capital from multinationals that would come to set up plants for re-export, either to the region or to the wider US market.

Current reforms and economic developments helped to bring a substantial turnaround in the economic situation. However, Jordan is expected to continue to face a difficult external environment, particularly as a result of a turbulent regional political situation, and will therefore still require external financial support, given its heavy external debt burden, estimated at 90 per cent of GDP in 2001. Continued efforts at fiscal adjustment will be needed in subsequent years to reduce the debt burden and free resources for private sector development. Excluding grants, the ratio of the budget deficit to GDP is expected to drop below 7 per cent in 2001.

Unemployment in the country is yet another major challenge facing the Jordanian authorities, particularly in light of the need to downsize bloated payrolls in public institutions as they move into private-sector hands. Unemployment statistics are highly controversial in the kingdom, with the official figure of 14.4 per cent in 2000. Moreover, population growth continues, resulting in lower per-capita GDP growth and delaying the alleviation of poverty in the kingdom.

## *GROWTH*

In November 2000, Jordan revised its GDP figures and GDP growth rates of the previous 10 years in light of the adoption of a new methodology for arriving at these important indicators, as recommended by the World Bank and the IMF. Growth rates were revised down for the years 1992–4 and revised up for the years 1995–9. Nominal GDP for the year 1999 is now set at JD5724 million, compared to the previous estimate of JD5293 million, while real GDP growth for 1999 and 1998 was revised to 2.9 per cent and 3.1 per cent, from 1.7 per cent and 1.6 per cent respectively.

Despite regional instability, the Jordanian economy recorded real GDP growth of a 3.9 per cent in 2000, compared to 3.1 per cent in 1999. Nominal growth in 2000 is set at 3.3 per cent. Real growth for the first three quarters of 2000 stood at 4.1 per cent, but had dropped to 3.5 per cent during the last quarter of the year. With the exception of the mining sector, all other economic sectors picked up momentum in 2000. According to Department of Statistics estimates, growth was fuelled by enhanced performance in four major economic sectors: retail, wholesale, hotels and restaurants; government services; manufacturing; finance, insurance, property and business; growth in value-added increased by 8.5 per cent, 6.9 per cent, 5.6 per cent and 5.2 per cent respectively. In order to boost investment in the country, the government is planning to adjust the income tax law.

The turnaround in the economy continued in 2001 as the effects of a more liberal economic environment and higher levels of investment, both domestic and foreign, spread across the economy. Real GDP growth in the first three quarters of

2001 was put at 4.2 per cent and growth for the year as a whole is likely to be close to 4 per cent. However, the drop in tourism following the 11 September attack on the US and the ongoing conflict in the Palestinian territories will dampen the forecast real growth in 2002 to 3.5 per cent.

## *MONETARY POLICY*

The Central Bank's monetary policy centres on reducing inflation and maintaining the stability of the dinar vis-à-vis the US dollar. To this end, it has adopted a policy of tight control since 1996 and succeeded in upholding monetary stability while reining in inflation and bolstering capital inflows.

Political pressures stemming from concerns over the late King Hussein's health in July 1998 forced the Central Bank to tighten monetary policy towards the end of 1998 and in the first quarter of 1999. Total foreign reserves fell from JD1200 million ($1693 million) in 1997 to a low JD829 million ($1170 million) at the end of 1998, and maintained that level in the following two months. Since then, total foreign reserves have climbed steadily to reach JD1959 million ($2763 million) at the end of 2000, constituting eight months of import coverage. Record high reserves, a stable currency, subdued consumer prices and the decline in the US dollar interest rates have prompted the Central Bank to adopt a more relaxed attitude to monetary policy in 2001.

## *EXCHANGE RATE*

After going through successive devaluation in 1989 and 1990, the Jordanian dinar is now one of two currencies in the Arab world officially pegged to the US dollar. Effective from 23 October 1995, the dinar' s exchange rate against the dollar is fixed at an average rate of JD0.709, and the monetary authorities have been able to maintain it at that level via a strict discipline of high interest rates and tight liquidity.

The Central Bank will do all that is needed to uphold the dinar, as was apparent in July 1998 when it had to dig into its foreign-reserve coffers to counter a short-lived run on the currency following fears over King Hussein's health, and again in February 1999 in the aftermath of his death. It was estimated that the Central Bank used over $400 million to defend the local currency. We expect the fixed JD/$ rate to prevail during the period between 2002 and 2005.

## *INFLATION*

Strict monetary discipline throughout the 1990s has enabled the government to reduce inflation rates, as measured by the cost-of-living index, from a high of 25.8 per cent in 1989 to an average of 2.8 per cent for the period 1992–7, except in 1996, when the removal of subsidies on food items pushed inflation up to 6.5 per cent.

Official figures place inflation in 1998 at 3.1 per cent, while in 1999 weak domestic demand coupled with low commodity prices kept inflation at 0.6 per cent despite an increase in the general sales tax from 10 per cent to 13 per cent. While inflation remained low at 0.9 per cent in 2000, higher commodity prices alongside the introduction of VAT in 2001 should put a slight upward pressure on price level, with inflation expected to rise to around 1.5 per cent.

Figure 9.1
Jordan: annual change in the cost-of-living index

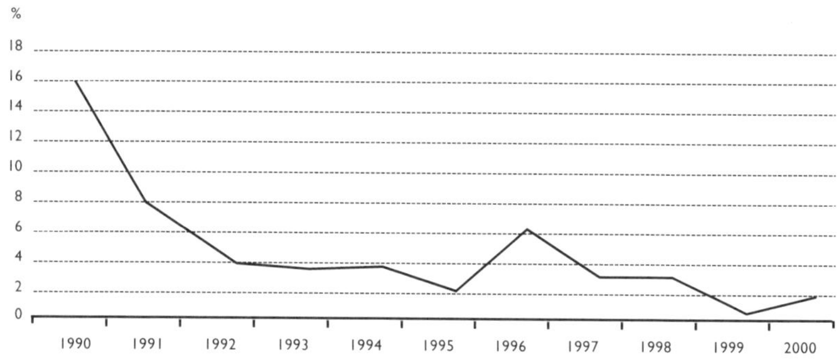


*Source: Central Bank of Jordan*

## *INTEREST RATES*

Interest rates on the dinar have been maintained at relatively high levels since 1996 to help bolster monetary stability, often at the expense of economic growth. In response to political pressures stemming from the king's health in late July 1998, the Central Bank tightened monetary policy and raised interest rates significantly, with the benchmark yield on three-month CDs increasing to 10.61 per cent in September 1998 from 6.25 per cent in December 1997, dropping slightly to 9.45 per cent by January 1999. Lending rates soared, and both the re-discount and the rate on advances to licensed banks rose to 9 per cent in September 1998 from 7.75 per cent in December 1997.

As a result of the strong recovery in the demand for the dinar, alongside the build-up in foreign reserves following the smooth transition of power to King Abdullah, the Central Bank started to ease interest rates up towards the second half of 1999. Rates on three-month CDs assumed a declining trend, dropping to a monthly average of 6 per cent by December 1999, from 9.45 per cent in January, and further down to 5.85 per cent in September 2000. At the end of 2000 the interest rate on three-month CDs had rising back to 6 per cent. The re-discount and the rate on advances to licensed banks dropped to 8 per cent by the end of 1999, and to 6 per cent by the end of 2000.

In December 2000, the Central Bank announced its intentions to lower the compulsory reserve requirements on deposits and savings accounts in commercial banks from 10 per cent to 8 per cent, in a move to spur economic growth in the country. This followed two similar cuts in June 2000 that brought the requirement down from 14 per cent. The new percentage, effective at the beginning of 2001, will release an estimated JD160 million for potential lending. The lower reserve requirement should give local banks an incentive to streamline the additional funds towards more loans and investment projects. The Central Bank has progressively reduced interest rates in Jordan over 2000 and 2001. Interest rates on three-month certificates of deposits fell from 8 per cent in 1998 to 5 per cent in December 2000 and to 4 per cent in December 2001. This led the Arab Bank (the market leader) to reduce its prime rate to 8 per cent, effective from January 1 2002.

The Central Bank will continue to manage interest rates cautiously, taking into account the country's growth objective. Interest rates are likely to continue on a declining trend in the first few months of 2001, in line with the decline in US rates. However, the monetary authority stands ready to implement upward interest-rate adjustments if the need arises to maintain confidence in the dinar.

## *FISCAL POLICY*

Jordan's fiscal performance deteriorated sharply over the period 1996–8, with the budget deficit reaching a high 9.9 per cent of GDP in 1998 (7.2 per cent including grants). Despite the fact that total revenues in 1999 fell 6.2 per cent short of budgeted figures, the deficit for the year came well within target, at 7.4 per cent of GDP (4.3 per cent including grants), compared to a target of 8 per cent. This was primarily due to effective fiscal constraint, with total expenditure for the year equal to JD2007 million, 6.3 per cent below budget and marginally lower than 1998 spending.

According to official estimates, revenues in 2000 amounted to JD1850 million, well below initial government projections. In order to meet the budget-deficit target, expenditures were cut to JD2015 million, down from an initial estimate of JD2210 million. As a result, the deficit in 2000, excluding grants, stood at JD410 million, 7 per cent of GDP. Including grants, the deficit was JD165 million, 3.0 per cent of GDP.

Total revenues (including JD237 million in grants) in the 2001 budget plan were projected at JD2142 million, almost 16 per cent above 2000 revenues, while total expenditure in 2001 is JD2300 million, 14 per cent higher than the previous year. The government has earmarked JD470 million for capital investments, a 50 per cent increase on the 2000 figure, and current expenditure is set to rise by 7.5 per cent to JD1830 million. The budget deficit, excluding grants, is projected at JD400 million, equivalent to 6 per cent of GDP, that is a one per cent drop on the year before. Including grants, the deficit forecast drops to JD158 million, 2.7 per cent of GDP.

Table 9.2
Jordan: summary of central government budget (JD million)

| | 1998 | 1999 | 2000 | 2001B |
|---|---|---|---|---|
| Total revenues | 1699.5 | 1815.9 | 1850.0 | 2142.0 |
| Domestic revenues | 1496.5 | 1585.3 | 1576.4 | 1830.0 |
| Grants | 203.0 | 195.0 | 240.0 | 237.0 |
| Capital revenues (including technical grants) | – | 35.6 | 33.6 | 75.0 |
| Total expenditure | 2055.1 | 2039.4 | 2015.0 | 2300.0 |
| Deficit/surplus (excluding grants) | −558.6 | −422.0 | −410.0 | −400.0 |
| (as percentage of GDP) | −9.9 | −7.4 | −7.0 | −6.0 |
| Deficit/surplus (including grants) | −355.6 | −223.5 | −165.0 | −158.0 |
| (as percentage of GDP) | −7.2 | −4.3 | −3.0 | −2.7 |

*B: Budget*

*Source: Ministry of Finance*

## *EXTERNAL PUBLIC DEBT*

In the late 1980s, Jordan was one of the most indebted countries in the world, but since then its debt-management programme has received substantial assistance from major industrial countries. Jordan's total outstanding external debt at the end of 2000 stood at JD4795 million ($6761 million), or 81 per cent of GDP, compared to JD 6052.5 million ($9121 million) in 1990. Its largest creditors are industrial countries such as Japan, Germany, France and the UK in addition to multilateral institutions including the IMF and the World Bank.

At the conclusion of the G7 summit in June 1999, the G7 nations called on Jordan's international creditors to provide economic support to the country, including debt relief. Although the statement did not commission particular steps to reduce the kingdom's debt, it paved the way for Jordan to contact individual nations in order to secure assistance and debt relief. The government has negotiated with major donor countries for debt rescheduling, in addition to debt forgiveness and the swapping of some debt into local investment.

## *INTERNAL PUBLIC DEBT*

Jordan's internal debt stood at JD1203 million at the end of 2000, up slightly on its level of JD1024 million in 1999. Internal public debt outstanding as a percentage of GDP has fluctuated at approximately 20 per cent of GDP over the past three years. Approximately 42 per cent of total internal debt were held by the Central Bank, 48 per cent by licensed banks, the remainder by non-bank sources.

## EXTERNAL SECTOR

Jordan's trade deficit widened by 40 per cent in 2000 to JD1.86 billion, compared to a deficit of JD1.32 billion the year before. This was mainly a result of subdued export growth, with exports up 3.6 per cent to JD1.35 billion, compared to strong import growth of 22 per cent to JD3.2 billion.

This followed a steady path of decline in the trade deficit over the 1998/99 period, one which reflected not an improvement in exports, but slack economic activity and weakening domestic demand. The trade account recorded a deficit of JD1.34 billion in 1999, down 7 per cent on its 1998 level, immediately following a steep 10.6 per cent retraction in the deficit in 1998. Much of the credit for the smaller trade deficit goes to lower import activity each year. Imports fell by 3 per cent in 1999, following declines of 6.7 per cent and 4.5 per cent in 1998 and 1997 respectively. Imports failed to achieve the 4 per cent growth anticipated by the IMF reform programme, reflecting a sharp, broad-based fall of 11 per cent in the first half of 1999. However, import growth returned to a healthier pace in the second half of the year reflecting some return of confidence as well as a sharp upturn in food imports due to the drought. Total exports (including re-exports) remained sluggish, rising by 1.6 per cent in 1999 following a drop of 1.8 per cent in 1998 and a modest increase of 1 per cent in 1997.

Table 9.3
Jordan: balance of payments (JD million)

| | 1997 | 1998 | 1999 | 2000 |
|---|---|---|---|---|
| Current account | 20.8 | 15.5 | 287.1 | 94.3 |
| (as percentage of GDP) | 0.4 | 0.3 | 5.0 | 1.6 |
| Trade balance | –1605 | –1435 | –1324 | –1859 |
| Exports | 1301 | 1278 | 1299 | 1345 |
| Imports | 2907 | 2712 | 2623 | 3204 |
| Services balance | 1345 | 1191 | 1217 | 1458 |
| Current transfers | 281 | 259 | 394 | 495 |
| **Capital account** | **212** | **205** | **133** | **386** |
| **Errors and omissions** | **–39** | **–305** | **21** | **193** |
| **Overall balance** | **194** | **–84** | **441** | **673** |

*Source: Central Bank of Jordan*

The current account registered a modest surplus equal to JD94 million in 2000, or 1.6 per cent of GDP, down from a surplus of JD287 million in 1999, mainly reflecting the increase in imports, given the reductions in customs duties required by Jordan's WTO membership. The overall balance of payments showed a healthy surplus of JD673 million, supported by a strong increase in the capital account compared to the year before.

# LEBANON

Table 9.4
Lebanon: main economic indicators

| | 1996 | 1997 | 1998 | 1999 | 2000 | 2001 |
|---|---|---|---|---|---|---|
| Nominal GDP (LBP trillion) | 21.10 | 22.90 | 24.50 | 23.80 | 24.10 | 24.80 |
| Nominal GDP ($ billion) | 13.00 | 14.90 | 16.20 | 15.80 | 16.00 | 16.48 |
| Nominal GDP growth | 12.80% | 8.60% | 7.10% | –2.80% | 1.30% | 3.00% |
| Real GDP growth | 4.00% | 3.50% | 2.00% | –1.00% | 0.00% | 1.50% |
| Inflation | 8.90% | 7.80% | 5.00% | 1.40% | 0.50% | 1.20% |
| **Fiscal indicators (LBP billion)** | | | | | | |
| Revenues | 3534 | 3722 | 4430 | 4872 | 4552 | 4891 |
| Expenditures | 7288 | 9155 | 7815 | 8458 | 10,424 | 9963 |
| Budget deficit | 3754 | 5433 | 3385 | 3586 | 5872 | 5072 |
| (as percentage of GDP) | 18.6 | 23.9 | 14.0 | 15.0 | 23.7 | 20.4 |
| External debt ($ million) | 1898 | 2434 | 4200 | 5538 | 6968 | 8968 |
| Domestic debt | 13,358 | 18,381 | 19,543 | 21,535 | 24,530 | 26,590 |
| **External indicators ($ billion)** | | | | | | |
| Exports | 0.78 | 0.65 | 0.72 | 0.73 | 0.75 | 0.77 |
| Imports | –7.00 | –6.90 | –6.53 | –6.51 | –6.60 | 6.80 |
| Current account | –4.62 | –4.19 | –3.41 | –3.38 | –3.35 | –3.50 |
| (as percentage of GDP) | –35.50 | –28.00 | –21.10 | –21.40 | –20.90 | –21.20 |

*Sources: Central Bank of Lebanon, IIF*

## *ECONOMIC OVERVIEW*

Lebanon today has one of the highest debt levels in the world, with total public debt standing at LBP35,071 billion at the end of 2000, equivalent to over 140 per cent of GDP. On the fiscal front, the deficit in 2000 was equivalent to more than 52 per cent of spending and 24 per cent of GDP, compared to a target of 36.2 per cent and 12.7 per cent respectively in the original budget plan. The deficit target for 2001, of $3.36 billion, is equivalent to 20.4 per cent of GDP, and the debt-to-GDP ratio may rise to over 160 per cent. Currently the main challenge of economy policy in Lebanon is finding a feasible solution to the sharply deteriorating fiscal situation and the mounting public debt, both of which threaten to undermine confidence in the domestic currency and in the economy as a whole.

In late September 2000, Standard & Poor's downgraded Lebanon's long-term foreign-currency-debt-rating to 'B+' from 'BB–', and its long-term local currency debt rating to 'BB–' from 'BB', while maintaining its 'stable' outlook. According to the agency, the lower ratings reflect the country's precarious fiscal position, the possibility that the government will fail to pass the VAT law in time, and the government's decision to reject the $2.7 billion licence offer from the country's mobile telecommunications operators.

International rating agency Fitch also lowered its credit rating for Lebanon in 2001, due to the country's failure to control public finances. The agency lowered the long-term ratings for both foreign and local currency Lebanese debt to B+ and BB respectively, which are below investment grade. The reasons for the lower rating were, again, the country's heavy debt burden and worsening fiscal situation. Fitch believes that the public debt as a percentage of GDP could rise to 180 per cent by the end of 2002. However, Fitch assigned an outlook of 'stable' on the new rating, to reflect the government's plans to modernize and liberalize the economy and to introduce a number of fiscal measures.

The tone of economic policy of the present government that took office in late 2000 is expansionist, in direct contrast to the previous government's austerity measures, which were designed to bring the escalating budget deficit under control. The government's economic strategy is focused on stimulating private-sector growth, increasing trade and attracting higher levels of investment to the country. The hope is that over the medium term, the increased economic activity will generate higher government revenue, thus addressing the country's fiscal deficits and mounting debt problems.

As part of the its liberalization programme, the Lebanese government took the decision to lower custom duties, effective from January 2001, from a range of 6–105 per cent to 0–70 per cent in a bid to increase consumer spending, revive the ailing economy and turn the country into a regional trading and shopping centre. Custom duties on raw materials and semi-finished materials not manufactured in Lebanon were eliminated, along with duties on computer software and hardware. The decree also reduced by 25 per cent tariffs on imported goods that compete with Lebanese-made products, and all rates above 100 per cent were cut to 70 per cent. Other imported finished products that were previously subject to custom rates between 10 per cent and 100 per cent have had tariffs reduced to rates ranging from 5 per cent to 70 per cent. Tariffs on the agricultural sector and duties on tobacco, gas, fuel oil, cement and automobiles were left unchanged.

The government has also taken many steps to make investment in the country easier. FDI represented just 1.2 per cent of GDP in 2000, compared to 5.7 per cent in the region. A recently passed law on land ownership allows foreign companies and individuals to buy large plots across the country and use them to establish companies. The government also reduced property registration fees for foreigners from 16 per cent to 5 per cent. Other investment-friendly legislation includes the recent revitalization of the Investment Development Authority (IDAL) as a one-stop shop to help investors quickly obtain all licenses and approvals to start local businesses. A new investment law also offers a range of tax incentives to encourage investors to set up projects in rural areas such as the Bekaa and the south.

The new government's initial response to a widening fiscal deficit has been to cut taxes, ease capital-spending controls and further liberalize the economy. However, more recently, there has been a clear shift of emphasis in the government's economic strategy towards cost-cutting measures in an effort to slow the rate at which the fiscal deficit is growing. This reflects the growing awareness that unless the gaping budget deficit is brought under control, the ensuing imbalances will pressure the stability of the entire economy and preclude the return of local and international confidence.

Bringing the overwhelming fiscal deficit under control will not be an easy task. The budget plan for 2002 forecasts a deficit equivalent to 20.4 per cent of GDP, compared to an equivalent of 24 per cent of GDP in 2001. The government will have a difficult time raising revenues by the 7.4 per cent outlined in the 2002 budget plan, especially in light of the impact that recent tariff cuts have had on customs earnings. Moreover, the still-weak economic growth forecast for 2002 will likely dampen tax revenues. Nonetheless, the government remains optimistic, with the Ministry of Finance forecasting a lower-than-targeted budget deficit for 2002 as a result of a government reduction in expenditure on different fronts, such as the reduction of civil servants' salaries, the redundancy of unnecessary state employees, and the restructuring of the national TV station.

In order for the new government successfully to build the confidence of the local and international community and maintain access to the debt market, it must give the long-promised privatization programme high priority. If the privatization proceeds were used exclusively to reduce public debt, this would create a virtuous circle, whereby interest rates would be allowed to fall further, reducing in the process government spending and the need to borrow. The obvious assets to sell are the telecommunications licences, followed by the fixed-line telecommunications network and third-generation licences. The previous government refused offers from the mobile operators to convert their BOT contracts into full licences, forfeiting revenues that would have reduced the debt, injected some confidence in the market and increased the scope for interest-rate cuts.

The present government has had more success than its predecessor in slimming down the public sector and pushing ahead with privatization. The loss-making Tele-Liban has been closed. The fixed-line telecommunications sector is being privatized, and the government has also appointed French investment bank BNP Paribas to prepare Electricité du Liban for sale to a strategic investor. Even the budget for the security forces has become a matter for debate.

The Lebanese government remains committed to the current value of the Lebanese pound. According to the government, a devaluation of the Lebanese pound would destroy savings, lead to a rise in inflation, and significantly hurt the banking sector. There have been continued worries about the strong demand for the dollar compared to the demand for the Lebanese pound, but the Central Bank has strongly defended the pound, losing $4 billion of its reserves by the end of 2001.

A real turnaround in the economy is not expected before 2004. The political uncertainties on the local and the regional scenes, along with the proposed new fiscal measures, will overshadow Lebanon's economic outlook in 2002. It remains to be seen whether the new investment initiatives in the country will succeed in driving up private investment. Sluggish private consumption will dampen the prospects of economic recovery, keeping real GDP growth for 2001 and 2002 at 1.5 per cent, while still containing the rise in inflation to less than 2 per cent.

Notwithstanding the ongoing fiscal woes, the stability of Lebanon's financial markets continues to be supported by the country's strong foreign reserves and gold holdings, the demonstrated ability of the Central Bank to manage past financial stress and regulate the local banking system, and the solid financial backing of the country's resident and expatriate nationals, as reflected in the success of the recent eurobond issues.

## *GROWTH*

Stabilization and reform measures have laid the groundwork for healthy economic growth since 1993. On the back of the boom in the construction sector, economic activity surged in 1994, registering record growth-rates of 8 per cent, and 7.5 per cent in 1995. However, economic expansion was short-lived and growth rates started faltering in subsequent years amid rising hostilities in South Lebanon, sluggish growth in construction activity, and high interest rates that crowded out private investment and discouraged borrowing.

Real GDP growth rate was 4 per cent in 1996, 3.5 per cent in 1997, 2 per cent in 1998 and –1 per cent in 1999. Weak growth conditions were induced by subdued domestic demand, slower remittances and a decline in direct investments from abroad. Most sectors of the economy suffered a second year of recession in 2000, with only the tourism industry posting a good performance – especially in the first half of the year. Real GDP growth for 2000 came at virtually 0 per cent. Growth is expected to pick up to 1.5 per cent in 2001 and 1.8 per cent in 2002, driven mainly by a recovery in the services sector.

## *INFLATION*

Lebanon's tight monetary policy has been geared towards taming inflation. The Central Bank's policy of stabilizing the exchange rate and managing interest-rate movement has brought inflation under control, from a high of 100 per cent in 1992 to approximately 5 per cent in 1998, 1.5 per cent in 1999. Weak domestic demand and low import prices kept inflation at check in 2000 at approximately 0.5 per cent. Inflationary pressures are expected to increase modestly in 2001 to around 1.2 per cent.

## *EXCHANGE RATE AND FOREIGN RESERVES*

The Central Bank has adopted a prudent monetary policy anchoring the Lebanese pound to the dollar and intervening on the foreign exchange market on a daily basis, either absorbing surpluses or supplying shortages of foreign currencies in order to dampen speculative activities on the local currency. The monetary authorities maintained an average weekly appreciation of the pound of around LBP0.5 against the dollar during the period 1992–9. This succeeded in raising the value of the currency relative to the dollar from LBP1838 at the end of 1992 to LBP1527 in 1997, LBP1508 in 1998, and LBP1507.5 in 1999. The country's gross foreign-currency reserves increased from $2.2 billion in 1993 to $7.6 billion in 1999, providing 14 months of import cover.

The exchange rate came under repeated pressure in 2000 and 2001 as confidence in the economy dipped, forcing the Central Bank to intervene in the foreign exchange market on several occasions and pulling gross foreign reserves down by 24 per cent to $5.75 billion by the end of 2000. Foreign reserves rose back up to $5.88 billion in the first two months of 2001, only to drop back down to $4 billion at the end of 2001. The Lebanese pound is expected to stay within its trading range of LBP1501–1514 to the dollar till the end of 2002, and defence of the peg will remain the focus of monetary policy in the foreseeable future. However, pressure on the currency will build up sharply if the reform measures adopted by the new government fail to bear fruit, or in the case of a marked deterioration in the fiscal situation.

## *FISCAL POLICY*

The Lebanese economy's most vulnerable point and the most volatile source of investor uncertainty has been the unstable state of public finances. The launching of the reconstruction process in 1992 induced a sharp increase in public investment, which in turn led to higher domestic borrowing and a heavy reliance on treasury bills for relatively non-inflationary financing of the budget deficit. Consequently, Lebanon accumulated successive large budget deficits, which reached a high of 59.3 per cent of expenditure in 1997. The deficit to expenditure ratio was brought down to 42.4 per cent by 1999, but jumped back up to 56.3 per cent in 2000 reviving worries over the country's precarious fiscal position.

Figure 9.2
Lebanon: gross foreign-exchange reserves

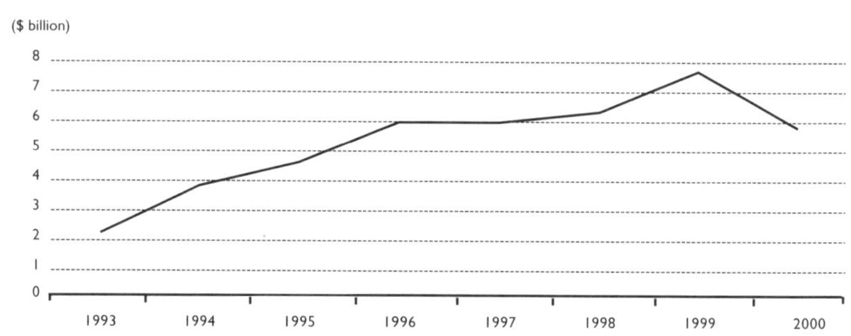


*Source: Central Bank of Lebanon, IMF, IIF*

Table 9.5
Lebanon: public finance conditions (LBP billion)

| | 1998 | 1999 | 2000 | 2001B | percentage change 2000/01 |
|---|---|---|---|---|---|
| Revenues | 4430 | 4868 | 4552 | 4891 | 7.4 |
| Expenditures | 7815 | 8454 | 10,424 | 9963 | –4.5 |
| Debt service | 3637 | 3662 | – | – | – |
| Budget deficit | 3385 | 3586 | 5872 | 5072 | –13.7 |
| Deficit/expenditure | 43.3% | 42.4% | 56.3% | 50.9% | – |
| Deficit/GDP | 14.0% | 15.0% | 23.7% | 20.4% | – |

*B: Budget draft*

*Source: Ministry of Finance*

The 2001 budget projected total spending of LBP9963 billion and revenues of LBP4891 billion. That leaves a deficit of about LBP5072 billion, equivalent to 50.87 per cent of spending. The deficit in 2000 rose by more than 60 per cent on its level the previous year, to LBP5872 billion, equivalent to 56 per cent of spending and 24 per cent of GDP – compared to targets of 36.2 per cent and 12.7 per cent respectively in the original budget plan – underlining the tough task the government has in controlling the public finances. The budgets for 2001 and 2002 suggest that Rafik Hariri's government is emphasizing economic growth rather than fiscal austerity.

The budget projects a drop in the revenues from customs duties to $640 million in 2001, compared to $817 million in 2000. This follows wide-ranging cuts in import duties introduced in 2001, the largest single source of government income, in an attempt to stimulate growth. The government is hoping that it will be able to increase its revenues from tax collection once growth is achieved. The budget made no mention of privatization or VAT, which were introduced in late 2001.

The budget for 2001 projected a rise in the revenues from income and corporate taxes to $505 million from $344 million in 1999, an increase of $161 million. Excluding privatization revenues, the government expects to increase total tax revenues to $2.2 billion from $1.6 billion in 1999. To help boost investments, the budget called for a 50 per cent cut in the registration fees of intellectual properties and trademarks. The government also offered a variety of small cuts in the fees of Finance Ministry stamps and other fees and taxes.

## *DOMESTIC DEBT*

Since the end of hostilities in 1990, Lebanon's internal debt has been rising – by 58.1 per cent in 1994, 44 per cent in 1995 and 38 per cent in 1997, reaching LBP18,381 billion ($12.2 billion). Growth in domestic debt decreased during the 1989–2000 period, to an average of 10.1 per cent annually, with net domestic debt reaching LBP24,530 billion ($16.27 billion) by the end of 2000, equivalent to 102 per cent of GDP. Domestic debt rose by around 5 per cent in 2001, to LBP25,438 billion ($16.8 billion). Domestic debt is mainly financed by the issuance of treasury bills (98 per cent of the total), which has increased considerably in recent years. The government raised interest rates during times of political uncertainty to finance internal imbalances, and resorted to cheaper external borrowing to reduce the debt-service bill. In 1999 the Central Bank gradually started cutting interest rates in its efforts to ease the pressure on the debt-service burden without causing any pressure on the local currency. The slow-down in the growth of internal debt over the past few years was aimed at reducing government reliance on the local market debt financing through reducing the sales of locally denominated treasury bills and partially allocating bids on the weekly auctions. However, the debt ratios are still high, with the domestic debt reaching 102 per cent of the GDP in 2000 and accounting for 70 per cent of the total debt.

## *EXTERNAL DEBT*

Lebanon's external debt began to rise in 1993 in light of high financing needs for large reconstruction projects. Lebanon tapped international markets in September 1994 with the launch of its first eurobond, providing the government with access to non-resident Lebanese, Arab and foreign capital. Following a series of eurobonds, external debt rose from $772 million in 1994 to $2434 million in 1997 and $4199 million in 1998. Although the stock of foreign liabilities had grown in nominal terms to $6992 million by the end of 2000, it continues to represent only 43.5 per cent of the GDP and 27 per cent of the total debt, placing Lebanon at an acceptable level compared to other developing countries. Over the medium term, public external debt is expected to grow due to the refinancing of public debt denominated in Lebanese pounds. Total foreign debt at the end of 2001 stood at $9100 million.

Table 9.6
Lebanon: domestic and external debt

| | Net domestic debt LBP billion | External debt $ million | Net total debt LBP billion |
|---|---|---|---|
| 1993 | 4415 | 327 | 4974 |
| 1994 | 6712 | 772 | 7983 |
| 1995 | 9287 | 1343 | 11,431 |
| 1996 | 13,358 | 1898 | 16,319 |
| 1997 | 18,381 | 2434 | 22,098 |
| 1998 | 19,543 | 4200 | 25,877 |
| 1999 | 21,535 | 5538 | 29,910 |
| 2000 | 24,530 | 6992 | 35,071 |
| 2001 | 25,438 | 7155 | 36,224 |

*Source: Central Bank of Lebanon*

The draft budget for 2002 calls for the government to issue up to $2 billion in new eurobonds and more than $1 billion in domestic treasury bills to help finance budget deficit. Debt servicing costs for 2001 are put at $2.8 billion, the largest single spending item in the budget. Worsening public finances could make it more expensive for Lebanon to issue new eurobonds. Lebanon's foreign debt, most of which is dollar-denominated, has longer maturities and lower interest rates than domestic treasury bills.

## *EXTERNAL SECTOR*

The external sector has historically exhibited large current-account deficits, which reflect Lebanon's heavy reliance on imports and a relatively weak export base. Over the five years to 1999, the current account deficit averaged 27 per cent of GDP. However, this masks a strong declining trend; the current-account deficit has fallen steadily from 49 per cent of GDP in 1993 to 25 per cent of GDP in 1998 and to 19 per cent of GDP in 2000. The narrowing of the current account over the past few years is attributed to both an improvement in the trade balance and an increase in the services, income and transfer surplus, resulting from improved tourism revenues and higher workers' remittances.

Table 9.7
**Lebanon: balance of payments* ($ billion)**

| | **1996** | **1997** | **1998** | **1999** | **2000** |
|---|---|---|---|---|---|
| Current account | –5.00 | –4.80 | –4.03 | –3.12 | –3.09 |
| (as percentage of GDP) | –38.50 | –32.10 | –24.90 | –19.70 | –19.30 |
| Trade balance | –6.60 | –6.90 | –6.40 | –5.50 | –5.60 |
| (as percentage of GDP) | –50.70 | –45.90 | –39.80 | –34.90 | –34.90 |
| Exports | 1.01 | 0.64 | 0.66 | 0.68 | 0.71 |
| Imports | –7.60 | –7.50 | –7.10 | –6.20 | –6.30 |
| Balance of service, Income and transfers* | 1.59 | 2.06 | 2.41 | 2.40 | 2.50 |
| Balance of payments | 0.79 | 0.42 | –0.49 | 0.27 | –0.29 |

** IIF estimates*

*Sources: Banque du Liban and IIF*

The Lebanese external balance suffers from a large trade deficit, equivalent to a high of 51 per cent of GDP in 1996 but declining gradually to 35 per cent in 2000. Average annual imports between 1995 and 2000 amounted to $6.96 billion, compared to less than $756 million in exports. Import growth was particularly strong in the first half of the 1990s as a result of the then booming reconstruction programme, but has since then declined, dropping by 18 per cent between 1996 and 2000. Exports reached a high of $1.01 billion in 1996, but dropped to $642 million in 1997. Over the years to 2000, exports recorded modest growth rates, reaching $714 million.

Large current-account deficits have traditionally been covered by equally large surpluses in the capital account resulting in an overall surplus in the balance of payments in the five-year period to the end of 1999 (with the exception of 1998) and a strong buildup in reserves. Weaker-than-anticipated capital flows in 2001 failed to cover the gap in the current account, resulting in a negative balance of payments equal to $289 million.

## PALESTINIAN TERRITORIES

Table 9.8
Palestinian territories: main economic indicators

| | 1995 | 1996 | 1997 | 1998 | 1999 | 2000 |
|---|---|---|---|---|---|---|
| Nominal GDP ($ million) | 3575 | 3896 | 4173 | 4485 | 4837 | 4111 |
| Nominal GDP growth | 20.2% | 9.0% | 7.1% | 7.5% | 7.8% | –15.0% |
| Real GDP growth | 2.0% | 0.5% | 1.0% | 4.1% | 6.0% | –5% |
| Inflation | 10.8% | 7.9% | 7.6% | 5.5% | 6.3% | 10.0% |
| Unemployment | 29.0% | 24.0% | 20.3% | 16.0% | 12.7% | 27.0% |
| **Fiscal indicators ($ million)** | | | | | | |
| Total revenue | 425 | 670 | 954 | 1084 | 1136 | 1164 |
| Total expenditure | 682 | 995 | 1113 | 1194 | 1193 | 1364 |
| Budget deficit | –257 | –325 | –159 | –110 | –57 | –200 |
| (as percentage of GDP) | –7.2 | –8.3 | –3.8 | –2.5 | –1.2 | –4.9 |
| **External Indicators ($ million)** | | | | | | |
| Exports | 550 | 582 | 883 | 1034 | 1291 | 1068 |
| Imports | 2012 | 2369 | 2651 | 3712 | 4573 | 3773 |
| Trade balance | –1463 | –1786 | –1768 | –2678 | –3282 | –2905 |
| (as percentage of GDP) | 40.9 | 45.9 | 42.4 | 59.7 | 67.9 | –70.7 |
| Current-account deficit | –574 | –708 | –755 | –800 | –1010 | –1500 |

*Sources: IMF, Palestinian Monetary Authority, Ministry of Finance*

### *ECONOMIC OVERVIEW*

The harsh measures taken by Israel in its attempt to crush the new *Intifada*, which started in late September 2000, have devastated the Palestinian economy. While the destruction of physical assets is difficult to estimate, more tangible losses due to the disruption of productive activities are estimated by the Palestinian authority at $20 million a day or $1.8 billion till the end of 2000. These losses are five times bigger than the donor disbursements of $360 million for infrastructural projects in 1999. The total losses of the Palestinian economy in 2001 are put at $8 billion.

Before the uprising, the young Palestinian economy had been growing at an annual rate of 7 per cent. The performance of the Palestinian economy surpassed expectations in 1999, with the Ministry of Finance and the IMF revising earlier estimates of real GDP and GNP growth from 4.5 per cent and 4.6 per cent to 6 per cent and 7 per cent respectively, making 1999 the second consecutive year of rising real per-capita income since the recession of the mid-1990s. There were positive trends in planned business construction and credit expansion by the banking system, and relatively stable prices. A 32 per cent increase in bank credit to the private sector was recorded in 1999; a 15 per cent increase in labour flows to Israel; a 14 per cent increase in planned construction; substantial growth in new company registrations; a 12 per cent rise in donor assistance and the lowest incidence of border closures since 1993. Local job creation was also up, with the standard unemployment rate declining from an average of 15.6 per cent in 1998 to 12.7 per cent in 1999 according to the UN Special Commission (UNSCO), its lowest level since the early 1990s.

The picture has been reversed, and the economy shrank by 4.9 per cent in 2000 and is provisionally estimated to have recorded a negative growth of 30 per cent in 2001.

The Palestinian territories, home to three million people, with a historic unemployment rate of 15 per cent and one-quarter of the population living below the poverty line, have now come to a complete standstill. Unemployment is estimated to have risen to 35 per cent in Gaza and 25 per cent in the West Bank. Most of the 125,000 Palestinian workers previously employed in Israel are now without jobs. This amounts to a loss of household income of more than $105 million a month. Israel withheld the monthly payments in tariffs and custom duties collected on behalf of the Palestinian Authority during the uprising. In the first 10 months of 2000, the monthly rebate averaged around $55 million, more than enough to cover the civil service and police payroll. The budget deficit for 2001 could exceed $400 million.

Some employees in the private sector have been given extended non-paid leave. If such a situation persists, and is accentuated with the possible disruption in payment to civil service employees, it would lead to a noticeable drop in household income. This will have a multiplier effect on the economy by reducing domestic purchases of goods and services, leading to more unemployment and further decline in income. The problem is compounded by the disruption in institutional development programmes and the halting of infrastructural projects, many of which are financed by multilateral sources. Israel controls the borders of the Palestinian territories, allowing it to restrict the flows of exports and imports, and is also in a position to cut the supply of electricity, water and fuel to Palestinian population centres.

The agricultural sector, which accounted for 10 per cent of GDP in 1999, has been seriously affected. Palestinian exports of agricultural products to Israel, Egypt and Jordan have also been severely restricted. Total Palestinian imports in 1999 amounted to $4.6 billion, at a daily average of $12.5 million, with 90 per cent of that coming from Israel. Another hard-hit sector is construction, which accounted for 7 per cent of GDP in 1999. Work on infrastructural projects has stopped, including the Gaza power plant and port and various other construction activities in the West Bank. This has reflected negatively on construction-related industries such as cement tiles, glass, doors and aluminum. The industrial sector, which accounts for 11 per cent of GDP, is dominated by subcontracting agreements with Israeli firms to produce semi-finished products. The vulnerability of the sector regarding raw material inputs from Israel suggests that huge losses have also been incurred in this sector because of closure of the borders.

Tourism, which was poised to be one of the fastest-growing sectors in the Palestinian territories, has also suffered. Hotels, restaurants, travel agents, transport companies and tourist guides have all seen business come to a standstill. Numerous hotel buildings were seriously hit by rocket fire, and various handcraft businesses closed down. Banks in the Palestinian territories had been doing quite well until the beginning of the Israeli blockage, but have suffered since then. The strict Israeli measures have led to severe bank liquidity shortages, raised the number of bad debts, and brought credit expansion to a halt. Savings deposits have been drawn down to supplement income.

The current crisis will carry a long-term cost to the Palestinian territories and the region, as domestic and foreign investors reassess their risk perception of the area. This could lead to capital outflows and threaten the short- and long-term growth prospects of the Palestinian economy at a time when a number of major aid-financed infrastructural schemes are poised to go ahead. Without a lasting peace settlement, it would be difficult to convince nervous investors to return, and the cloud of uncertainty that is hovering over the region as a whole will continue to undermine economic growth prospects and stock markets' performance.

## *GROWTH*

Since the initiation of the peace talks with Israel in 1993 and 1998, real growth in the Palestinian territories ranged between 0.5 per cent and 2 per cent annually, lower than the population growth rate of 3.5 per cent, resulting in a marked deterioration in living standards. A recovery started in 1998 with an estimated real GDP growth rate of 4.1 per cent. This was sufficient marginally to advance West Bank and Gaza Strip per-capita income levels for the first year since the beginning of the five-year interim period.

**Table 9.9**
**Palestinian territories: GDP growth ($ million)**

| | 1997 | 1998 | 1999 | 2000 | 2001E |
|---|---|---|---|---|---|
| Nominal GDP | 4173 | 4485 | 4373 | 4226 | 2746 |
| Nominal GDP growth | 7.1% | 7.5% | 10.9% | –15.0% | –35.0% |
| Real GDP | 1.0% | 4.1% | 6.0% | –5.0% | –30.0% |

*E: Jordinvest estimates*

Palestinian Ministry of Finance and IMF figures suggest that the Palestinian economy continued its recovery in 1999. Real GDP is grew by about 6 per cent, based on strong growth in employment both internally and in Israel, higher domestic consumer demand and an expansion in bank credit to the private sector. Higher growth was also encouraged by the reduced severity of comprehensive closures of crossing routes to Israel in 1998 and 1999, which have seriously impeded economic activity in the past.

Prior to the start of the uprising in 2000, real growth was expected at around 4–5 per cent in real terms for the year. However, the substantial decline in GDP in the fourth quarter of 2000 saw total GDP (in nominal terms) for the year dropping by 15 per cent. Real GDP registered a decline of 5 per cent in 2000 and is provisionally estimated to have dropped by 30 per cent in 2001.

## *MONETARY POLICY*

The Paris Economic Protocol allowed for the establishment of the Palestinian Monetary Authority (PMA), which is endowed with most of the functions typical of a central bank. Yet the lack of a domestic currency, and therefore the Monetary Authority's inability to control the monetary base, undermines the effectiveness of traditional monetary policy instruments in influencing inflation and domestic liquidity.

The PMA can, however, help create a viable environment for growth by promoting financial stability through the development and maintenance of a healthy banking sector. Currently, the main thrust of the PMA lies in encouraging domestic lending and stemming the export of funds outside the West Bank and Gaza Strip. The total value of credit extended by the banking sector in the area increased by 36 per cent in 1998 to $822 million, compared to $613 million in 1997. Credit facilities of the Palestinian banking sector had risen by 19 per cent to $979 million by the end of October 1999, with the bulk of the increase going to the private sector.

Figure 9.3
Palestinian Territories: consumer price inflation

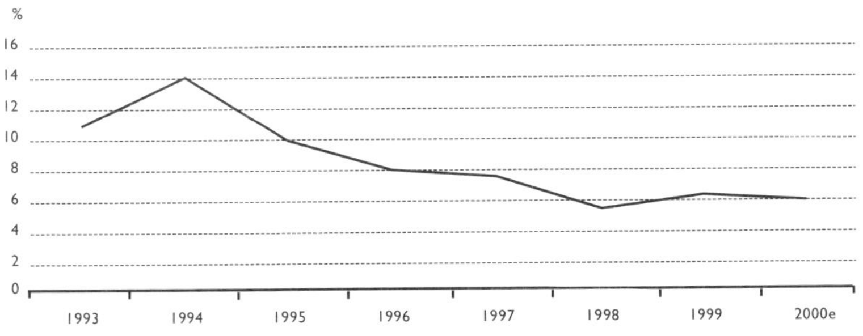


*Sources: Palestinian Central Bureau of Statistics and the World Bank*

## *INFLATION*

There has been an obvious disinflationary trend in the Palestinian economy over the past few years. The inflation rate averaged almost 12 per cent per year during the period 1993–5, but fell steadily after that to reach an estimated 7.6 per cent in 1997 and 5.5 per cent in 1998, before rising to 5.5 per cent in 1999. Inflation is estimated at around 2.8 per cent in 2000 and 0.9 per cent in 2001.

Table 9.10
**Palestinian territories: fiscal operations of the Palestinian Monetary Authority ($ million)**

| | 1998 | 1999 | 2000B |
|---|---|---|---|
| **Total Revenue** | **1084** | **1136** | **1363** |
| Domestic revenue | 754 | 901 | 963 |
| Tax revenue | 616 | 782 | 847 |
| Income tax | 76 | 86 | 80 |
| Custom duties | 247 | 302 | 326 |
| VAT and excises | 291 | 393 | 440 |
| Other taxes | 2.2 | 1.4 | 1.4 |
| Non-tax revenue | 138 | 119 | 116 |
| **Grants** | **330** | **235** | **400** |
| **Total expenditure** | **1194** | **1194** | **1364** |
| Current expenditure | 819 | 927 | 925 |
| Capital expenditure | 34 | 26 | 15 |
| Development expenditure | 341 | 241 | 424 |
| **Budget balance** | **–110** | **–58** | **–1** |

*B: Budget*

*Source: Ministry of Finance*

## *FISCAL POLICY*

In the Palestinian context, the role of fiscal policy is of paramount importance given the limitations on monetary policy tools. The Palestinian authority has been relatively successful in securing a solid revenue base within the constraints placed by the Oslo Accords, despite continued strong increases in current expenditure.

The Palestinian authority budget has exhibited considerable growth over the past few years. Total expenditure in 1999 was maintained at their 1998 level of $1194 million, while total revenues (including grants of $235 million for financing development projects) rose by 5 per cent to $1136 million, driven by a substantial increase in tax revenues to $782 million from $616 million in 1998. This translated into an overall deficit of $58 million, down from $110 million in 1997.

The 2000 budget projects almost balanced figures in 2000, supported by further increases in domestic revenues and substantially higher grants. Total revenues (including $400 million in grants) for 1999 are projected at $1363 million, while total spending is $1364 million. The actual budget deficit rose to $232 million, or 5.5 per cent of GDP in 2000 , and is estimated to have reached $400 million in 2001, or 12.5 per cent of GDP.

## *EXTERNAL SECTOR*

There is a pressing need to redress the imbalance in the Palestinian external sector and steer the economy towards a viable balance-of-payments position. The West Bank and Gaza Strip are currently in a precarious current-account position with a rapidly widening deficit. The current-account deficit, inclusive of grants, amounted to $754.6 million in 1997 (18.7 per cent of GDP), up from $708 million in 1996 and $240 million in 1993.

The large gap in the current account is due to an excessive trade deficit, which reached $3.28 billion in 1999 (68 per cent of GDP). During Israeli occupation, Palestinian merchandise trade exhibited continuous fluctuations, but steadily became overwhelmingly anchored to Israel. While exports grew steadily in the 1970s, they have been on a predominantly downward trend since then. Post-1993 trade patterns in the West Bank and Gaza Strip were largely dictated by the Economic Protocol of 1994, which created a trade regime between the Palestinian-authority controlled areas and Israel that is a hybrid between a free-trade arrangement and a customs union.

**Table 9.11**
**Palestinian territories: trade balance ($ million)**

| | 1996 | 1997 | 1998 | 1999 |
|---|---|---|---|---|
| Exports | 582 | 883 | 1034 | 1291 |
| Imports | 2369 | 2651 | 3712 | 4573 |
| Trade balance | –1786 | –1768 | –2678 | –3282 |
| (as percentage of GDP) | 45.9 | 42.4 | 59.7 | 67.9 |

*Source: Palestinian Monetary Authority (estimates)*

According to revised Palestinian Money Authority estimates, the post-1993 policy environment neither reversed the long-term decline in the Palestinian export sector nor dampened strong growth in imports. With the exception of a significant rise in 1995 (along with an equally significant rise in imports), the performance of Palestinian exports has been disappointing over the past few years, and exports actually dropped by approximately 25 per cent in 1998 to $500 million. This was accompanied by a mounting import bill, with imports rising from $1.1 billion in 1993 to $2.22 billion (54 per cent of GDP) in 1998. The trade deficit widened in 1999 to $3.2 billion (67.9 per cent of GDP).

# ARAB SYRIAN REPUBLIC

Table 9.12
Arab Syrian Republic: main economic indicators

| | 1995 | 1996 | 1997 | 1998 | 1999 | 2000 | 2001F |
|---|---|---|---|---|---|---|---|
| Nominal GDP | | | | | | | |
| (SL billion) | 570.98 | 690.86 | 745.57 | 795.73 | 795.47 | 827.3 | 868.67 |
| Nominal GDP ($ billion) | 16.62 | 17.65 | 16.61 | 16.69 | 16.68 | 17.35 | 18.22 |
| Nominal GDP growth | 12.8% | 21.0% | 7.9% | 6.7% | 0.0% | 4.0% | 5.0% |
| Real GDP growth | 5.8% | 4.4% | 1.8% | −1.5% | −1.2% | 1.5% | 2.6% |
| Inflation | 8.0% | 8.2% | 8.3% | 2.2% | 1.0% | 1.0% | 1.5% |
| **Fiscal indicators (SL billion)** | | | | | | | |
| Revenues | 125,393 | 156,913 | 180,494 | 213,036 | 217,909 | 239,499 | 283,759 |
| Expenditure | 162,040 | 188,050 | 211,125 | 237,300 | 255,300 | 275,400 | 322,000 |
| Deficit | −36,647 | −31,137 | −30,631 | −24,264 | −37,391 | −35,901 | 38,241 |
| (as percentage of GDP) | −6.4 | −4.5 | −4.1 | −3.0 | −4.7 | −4.3 | −4.4 |
| **External indicators ($ million)** | | | | | | | |
| Exports | 3858 | 4178 | 4057 | 3142 | 3806 | 4700 | 4300 |
| Imports | -4004 | -4516 | -3603 | -3320 | -3590 | 3600 | 3800 |
| Current account | 263 | 40 | 461 | 58 | 201 | 1200 | 600 |

*F: Jordinvest forecasts*

*Sources: IMF World Economic Outlook Database, IFS, UN, and Jordinvest estimates*

## *ECONOMIC OVERVIEW*

The Syrian economy is currently in a transitional stage, moving from a state-dominated to a market economy. The reform process started in the mid-1980s with a law allowing for mixed private- and public-sector companies, a measure of trade liberalization, export encouragement and an easing of foreign-exchange controls. The next big step came in 1991 with Investment Law no 10, which opened the door for fully private investment in agriculture, industry and transport, new incentives, a further relaxation of import laws and access to foreign currency. However, the piece-meal reform measures that were implemented in the 1980s and early 1990s failed to unleash the full potential of the Syrian economy, mainly due to the lack of a conducive environment for private participation, exemplified in the lack of a modern banking system, limited private-sector access to credit, a still-rigid foreign-exchange regime, and a cumbersome regulatory structure.

Since the country's new president, Bashar Assad, came into power, the reform process has witnessed a rapid acceleration: the year 2000 marked the start of a new era in the country's development. A new council of ministers was appointed, headed by Prime Minister Muhammad Mustafa Miru. The new government has given economic reform top priority. With the new government and the new generation in power, there has been a more aggressive approach to economic reform. Both the young president and the government are aware of the serious economic challenges that face the country – this constitutes a good starting-point for reform.

Three key economic developments were set in motion before President Asad's death: the Syrian budget for 2000 was swiftly approved, the anti-corruption movement forced several senior political figures out of office, and new investment laws were put in place. Syria recently introduced a series of decrees to stimulate investment in the country. In particular, decree no 7 provides for additional advantages for investment projects. The decree tackled other investment issues, such as securing land for Arab and foreign investors, allowing the repatriation of foreign capital by foreign investors after a five-year time period, the establishment of joint stock companies and the reduction of their tax burden.

Putting in place the necessary infrastructure for the development of a market economy is now a top priority in Syria. This includes new copyrights and financial laws, banking reform and modern communications and transport-facility development. President Asad has initiated sweeping economic reforms for the country. In early 2001, Syria approved the unrestricted establishment of private banks in the country as part of the government's programme to reform the economy and attract foreign investment. This will end nearly 40 years of state monopoly of the banking sector. According to the new directives, banks can be either entirely owned by private investors or can have mixed private–public ownership. In the case of mixed ownership, the public sector can own a maximum of 25 per cent of a bank's capital. Foreign investors will have an ownership ceiling of 49 per cent of a commercial bank, with the other 51 per cent limited to Syrian individuals and/or institutional investors. Furthermore, the law calls for the creation of bank secrecy laws similar to those in Lebanon.

The reform programme drawn up for the Syrian financial sector also includes a plan to improve the role of the Central Bank of Syria in directing financial and monetary policy, to create a stock exchange, and to amend foreign-exchange laws for the Syrian pound so as to reflect free-market rates. Currently, there are at least three rates used to determine the price of the Syrian pound. In mid-February 2001, the council of ministers in Syria approved a draft law to set up the country's first stock exchange. The stock market will be established as a private institution, will enjoy full administrative and financial independence, and will be qualified to manage its own financial resources.

Earlier, in 2000, Syria gave permission for several Lebanese banks – including Fransabank, Banque Européenne pour le Moyen-Orient (BEMO) and Societé Générale Libano-Européenne de Banque – to operate in the country's free-trade zones. The Syrian government requires that banks provide $10 million in capital for their main bank branch in Syria before being granted licenses to operate, and another $1 million for each additional branch. Syria is hoping that the number of investors in the country's free-trade zones will grow substantially once private banks are established.

The decision to reform the banking sector and allow the establishment of private banks has been one of the most significant developments so far. The opening up of the sector is a crucial step to encourage foreign investment, to increase the number of development projects and to stimulate domestic economic growth. Foreign investment outside the oil sector has been virtually non-existent due to the lack of access to private debt financing. The banking sector in Syria has been under state control for the past four decades, and lacks the basic financial products that characterize a modern economy, such as loans, ATMs and credit cards. Total deposits in the Syrian banking sector are estimated at $5 billion, compared to more than $36 billion in Lebanon.

The Syrian government is also planning to reform the economy's industrial sectors and to lower customs duties in order to increase exports and boost the country's industrial competitiveness. The new reforms will centre on the private and public sectors as well as joint-development projects utilizing both state and private financing. The country has adopted reform measures aimed at making the public industrial sector more productive and profitable. The private sector will also soon be allowed to invest in industries previously limited to the public sector, such as the production and refining of sugar, the generation and distribution of electricity, the oil, gas and cement industries. In addition to the industrial reform measures, the government is also preparing a bill to cut customs duties on raw materials, to counter Lebanese competition.

Syria has for the time being ruled out the privatization of public-sector institutions – instead it plans to reform them. In fact, the government has already started a programme to reform and reactivate the public sector. One of the mainstays of the new reform programme is the separation of ownership and management in public-sector companies and the introduction of private sector management contracts, both Syrian and foreign, to these companies. The programme also requires that public-sector companies operate on the basis of profitability and economic feasibility, as the economic return of these companies will be the main benchmark in evaluating their performance. However, the government will not ignore the social implications of the reform programme, and will work on retraining employees to adapt to the new operating environment and to guarantee maximum levels of efficiency. The government will also continue to support the private sector and provide it with the necessary backing via the adoption of laws and regulations to enable it to play a greater role in the country's development process.

In a constructive move towards the liberalization of the Syrian economy, a law for the restructuring of public sector companies was finalized in May 2001. The new law plans to overhaul poorly managed public-sector companies by transforming them into holding companies or joint-stock companies. According to the new legislation, these companies will enjoy financial and economic independence within a legal framework independent of the existing commercial law, and will have the authority to make decisions without needing to obtain ministerial approval. The new firms will replace existing public sector firms, take on the assets and liabilities of their subsidiary companies and enjoy many freedoms, including the freedom to issue shares and borrow both domestically and externally without government guarantees. They will also be able to engage in investment activities and undertake financial management of company assets.

A special government committee is also discussing a new tax law to replace the existing tax regulations, some of which have remained unchanged since 1949. Income taxes in Syria are relatively high compared with neighbouring countries. The basic income-tax rate is 30 per cent, payable on all but the first SL100 ($2) of income, and profits exceeding SL1 million ($20,000) are taxed at a rate of 63 per cent. Not surprisingly, the high tax rate is the main reason for tax evasion and the decline in the volume of investment in the country. A revision of the tax laws will play an integral part in encouraging more Syrian expatriates to invest their money in the country.

Syria is also raising its profile as a tourist destination with promotional efforts, construction plans and deregulation. The government is facilitating the issue of permits to tour operators, sponsoring the construction of hotels and other tourism facilities, and is diligently promoting the country's many historical and natural attractions. The policy has yielded promising results, with an increase in the number of Arab tourists in the first half of 2000 to 883,000 (up 10 per cent) and a 43 per cent increase in non-Arab tourists Annual revenues from tourism have exceeded $1 billion in the late 1990s.

On a regional level, the signing of a free-trade agreement with Iraq and a $1 billion gas-pipeline deal with Egypt, Lebanon and Jordan, are also indicative of a further opening up to regional trading partners. The Iraqi–Syrian agreement is expected to raise trade between the two countries to $1 billion in 2001, compared to $500 million in 2000. The two countries also plan to build a new oil pipeline with a capacity of around 1.4 million barrels per day. Syria and Saudi Arabia have also signed an agreement establishing a free-trade zone to boost commercial co-operation between the two countries. The agreement will take effect from January 2003. The accords with Iraq and Saudi Arabia pave the way for the creation of an Arab free-trade zone by 2007: all Arab products traded within it would be free of custom duties and other restrictions.

The leaders of Jordan, Syria and Egypt met in Syria in March 2001 to attend the inauguration of the $145 million Jordan–Syria electricity-network project. The Syrian part of the project is estimated to have cost $115 million, compared to the $30 million it cost to set up the network in the Jordanian territory. The link-up required the erection of a 360km line connecting the Syrian and Jordanian networks, with a capacity of 400kv. The Jordanian and Egyptian networks were linked in March 1999 by an underwater cable as part of a project launched in 1996 aimed at connecting the grids of Egypt, Jordan, Syria, Lebanon, Turkey and Iraq. The next phases of the network should link Syria with Turkey and Lebanon. The 350km-long line between Syria and Turkey should be completed by the end of 2001, and that with Lebanon by the end of 2002. The Arab Fund for Economic and Social Development (AFESD) has put $300 million towards the project.

Syria is also looking to improve economic ties beyond its Arab neighbours. In particular, the European Commission president's visit to Damascus in February

2001 helped compress the timetable for negotiating a free-trade accord with the EU. The Syrian–EU Association Agreement should establish a free-trade zone by 2010 and give the EU preferential access to the relatively closed Syrian market. The signing of Syria's first copyright law is yet another clear signal that Damascus is prepared to pay greater heed to international business 'norms'. In February, the Syrian president endorsed a copyright law providing full protection for all written, performed, recorded or drawn material. The law prohibits unauthorized duplication of audiotapes, videotapes, CD-ROMs and printed material. The new regulations cover works by people residing in Syria, irrespective of nationality, as well as Syrian citizens living abroad. Illegal duplication of protected material carries a prison sentence of up to two years or a fine of up to $2000. The new law does not, however, apply to imported material such as trademarks, computer programs and films.

The changes that took place in 2000 and 2001 signal a new commitment to modernization and a move to a more market oriented economy. If these are pursued diligently, they should attract much-needed foreign investment to the country. Already a number of foreign firms have begun exploring new investments in the telecommunications, energy and power sectors. In a recent development, the Syrian–Egyptian joint venture SyriaTel and the Lebanese Investcom were granted a 15-year mobile telecommunications concession. With one of the world's highest population growth rates (in the range of 3.4 per cent annually), Syria will need around $4 billion in investment over the next decade in order to create the approximately 200,000 jobs needed annually to absorb the growing labourforce. Although the unemployment rate in the country was officially estimated at 5 per cent in 1998, private estimates place it at more than twice that level.

## *GROWTH*

The Syrian economy has been stagnant over the past few years, as a result of rigidities in production structures and institutions, widespread corruption, and the inflexible internal functioning of the economy. Signs of a slow-down in the Syrian economy first appeared in 1997 when real GDP growth dropped to a modest 1.8 per cent from approximately 4.4 per cent and 5.8 per cent in 1996 and 1995 respectively. The sharp decline in oil prices and revenues in 1998, in addition to falling prices of its cotton exports and reductions in financial assistance from GCC countries, forced the government to cut spending on investment projects. In light of the generally constrained role of the private sector in the development and growth of the Syrian economy, GDP contracted by an estimated 1.5 per cent in 1998.

Despite higher oil prices in 1999, real GDP growth slipped further, by 1.2 per cent, as the country was hit by its worst drought in over 25 years, with the total rainfall level down to almost half its annual average. Real GDP recovered to 1.5 per cent in 2000. The continuing drought adversely affected the agricultural sector, preventing the country from achieving a higher economic growth rate in 2000. The economic recovery picked up momentum in 2001 due to greater participation by the private sector and fresh aid and investment flows from Gulf states, with real growth at 2.6 per cent.

## *INFLATION*

Syria was able to reduce its inflation rate to an estimated 2.2 per cent in 1998, compared to approximately 8.2 per cent in the previous two years. Tight monetary policy, constrained expenditure by the government – which plays a leading role in the Syrian economy – lower import prices from East and Southeast Asian countries and weak economic growth helped to keep the inflation rate to approximately 1 per cent in 1999 and 2000, before edging slightly higher in 2001 as a result of a modest rebound in economic activity and higher import prices.

**Figure 9.4**
**Arab Syrian Republic: consumer price index, 1985–2000**

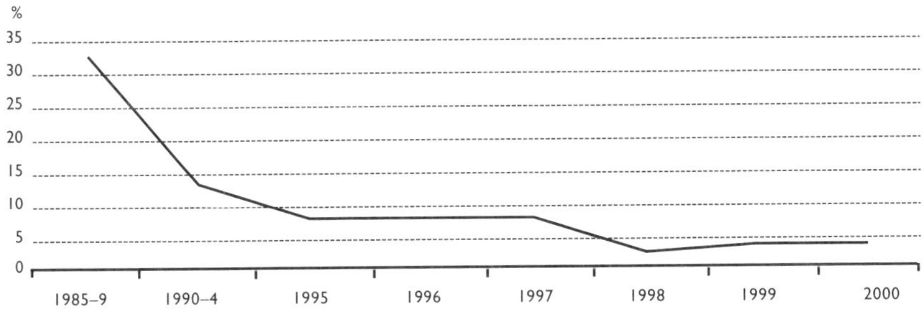


*Source: ESCWA*

## *EXCHANGE RATE*

Syria maintains one of the last remaining fixed multiple exchange-rate systems. There are at least four different government exchange rates for the local currency. There is the official exchange rate of SL11.2 to the dollar, the 'neighbouring country' rate of SL46, the customs rate of SL23, and finally, the 'export dollar' rate, which ranges between SL52 and SL57. The 'neighbouring country' rate accounts for approximately 85 per cent of the country's transactions. However, as part of the country's reform schedule for the financial sector, the government is planning to amend foreign-exchange laws for the Syrian pound so as to reflect free-market rates.

## *FISCAL POLICY*

The 2000 budget projected revenue growth across the board. Revenues from taxes and duties were set to increase by 3.9 per cent to SL85.91 billion ($1.87 billion), compared to SL82.69 billion ($1.80 billion) in 1999, while revenues from services and property were slated to increase by 31.1 per cent.

Table 9.13
Arab Syrian Republic: budgets, 1997–2001 (SL million)

| | 2001 | 2000 | 1999 | 1998 | 1997 |
|---|---|---|---|---|---|
| **Expenditure** | | | | | |
| Government services, including: | 171,325 | 150,060 | 144,088 | 127,432 | – |
| Justice | 41,268 | 33,125 | 31,503 | 30,816 | 28,965 |
| National security | 49,373 | 48,373 | 47,594 | 45,912 | 43,860 |
| Education | 8793 | 7336 | 7039 | 6801 | 15,471 |
| National debt | – | – | – | – | 14,436 |
| Agricultural, forest and fisheries | 27,487 | 26,123 | 24,581 | 25,059 | 24,220 |
| Extractive industries | 11,449 | 10,277 | 8635 | 8965 | 8471 |
| Manufacturing industries | 17,932 | 16,060 | 16,735 | 17,049 | 14,033 |
| Electricity, water and gas | 30,667 | 25,685 | 23,539 | 25,168 | 27,004 |
| Construction | 110 | 1079 | 1118 | 1225 | 1216 |
| Trade | 2752 | 2848 | 3370 | 3732 | 3435 |
| Transport, communications and storage | 35,549 | 21,970 | 20,289 | 17,680 | 11,012 |
| Banking, insurance and property | 2888 | 1590 | 1147 | 1389 | 1164 |
| Unallocated expenditure | 20,850 | 19,708 | 11,800 | 9600 | 4400 |
| **Total expenditure** | **322,000** | **275,400** | **255,300** | **237,300** | **211,125** |
| **Revenues** | | | | | |
| Taxes and duties | 115,932 | 85,913 | 82,686 | 75,516 | 69,296 |
| Services and property | 26,885 | 25,397 | 19,409 | 20,054 | 18,574 |
| Miscellaneous revenues, including: | 68,625 | 67,504 | 65,500 | 70,385 | 48,108 |
| Various revenues | | | | | 23,818 |
| Concessional loans | | | | | – |
| Surplus on state activities | 69,317 | 59,685 | 50,314 | 47,081 | 44,516 |
| Exceptional financing, including: | 38,241 | 36,901 | 37,391 | 34,264 | 30,631 |
| Foreign loans | – | – | – | – | 22,184 |
| Domestic loans | – | – | – | – | 8071 |
| **Total Revenue** | **322,000** | **275,400** | **255,300** | **247,300** | **211,125** |

*Source: Middle East Economic Survey*

Concerning expenditure, the 2000 budget concentrated on the development process and showed that efforts are underway to enhance infrastructure, support economic development, and activate the market. Total government spending was forecast to rise by 7.9 per cent to SL275.40 billion ($5.99 billion) in 2000 from SL255.30 billion ($5.55 billion) in 1999. Strengthening the economy's infrastructure and utilities figured highly in the budget, with the combined expenditure on transport, communication, electricity, water, and gas up 9 per cent on the year before. Expenditure on total government services, including justice, national security and education, increased by 4.1 per cent to SL150.06 billion ($3.26 billion) for 2000, up from SL144.09 billion ($3.3 billion) in 1999.

In December 2000, the Syrian government approved a SL332 billion balanced budget for 2001. Expenditures for 2001 increased by 16.9 per cent to SL322 billion ($7 billion). This increase mainly went towards covering the 25 per cent increase in government salaries approved in early 2001. SL37.3 billion ($0.81 billion) was allocated to cover repayment of foreign debt and to help preserve local prices at their current level.

## *EXTERNAL SECTOR*

According to data from the IMF's International Financial Statistics (IFS), Syria's current account was in credit from 1995 to 1999. Oil revenues account for around 60 per cent of Syria's exports: the collapse in oil prices in 1998 drove total exports down 23 per cent to $3142 million from $4057 million in 1997, pulling the trade balance into a deficit of $178 million following a generous surplus of $454 million in 1996. As a result, the current account narrowed to $58 million in 1997, significantly below the $461 million recorded in 1997. The slow-down in the economy over the past few years is witnessed by the decline in imports from $4604 million in 1994 to $3320 in 1998.

Table 9.14
Arab Syrian Republic: balance of payments, 1994–9 ($ million)

| | 1994 | 1995 | 1996 | 1997 | 1998 | 1999 |
|---|---|---|---|---|---|---|
| Current account | –791 | 263 | 40 | 461 | 58 | 201 |
| Trade balance | –1275 | –146 | –338 | 454 | –178 | 216 |
| Goods, exports | 3329 | 3858 | 4178 | 4057 | 3142 | 3806 |
| Goods, imports | –4604 | –4004 | –4516 | –3603 | –3320 | –3590 |
| Services balance | 252 | 362 | 237 | 93 | 175 | 39 |
| Income balance | –359 | –560 | –483 | –585 | –470 | –543 |
| Current transfers (net) | 591 | 607 | 624 | 499 | 531 | 489 |
| **Capital account** | **102** | **20** | **26** | **18** | **27** | **80** |
| **Financial account** | **1159** | **521** | **782** | **65** | **196** | **173** |
| **Net errors and omissions** | **96** | **35** | **139** | **–95** | **153** | **–195** |
| **Balance of payments** | **566** | **839** | **987** | **449** | **434** | **259** |

*Source: IFS*

The recovery in oil prices in 1999 drove exports up 21 per cent to $3801 million and placed the trade balance in positive territory again, with a surplus of $216 million. The improvement in the trade balance was moderated by a rise in imports that year, up 8 per cent to $3590. The current account registered a surplus of $201 million that year. The overall balance of payments has been in surplus over the past few years, and stood at $259 million in 1999. 2000 is likely to have recorded a further improvement in the external balance as even higher oil prices propel exports higher. The improvement in the trade balance will be moderated by the anticipated increase in imports and lower non-oil exports associated with the drought related fall in food production. The services balance and net transfers should improve as a result of higher growth in the Gulf, prompting an increase in visitors to Syria.

## *PUBLIC DEBT*

Syria is burdened by a large external debt, estimated at approximately $21.1 billion, around 120 per cent of GDP. Over the past few years, some progress has been made in reducing and rescheduling the debt burden. A large part of the debt was accrued through military purchases from the Soviet Union and Eastern European countries: more than half the country's external debt is owed to Russia alone.

In 1997, Syria and the World Bank negotiated an agreement for the settlement of the arrears, which by then had reached $550 million. Syria has fully complied with the agreement, and it is expected that all arrears will be cleared by September 2002. The government cannot seek World Bank loans until that issue is fully settled. In 2000, Syria settled a portion of its debt with Germany by writing off loans, while another part was diverted to cover social and environmental projects. The debt-rescheduling agreement with Germany requires Syria to repay $572 million in instalments over a 20-year period, with a five-year period of grace. Similar agreements have been reached with Italy, Belgium and France.

# 10

# THE GCC COUNTRIES

## SAUDI ARABIA

Table 10.1
Saudi Arabia: main economic indicators

| | 1996 | 1997 | 1998 | 1999 | 2000 | 2001 |
|---|---|---|---|---|---|---|
| Nominal GDP (SR billion) | 529.3 | 548.6 | 491.0 | 534.2 | 680.1 | 668.0 |
| Nominal GDP ($ billion) | 141.3 | 146.5 | 131.1 | 142.6 | 181.6 | 178.3 |
| Nominal GDP growth | 10.6% | 3.6% | −10.5% | 8.8% | 27.2% | −1.8% |
| Real GDP growth | 1.4% | 2.7% | 1.6% | 1.8% | 4.5% | 2.2% |
| Inflation | 0.9% | −0.4% | −0.2% | −1.2% | −0.9% | −0.8% |
| **Fiscal indicators (SR billion)** | | | | | | |
| Revenues | 179.1 | 205.5 | 141.6 | 147.0 | 248.0 | 230.0 |
| Expenditure | 198.1 | 221.3 | 190.1 | 181.0 | 203.0 | 255.0 |
| Deficit/surplus | −19.0 | −15.8 | −48.5 | −34.0 | 45.0 | −25.0 |
| (as percentage of GDP) | −3.6 | −2.9 | −9.9 | −6.4 | 7.3 | −3.7 |
| Internal debt | 417 | 447 | 493 | 540 | 600 | 605 |
| (as percentage of GDP) | 78.8 | 81.5 | 100.4 | 101.1 | 97.2 | 97.1 |
| **External indicators ($ million)** | | | | | | |
| Exports | 60,729 | 60,731 | 38,822 | 50,757 | 72,000 | 66,000 |
| Imports | 25,358 | 26,370 | 27,535 | 25,717 | 29,500 | 29,800 |
| Trade balance | 35,370 | 34,362 | 11,287 | 25,039 | 42,500 | 36,200 |
| Current-account balance | 681 | 305 | −13,150 | 412 | 14,800 | 8500 |
| (as percentage of GDP) | 0.5 | 0.2 | −10.0 | 0.3 | 9.0 | 5.1 |

*Sources: Saudi Arabian Monetary Authority and IMF*

### *ECONOMIC OVERVIEW*

A spirit of mild optimism surfaced in Saudi Arabia in 2000 and 2001, underpinned by the surge in oil prices and as a reflection of the new order expected to emerge from the recent package of liberalization measures. For the first time in years, the government and the private sector are discussing the economy in a positive way and are examining practical means of liberalizing the business arena and implementing new reforms which will give the kingdom an opportunity to 'roll back' the state sector, stimulate private business, bring in foreign investment – both direct and portfolio – and position the region on a higher growth path.

The Saudi government is using higher oil revenues to reduce internal and external indebtedness, boost foreign reserves and restore fiscal health rather than inflate domestic activities. With oil prices averaging $28.70 a barrel for Brent crude in 2000 and the prospect for prices to assume a new trading range of $18–28 in the coming few years, the kingdom is forecast to witness sustainable economic growth higher than the average prevailing between 1980 and 1999.

Despite massive oil wealth, the growth performance of Saudi Arabia over the past two decades has been disappointing. It recorded an average growth rate of 2.5 per cent during the period 1980–9, only half the average growth rate recorded by all developing countries. Given the kingdom's high population growth rate, this has translated into a decline in real per-capita income over the above period, compared to a 60 per cent rise for all developing countries. For example, in 1981 the US and Saudi Arabia both reported GDP per capita of $28,600; in 2000, US GDP per capita had risen to $40,000, while Saudi Arabia's had dropped to $8000.

There is little doubt that the Saudi economy has moved past the downturn of the late 1990s, with real growth in 2000 reaching 4.5 per cent, compared to 1.8 per cent and 1.6 per cent in 1998 and 1999 respectively. The government budget recorded a surplus in 2000 for the first time in almost two decades and the current account also showed a surplus of 9 per cent of GDP. However, despite the economy's strong performance in 2000, the major challenge facing the Saudi authorities in the coming years remains the heavy dependence of the Saudi economy on oil revenues, given the intermittent volatility of the oil market. The 1998 downturn in oil prices underscored the economy's vulnerability to oil-price fluctuations. The steep fall in oil prices in 1998 resulted in a deficit equal to 10 per cent of GDP and a sharp rise in domestic debt to 103 per cent of GDP. Moreover, the external position weakened, with the current account shifting into a deficit of 10 per cent of GDP that year. It is, therefore, only natural to conclude that unless the economy's dependence on oil revenues is addressed, imbalances will likely resurface.

The government is forging ahead with several far reaching measures to stimulate growth in and promote the role of the private sector, diversify the production base and address the underlying structural weaknesses in the budget. The reform agenda over the coming few years includes privatization, reform of the company, investment and tax laws, introduction of direct and indirect taxes, and strengthening the tax and customs departments.

In April 2000, the Saudi parliament passed a milestone foreign investment code aimed at relaxing foreign-investment restrictions. The main impetus behind the new law is the need to stimulate growth and job creation in the kingdom as part of a larger effort to make the private sector the main driving force behind the economy instead of the government. An additional goal is to attract home a large bulk of the substantial Saudi wealth invested outside the kingdom.

The law entails the creation of a new regulatory body, the General Investment Authority (GIA), the main responsibilities of which include reviewing investment laws and regulations, preparing government policies to promote investment further, studying investment opportunities in the kingdom and providing a wide range of information services to investors.. The GIA will be a 'one-stop-shop' to obtain the business license for approved projects within a maximum period of 30 days, and to incorporate new projects.

Under the new law, the top rate of taxation on foreign stakes in projects was cut from 45 per cent to 30 per cent – composed of 15 per cent income tax and 15 per cent withholding tax – which will apply to any new investment. Previously, foreign companies or equity stakes were taxed at a rate of 25 per cent on the first SR100,000 of profits, 35 per cent on profits between SR100,000 and SR500,000, 40 per cent on profits between SR500,000 and SR1 million, and 45 per cent on anything over that amount. The new law makes no mention of the tax holidays that were a feature of the old law. However, the new code is likely to include loss carry-forward provisions that have no time limit, consistent with tax laws in advanced economies.

The previous sponsorship system, under which foreign investors were required to involve a national partner in investment projects, has also undergone changes. Now, the foreign investor and its non-Saudi employees would be sponsored by the project itself. According to the new legislation, a licensed foreign project can apply to own property necessary to operate the project or house its workers on condition that they have invested a minimum of SR30 million ($8 million) in the country. Previously, only Saudi companies and individuals, or those from GCC states, were permitted to own property in the kingdom.

The new foreign-investment regulations assure foreign investors equal treatment with local investors in terms of incentives, guarantees and privileges. Previously, non-Saudi investors with stakes exceeding 49 per cent in local joint ventures were not eligible for tax holidays or soft loans from the Saudi Industrial Development Fund (SIDF) and were not treated on an equal footing with local companies when bidding for government contracts. The new capital-investment code holds that companies fully or partially owned by foreigners can apply for loans from the SIDF. Moreover, the foreign investor is assured that it has the right to transfer capital outside the country, and that the confiscation or the expropriation of part or all of the firm's assets is prohibited, unless done by judicial order or in the public interest.

The new investment regulations are expected to accelerate investments into the kingdom. However, some restrictions on foreign investment remain in place. The GIA issued a list identifying the sectors or business lines in which foreign investment is allowed. The dual taxation system – under which Saudi businesses only pay *zakat* (a religious tax) at a rate of 2 per cent of net income while foreigners are subject to much higher income-tax rates, albeit lower now under the new law –

remains in place, and contradicts the principle of non-discriminatory treatment of nationals and foreigners required under WTO guidelines.

Saudi Arabia's desire to join WTO, which it is expected to do in 2002, will act as a further stimulus for economic liberalization and streamlining of a number of outdated regulations. Moreover, accession to the WTO will boost the potential for international trade and expose domestic industries to increased competition, thereby enhancing domestic productivity.

The broad lines of the government's reform programme are contained in the new five-year development plan (2001–5). The plan forecasts average annual real GDP growth of 3.16 per cent, with most of the growth expected to be generated by the private sector, which is forecast to grow at an average annual real rate of 5.04 per cent. The plan also forecasts 4.01 per cent average non-oil GDP growth, which would lead to an increase in the contribution of the non-oil sector to GDP to 71.6 per cent by the end of 2005 from 68.4 per cent in 1999. The budget deficit as a percentage of GDP would be reduced from around 10.8 per cent in 1999 to near balance by the end of the plan.

The plan asserted that the kingdom would focus on privatization as a 'basic economic option'. Private-sector investments are expected to reach SR478.5 billion, accounting for nearly 71.2 per cent of total investment during the life of the plan. Realizing average real investment growth of 6.85 per cent annually during the plan would lead to an increase in investment as a percentage of GDP from 22.7 per cent in 1999 to 25.4 per cent by the end of the plan. The development plan forecasts an average annual growth of 8.29 per cent in the petrochemical sector, 8.34 per cent in the non-oil mining sector, 5.14 per cent in industry, 4.62 per cent in the electricity, gas and water sector and 3.44 per cent in the services sector.

The plan also aims to boost the Saudi workforce from 44.2 per cent (1999) to 53.2 per cent of the kingdom's total population. Under the new plan, some 817,000 job opportunities are to be created for Saudi nationals, including 488,600 jobs which would be made available through a 'Saudization' programme to replace foreigners working in the kingdom. The kingdom recently introduced new fees for the issuance and renewal of residency papers and work permits for foreigners, the receipts of which are to be channelled towards training Saudi workers.

## *GROWTH*

The downturn in oil prices in 1998 dealt a hard blow to the Saudi economy, with average Saudi oil export prices dropping by over 40 per cent to $10.5 per barrel, from $17.7 in 1997. Real GDP growth slowed to 1.6 per cent in 1998, from 2.7 per cent in 1997. The slow-down was primarily driven by a terms-of-trade shock, with exports dropping by over 34.5 per cent in 1998.

Following the strong improvement in oil prices, nominal GDP grew by 8.8 per cent in 1999 to SR534 billion ($143 billion), while real growth remained modest at

1.8 per cent. The oil sector remained weak as higher prices in 1999 were offset by lower production and export volumes, in line with OPEC's production cuts. Real GDP growth in the non-oil sectors, which accounted for 64 per cent of GDP, has more than offset the 7.9 per cent decline in oil production.

Still higher oil prices and production levels in 2000 boosted GDP to SR680 billion ($181.6 billion), a growth of 27.2 per cent. Growth in the Saudi oil sector is estimated at 39.4 per cent in 2000, while Saudi Arabia's real GDP growth in the year 2000 is put at 4.5 per cent. Real growth is estimated at 2.2 per cent in 2001, supported by stable oil prices and the numerous measures recently adopted by the government to promote the role of the private sector and attract foreign investment. Nominal GDP is estimated to have declined by 1.8 per cent in 2001, due mainly to the decline in oil prices, which averaged $23 per barrel for Brent crude.

## *MONETARY POLICY AND INTEREST RATES*

Exchange-rate and price stability continues to be the strategic focus of monetary policy in Saudi Arabia. The use of monetary tools in Saudi Arabia is circumscribed by the institutional setting – an open economy with a pegged exchange rate – along with several requirements, including a 100 per cent foreign-exchange cover for Saudi Arabian Monetary Authority's (SAMA) domestic currency issue, and a prohibition on central-bank lending to the government.

During periods in which there is little or no speculation against the Saudi riyal, interest rates on local-currency deposits tend to move in tandem with corresponding dollar-rates. However, in 1998 and early 1999, domestic interest rates were allowed to rise above those on equivalent dollar deposits in response to tight liquidity conditions amidst strong credit demand and intermittent speculative attacks against the riyal.

Saudi riyal three-month deposit rates rose steadily in 1998 to average 6.21 per cent for the year, compared to averages of 5.47 per cent and 5.79 per cent in 1996 and 1997 respectively. Domestic interest rates continued to rise in the first quarter of 1999, Saudi riyal three-month deposit rates reached a high of 6.85 per cent in March 1999 from less than 6 per cent in November 1998. Interest-rate differentials between Saudi riyal and dollar deposits rose from a low of 0.35 per cent in January 1998 to a high of 1.95 per cent in March 1999. The widening spreads were a reflection of heightened speculative pressure against the riyal at a time when oil prices were weak.

Following the recovery in oil prices since the second quarter of 1999, the interest rate differential with dollar assets declined, and speculative pressure on the riyal subsided. Interest rates in Saudi Arabia rose throughout the year 2000 in line with rising interest rates in the US. The spread between Saudi interest rates and dollar-rates shrunk to an average of 0.25 per cent in 2000. As rates in the US declined in 2001, riyal rates followed suit, with three-month riyal deposit rates ending the year at 2.5 per cent – close to the corresponding dollar rates.

## *INFLATION*

Inflation has remained well bellow the 1 per cent level for most of the 1990s, with the exception of a steep rise at the beginning of the decade due to strong demand pressure, and in 1995 when an upward adjustment of some of the government-subsidized prices led to a 5 per cent increase in the CPI. The rate of increase in consumer prices decelerated to 0.9 per cent in 1996, and fell to –0.4 per cent and –0.2 per cent in 1997 and 1998 respectively. Continued low import prices and subdued domestic demand kept price levels in check in 1999, with the CPI falling by an estimated 1.2 per cent despite the increase in petrol prices earlier in the year. In 2000 and 2001, the cost-of-living index continued to be negative at –0.9 per cent and –0.8 per cent respectively.

## *EXCHANGE RATE*

Since June 1986, the riyal has effectively been pegged to the dollar at the fixed exchange rate of SR3.745. The exchange rate has occasionally come under pressure, particularly following prolonged drops in oil prices. SAMA's determination to uphold the exchange-rate peg was tested in August–September 1998 and later in early 1999, when the riyal came under strong speculative pressure as a result of the sharp decline in oil prices, and the associated worsening of the kingdom's current-account and fiscal imbalances. SAMA's intervention in the foreign-exchange market was successful (reportedly involving some $1 billion in August 1999), attesting to the monetary authority's commitment to the riyal/dollar peg. Higher oil prices in 2000/01 eliminated the speculative pressure on the currency.

The exchange-rate peg against the dollar is well suited to the Saudi economy, especially as the country's main export commodities – oil and petrochemicals – are priced in the dollar, and a large portion of both public and private financial wealth abroad is dollar-denominated. Therefore, devaluation will not make the country's exports more competitive. The current exchange-rate system provides the country with a useful nominal anchor, manages to keep inflation in line and lends credibility to the country's investment regime.

## *FISCAL POLICY*

Saudi Arabia has adopted a balanced budget for the year 2001, following the $12 billion surplus in 2000 – the first in 18 years – thanks to strong oil prices. Revenues and expenditures were estimated at SR215 billion ($57.33 billion). According to Finance Ministry estimates, actual spending in 2001 amounted to SR255 billion ($68 billion) against revenues of SR230 billion ($61.3 billion), leaving a deficit of SR25 billion ($6.6 billion).

The government has allocated $10.1 billion in 2001 to create more than 27,000 new jobs in the education, communications, public services and health sectors, $14.2 billion is to be spent on the education and vocational training sectors, the health and social development sector is allocated $5.8 billion, and $2.98 billion has been set aside for the industrial and agricultural sectors.

The budget results for the year 1998 highlight the persistent vulnerability of the kingdom's fiscal position to the volatility of oil prices, with the budget deficit that year reaching SR48.5 billion ($13 billion), equivalent to almost 10 per cent of GDP. The upturn in oil prices in 1999 offered some relief to budgetary pressures, slashing the budget deficit to 6.4 per cent of GDP.

Table 10.2
Saudi Arabia: budget overview (SR billion)

| | 1998A | 1999A | 2000A | 2001A | 2002B |
|---|---|---|---|---|---|
| Revenue | 141.6 | 147.0 | 248.0 | 230.0 | 157.0 |
| Oil revenue | 80.0 | 100.0 | – | – | – |
| Non-oil revenue | 61.6 | 47.0 | – | – | – |
| Expenditure | 190.0 | 181.0 | 203.0 | 255.0 | 202.0 |
| Deficit/surplus | –48.5 | –34.0 | 45.0 | –25.0 | –45.0 |
| Deficit (as percentage of GDP) | 9.9 | 6.4 | 7.3 | –3.7 | –6.5 |

*A: Actual*
*B: Budgeted*

*Source: Saudi Arabian Monetary Authority*

Expenditures in 1999 declined by 4.7 per cent on their 1998 level, to SR 181 billion ($48.3 billion), but were unexpectedly higher than the budgeted SR165 billion ($44.1 billion). Total revenue in 1999 increased by a modest SR5.4 billion ($1.4 billion), or 3.8 per cent, to SR147 billion ($39.3 billion), despite the average oil price increase of $5 per barrel – a rise of almost 40 per cent. The 1999 revenue figure reported in the budget results took many by surprise, falling well below expectations inspired by the substantial rise in oil prices during the year. The most likely explanation for the discrepancy between the actual revenues and those reported in the budget results is that Saudi Aramco retained a larger portion of oil earnings in 1999 to finance its capital spending in 2000 and settle part of the foreign debt accrued in 1998.

Unless the Saudi government addresses its structural fiscal imbalances, fluctuations in the oil market will continue to play havoc with government finances. Despite recent attempts at reform, several structural weaknesses remain, including persistent and excessive dependence on oil income, lack of a stable revenue-base and of smooth and sustainable growth in non-oil receipts, and an inability to adjust expenditure patterns, given the high proportion of incompressible spending in the form of wages, entitlements and interest payments. Therefore, strengthening the budget structure must involve work on two fronts: building up a strong non-oil revenue-base and rationalizing expenditures.

## *DOMESTIC DEBT*

Until 1988, Saudi Arabia financed its deficits through a drawdown of government deposits. The Saudi internal debt built up rapidly in the 1990s, from SR237 billion in 1992, or 51 per cent of GDP, to an estimated SR493 billion in 1998, equal to 103 per cent of GDP. The SR39 billion budget deficit of 1999 raised the existing domestic debt to SR540 billion, equivalent to 104 per cent of GDP. By the end of 2001, public debt in Saudi Arabia had exceeded SR605 billion.

The authorities have not ruled out the possibility of reducing the stock of debt through the use of privatization receipts. In the meantime, the government must allow borrowing carefully among its different sources of financing so as to avoid excessive dependence on bank financing, as this runs the risk of crowding out private-sector borrowers.

## *EXTERNAL SECTOR*

The oil-price crash in 1998 led to a sharp deterioration in the Saudi external sector, with the current account falling from a modest surplus of $305 million in 1997 to a deficit of around $13.15 billion, or 10 per cent of GDP. However, the revival in oil prices in 1999 and 2000 drastically improved the current-account balance, which registered surpluses equivalent to 0.3 per cent of GDP in 1999 and an impressive 9 per cent of GDP in 2000, its highest level in almost two decades.

The weakening in the current account in 1998 reflected the sharp drop in the kingdom's trade surplus. The loss of oil-export earnings and the drop in non-oil exports pushed Saudi Arabia's trade balance down from $34.4 billion in 1997 to $11.3 billion in 1998. Oil export revenues declined by $19.8 billion to $33.4 billion. Non-oil exports also weakened in 1998, dropping by 15 per cent on their 1997 level to $6.3 billion, and thus breaking the trend of rapid growth that prevailed during most of the 1990s. In particular, petrochemical exports fell by an estimated 35 per cent, to $1.7 billion, due to the significant decline in the international prices of fertilizers and petrochemicals that year.

Table 10.3
Saudi Arabia: balance of payments ($ million)

| | 1995 | 1996 | 1997 | 1998 | 1999 | 2000 |
|---|---|---|---|---|---|---|
| Exports | 50,041 | 60,729 | 60,731 | 38,822 | 50,757 | 72,000 |
| Imports | 25,650 | 25,358 | 26,370 | 27,535 | 25,717 | 29,500 |
| Trade balance | 24,391 | 35,370 | 34,362 | 11,287 | 25,039 | 42,500 |
| Services balance | −15,603 | −21,523 | −21,706 | −12,152 | −13,476 | −14,000 |
| Investment balance | 2803 | 2446 | 3156 | 2642 | 2994 | 600 |
| Transfers | −16,916 | −15,613 | −15,134 | −15,053 | −14,076 | −14,300 |
| Current account | −5325 | 681 | 305 | −13,150 | 412 | 14,800 |
| (as percentage of GDP) | −4.2 | 0.5 | 0.2 | −10.0 | 0.3 | 9.0 |

*Source: IMF, Finance and National Economy Ministry*

The impressive improvement in the trade surplus in 1999 takes much of the credit for the turnaround in the external position in 1999. The trade balance rose from a low $11.3 billion in 1998 to $25.0 billion in 1999. Exports in 1999 recovered to $50.8 billion, but still remained significantly below the $60.7 billion export receipts recorded in 1996 and 1997. The Kingdom's import bill declined by $1.8 billion, or 6.6 per cent, in 1999, to $25.7 billion. Merchandise imports have remained relatively steady in recent years, averaging around $25.4 billion over the period 1993–9. This stability is the result not only of favourable import prices but also of successful import substitution efforts in the production of several categories of goods.

2000 witnessed further improvements in the Saudi external sector: export receipts rose to $72 billion supported by strong growth in oil exports. Non-oil exports also picked up in 2000 particularly in light of the improvement in the international prices of fertilizers and petrochemicals. Strong growth in imports, to $28.5 billion, was also anticipated, given improved economic prospects and higher domestic demand. As a result, the current account recorded a healthy surplus in 2000, estimated at around $14.8 billion. Lower oil earnings in 2001 eroded the current-account surplus with a deficit projected for the year.

## KUWAIT

### *ECONOMIC OVERVIEW*

The Kuwaiti economy suffered in 1998 as oil prices fell, shifting Kuwait's fiscal balance to a deficit of 16 per cent of GDP in 1998/99, while the external current account surplus was reduced by over 70 per cent, nominal GDP declined by almost 14 per cent, and real GDP growth fell by 1.8 per cent. In 1999, despite modest real GDP growth of 0.5 per cent, the upturn in oil prices substantially improved the country's financial situation, with export earnings recovering by approximately 28 per cent and the current account surplus reaching 17 per cent of GDP.

Economic conditions improved markedly over 2000, reflecting the strong recovery in oil prices. The fiscal balance recorded healthy surpluses in both 1999/2000 and 2000/01, equivalent to 13.6 per cent and 14.8 per cent of GDP respectively. Nonetheless, Kuwait's long-term fiscal problem, generous public transfers in the context of strong population growth, extensive subsidies and a bloated public-sector payroll all remain unresolved. Fiscal and structural reforms are needed to curb demands on government revenues and bring forth a more diversified and balanced economy.

The medium-term challenge for Kuwait consists of raising economic growth and providing increased employment opportunities for its nationals. The government has historically used its oil wealth to maintain an open-handed welfare state in the form of generous transfers, subsidies and almost-guaranteed employment for

Table 10.4
Kuwait: main economic indicators

| | 1996 | 1997 | 1998 | 1999 | 2000 | 2001 |
|---|---|---|---|---|---|---|
| Nominal GDP (KD million) | 9178 | 8985 | 7742 | 9075 | 11,590 | 12,169 |
| Nominal GDP ($ million) | 30,141 | 29,507 | 25,425 | 29,803 | 38,062 | 39,965 |
| Nominal GDP growth | 15.4% | −2.1% | −13.8% | 17.2% | 27.7% | 5.0% |
| Real GDP Growth | 2.7% | 5.7% | −1.8% | 0.5% | 4.% | 1.7% |
| Inflation | 3.6% | 0.7% | 0.2% | 3.0% | 1.8% | 2.0% |
| **Fiscal indicators (KD billion)** | | | | | | |
| Revenues | 4391 | 3608 | 2798 | 5241 | 5003 | 3832 |
| Expenditure | 3889 | 3978 | 4040 | 4010 | 3290 | 5274 |
| Deficit/surplus | 502 | −370 | −1243 | 1231 | 1713 | −1443 |
| (as percentage of GDP) | 5.5 | −4.1 | −16.1 | 13.6 | 14.8 | −11.2 |
| Internal debt | 5339 | 4623 | 4271 | 4268 | – | |
| (as percentage of GDP) | 58.20 | 51.50 | 56.10 | 47.90 | – | |
| **External indicators ($ billion)** | | | | | | |
| Exports | 4475 | 4332 | 2931 | 3737 | 6005 | – |
| Oil exports | 4231 | 4085 | 2582 | 3357 | 5572 | – |
| Imports | −2380 | −2350 | −2351 | −2042 | −2100 | – |
| Current-account balance | 2128 | 2407 | 675 | 1540 | 4561 | – |
| (as percentage of GDP) | 23.20 | 26.40 | 8.70 | 17.00 | 26.20 | – |

*Sources: Central Bank of Kuwait and National Bank of Kuwait*

Kuwaiti citizens. Although the fiscal account is supported by substantial oil revenues, these generous benefits are not only unsustainable in the long run but are also leading to inefficient resource allocation and distortions in the economy.

The rapid growth in the Kuwaiti population makes matters worse, as each year brings increased numbers of citizens expecting free education, free healthcare, subsidized housing and cheap utilities. In addition, over half of the population is under the age of twenty, meaning that an increasing number of Kuwaiti citizens will be seeking comfortable high-paying public-sector jobs over the next two decades. Despite attempts by the government to encourage employment of nationals in the private sector, approximately 93 per cent of working Kuwaitis hold public-sector posts.

The government has been actively pushing for a reform programme that will scale down the welfare state and cut state subsidies and public-sector employment in the medium term. There are currently several laws under debate in the Kuwait parliament which are based on a series of proposed reform measures issued in late 1998. Specifically, the reform package was focused on privatization (of utilities, telecommunications and transportation), foreign investment, opening up oil activities to foreign participation under service-contract agreements, labour-market reforms, fiscal restructuring and reform of company law.

The Kuwait Investment Authority (KIA), which is responsible for managing the country's foreign investment, has announced plans to divest $2.7 billion-worth of shares in 19 local companies as of the beginning of 2002 as part of its privatization drive, which originally started in 1994 but slowed down in the following few years when the stock market started to decline. The organization will use the proceeds of the sales to establish investment funds and portfolios. It is estimated that the KIA is in charge of assets worth around $60 billion. Between 1994 and 1997, Kuwait divested around $3 billion-worth of local shares. KIA's holdings in local firms range from 5.3 to 87.7 per cent and are valued at KD826 million ($2681 million), or 12.9 per cent of total market capitalization, as of the end of October 2000. KIA is currently trying to encourage foreign fund managers to enter the local market, and there is speculation surrounding the creation of five foreign funds worth $500 million, 20 per cent of which would come from foreign investors.

The government's agenda has been met with strong resistance from the national assembly, and it has yet to be seen whether the government will be able to overcome parliamentary opposition and proceed with its much-needed reform agenda. In an encouraging step, the Kuwaiti parliament approved a draft law in 2001 that will allow foreigners – including non-GCC nationals – to invest in the Kuwait Stock Exchange (KSE). Previously, only GCC nationals were allowed to trade directly on the KSE, although foreign residents could invest in local shares through mutual funds.

The problems caused by the oil crisis in 1998 and early 1999 have made it clear that the country's inefficient system of state patronage is unsustainable. Unless more decisive steps are taken, the country's outlook will remain constrained by slow movement on structural reforms. Barring developments in the oil market, government action to solve structural weaknesses in the budget and address the inefficiencies of the economy is a crucial determinant of the country's economic prospects in the longer term.

## *GDP GROWTH*

Economic growth decelerated sharply in 1998 on the back of lower oil prices. Nominal GDP that year fell by over 15 per cent to KD7742 million, down from KD8985 million in 1997. The rebound in oil prices through most of 1999 initiated a recovery, with GDP up 17 per cent to KD9075 million. This was driven mainly by a 38.9 per cent growth in oil GDP, while growth in the non-oil sector (at purchaser's value) decelerated to 3.4 per cent, following growth rates of 7.4 per cent and 4.1 per cent in 1998 and 1997 respectively. However, real GDP growth in 1999 remained subdued, rising by a modest 0.5 per cent due both to the cut in crude oil production in line with the OPEC quota and the sluggish growth in the non-oil sector.

Strong growth continued in 2000, with nominal GDP up by an impressive 27.7 per cent and real GDP rising by 4 per cent. The economy remained on a positive growth-path in 2001, with real GDP growth estimated at 17 per cent. So far, the Kuwaiti private sector is not equipped to boost economic growth, which will remain tied to government spending, especially on large-scale projects, and developments in the oil sector. However, assuming the government's reform schedule falls through, stronger foreign-investment flows and greater private-sector initiative via privatization could translate into substantially higher real private-sector-led growth over the next few years.

## *MONETARY POLICY*

Liquidity, as measured by M2, increased by 1.6 per cent in 1999, following a tightening of 0.8 per cent the year before. However, M1 increased by almost 20 per cent in 1999, following a decline of 8.3 per cent in 1998. Tighter liquidity conditions forced commercial banks to finance part of their lending activities by repatriating foreign assets. M2 growth in 2000 reached 6.3 per cent, its highest level in five years, with most growth in dinar deposits.

The past few years witnessed a notable deceleration of credit growth in the private sector, following years of rapid credit expansion when the country was rebuilding the economy after Gulf-War damages. This was partly a result of tighter credit policies put in place by the Central Bank in late 1997 and the introduction of more stringent liquidity requirements in 1998, but also a natural response to the decline in economic activity since then and the depressed state of the stock exchange.

## *INFLATION*

Prices in Kuwait largely remained stable in 1997 and 1998, with modest rises in the CPI of 0.7 per cent and 0.2 per cent respectively. This was largely a reflection of lower import prices from crisis-hit trading partners in Asia. In light of the openness of the economy, domestic price levels are largely determined by prices of the country's major trading partners. The stability of the exchange rate has also worked towards keeping inflation in check, although inflation did rise to 3 per cent in 1999. Higher non-oil commodities and manufactured-goods prices put upward pressure on prices. Inflation remained subdued in 2000 and 2001, averaging around 1.8 per cent and 2 per cent respectively. Pressures will increase if the government begins to phase out planned reductions on subsidies for public services and utilities.

## *EXCHANGE RATE*

The stability of the exchange rate is the mainstay of monetary policy in Kuwait. The dinar exchange rate policy follows the weighted currency-basket approach. This policy bases the determination of dinar exchange rate on a specially weighted basket of currencies of Kuwait's major trading partners, in which the dollar is thought to account for about 80 per cent, although the weights are not officially disclosed.

The pegged exchange-rate arrangement is backed by sizable official foreign assets, estimated in the range of $60–65 billion and growing by around $3–5 billion per annum. As a result, the dinar held strong in 1998 in the wake of the oil crisis of that year, in contrast to the pressures on other regional currencies at the time.

The dinar/dollar exchange rate depreciated significantly in the early 1990s, but has since then remained relatively stable. By the end of 1999 the dinar had depreciated by 1 per cent against the dollar to 0.304, compared to 1998; however, the average rate for the whole year was almost unchanged from the 1998 average. The exchange rate held steady in 2000 and 2001. The exchange rate is expected to remain stable in the foreseeable future.

## *FISCAL POLICY*

The Kuwaiti budget has shown a surplus over the two years 1999/2000 and 2000/01. The 1999/2000 budget posted a surplus of KD1.23 billion, equivalent to 13.6 per cent of GDP. Similarly for the year 2000/01, the budget recorded a surplus of KD1.7 billion, or 14.8 per cent of GDP, compared to a budgeted deficit of KD1.29 billion. This is quite impressive taking into account the fact that the 2000/01 period covered only the nine months from July 2000 to March 2001, following the government's decision to change its fiscal year to run from April to March. The annualized surplus is equivalent to KD2.3 billion, the largest surplus achieved in 20 years. The improved fiscal position, however, does not appear to have diluted the government's determination to implement the much needed fiscal reform.

Achieving a viable fiscal structure is one of the main challenges facing the Kuwaiti authorities. Like the other Gulf countries, the government relies heavily on oil as a source of income. In fact, with practically no tax system to speak of (Kuwait has no personal income tax, nor any VAT or sales tax, while corporate taxes are collected only from foreign companies), revenues in the Kuwaiti budget consist almost entirely of oil income. The contribution of oil revenues to the budget has averaged 86 per cent over the past five years.

On the other hand, government expenditures are high, consisting mainly of wages and salaries, subsidies, spending on goods and services, and subsidies to loss-making public entities. The proportion of public spending going to pay wages and salaries has been rising steadily, reaching 32 per cent in the 2000/01 budget, compared to 24 per cent five years earlier. Including allowance, they constitute more than 50 per cent of expenditures. If public employment continues to be viewed by Kuwaiti citizens as a constitutional right, as is the case now, the public payroll will keep on rising.

The slump in oil prices in 1998 demonstrated the risk involved in maintaining high expenditure levels on such a narrow revenue base. Total revenues fell by 22.5 per cent, to KD2.8 billion in 1998/99 following a 30 per cent decline in receipts from oil sales. The budget deficit rose sharply to KD1243 million in 1998/99, equal to almost 14 per cent of GDP, from KD370 million in 1997/98, which was 4.8 per cent of GDP.

Table 10.5
Kuwait: government budget (KD million)

| | 1998/99 | 1999/00 | 2000/01 | 2001/02B |
|---|---|---|---|---|
| Total revenues | 2798 | 5241 | 5003 | 3832 |
| Oil revenues | 2254 | 4794 | 4623 | 3263 |
| Other receipts | 543 | 447 | 380 | 569 |
| Total expenditure | 4040 | 4010 | 3290 | 5274 |
| Wages and salaries | 1300 | 1339 | 1034 | 1557 |
| Requirements of goods and services | 309 | 338 | 342 | 565 |
| Means of transport and equipment | 29 | 23 | 25 | 35 |
| Projects and maintenance | 377 | 315 | 280 | 583 |
| Miscellaneous and transfer payments | 2027 | 1995 | 1609 | 2534 |
| Deficit | –1243 | 1231 | 1713 | –1443 |
| (as percentage of GDP) | –16.1 | 13.6 | 14.8 | –11.2 |

*B: Budget figures*

*Source: Central Bank of Kuwait*

In response to the threat of low oil prices, the Kuwaiti government managed to boost non-oil revenues by an impressive 36 per cent in 1998/99, while keeping the growth in expenditure low at 1.6 per cent, compared to 2.3 per cent the year before. However, spending control was mainly achieved at the expense of allocations for development projects, down 9 per cent, while current expenditure rose by 4 per cent to KD2.7 billion.

The budget plan for the year 2001/02, which runs from April 2001 to March 2002, projects a 10 per cent increase in spending on the annualized expenditure budgeted for the year 2000/01 to KD5.27 billion. The budget remains conservative with an oil-price assumption of $15 per barrel, setting total revenues at KD3.83 billion. As a result, the draft budget shows a large deficit equal to KD1.44 billion, equivalent to around 11 per cent of GDP.

The Kuwaiti government is aware of the need to address structural weaknesses in the budget; however, this requires the implementation of socially and politically unwelcome measures. Fiscal restructuring requires cutting down the various allowances, subsidies, and transfers provided to citizens and government employees, in addition to curtailing new government employment. On the revenue side, non-oil revenues can be bolstered through additional fees, charges on government services, the introduction of indirect taxes and widening the base of direct taxation.

The government has already introduced a series of measures aimed at raising non-oil revenues; however, still more needs to be done. Expatriates are now required to take out health insurance before their residency is confirmed, and a charge for the use of government hospitals and clinics by expatriates has been introduced. Together these measures are expected to generate between KD60–70 million in revenues. The price of petrol was also raised by between 30 and 50 per cent, promising an additional KD90 million to government coffers annually.

The issue of introducing income taxation was met with strong resistance from parliament when proposed by the government. Other fiscal reforms being considered include increasing electricity and water charges, tariffs on telephone services and rental rates on state property.

## *DOMESTIC DEBT*

Total domestic public debt reached KD3.96 billion at the end of 2000, equivalent to 34.2 per cent of GDP. This is considerably lower that its level of KD6.2 billion (almost 80 per cent of GDP) in 1995, testifying to the government's efficient debt-management policy. At the end of 2000, over 95 per cent of the government's domestic debt was held by local banks. Around 38 per cent of the debt is in the form of debt-purchase bonds, which were issued in 1992 when the government assumed the banks' loan portfolio to Kuwaiti citizens, including non-performing loans, in the aftermath of the Gulf War. The rest of the domestic debt comprises KD1.98 billion in treasury bonds and KD0.49 billion in treasury bills.

Table 10.6
Kuwait: public domestic debt (KD million)

| | 1996 | 1997 | 1998 | 1999 | 2000 |
|---|---|---|---|---|---|
| Total domestic debt | 5339 | 4623 | 4271 | 4268 | 3964 |
| (as percentage of GDP) | 58.2 | 50.8 | 55.3 | 47.3 | 34.2 |
| Treasury bonds | 1327 | 1285 | 1238 | 1758 | 1983 |
| Treasury bills | 1167 | 949 | 787 | 579 | 490 |
| Debt purchase bonds | 2845 | 2389 | 2246 | 1931 | 1491 |

*Source: Central Bank of Kuwait*

With regard to public external debt, the only remaining sovereign or sovereign-guaranteed debts are borrowings from the US Eximbank and other export credit agencies, which totalled $213 million at the end of 1998 and are estimated to have dropped to $140 million in 1999. On the other hand, Kuwait's total external debt, including private-sector debt, was estimated to be approximately $8 billion at the end of 1999.

## *EXTERNAL SECTOR*

The current account balance improved dramatically in 1999 and 2000 due to higher oil exports. Oil exports dropped by 37 per cent in the wake of the oil crisis in 1998, driving the merchandise trade balance down to KD580 million from KD2 billion in 1997. The recovery in oil prices in 1999 supported higher export receipts and drove the merchandise trade balance back up to KD1.7 billion. As a result, the current account surplus rose by over 120 per cent, to KD1.54 billion in 1999, equivalent to 17 per cent of GDP, up from KD675 million in 1998 (8.7 per cent of GDP), but has yet to recover its 1997 level of KD2.4 billion, or 26.4 per cent of GDP. The final balance of payments also showed a healthy surplus in 1999, equivalent to 3.1 per cent of GDP.

Table 10.7
Kuwait: balance of payments (KD million)

| | 1997 | 1998 | 1999 | 2000 |
|---|---|---|---|---|
| Current account | 2407 | 675 | 1540 | 4561 |
| (as percentage of GDP) | 26.4 | 8.7 | 17.0 | 39.3 |
| Goods and services | 960 | –572 | 596 | 3017 |
| Merchandise trade | 1982 | 580 | 1695 | 3905 |
| Exports | 4332 | 2931 | 3737 | 6005 |
| Oil exports | 4085 | 2582 | 3357 | 5572 |
| Import | –2350 | –2351 | –2042 | -2100 |
| Services | –1022 | –1152 | –1099 | -888 |
| Income (net) | 1904 | 1788 | 1555 | 2122 |
| Current transfers | –457 | –541 | –610 | -578 |
| Capital account | –1913 | –866 | –1523 | -3757 |
| Others | –511 | 252 | 264 | -109 |
| Overall balance | –17 | 61 | 282 | 695 |
| (as percentage of GDP) | –0.2 | 0.8 | 3.1 | 5.9 |

*Source: Central Bank of Kuwait*

The continued strength of oil prices in 2000 drove total exports up 60 per cent, which, coupled with a modest rise of 2.1 per cent in imports that year, more than doubled the trade balance from KD1.7 billion in 1999 to KD3.9 billion. The services balance also recorded an improvement in 2000, and investment income rose by an impressive KD567 million to stand at KD2.12 billion. As a result, the current account almost tripled to KD4.56 billion, equivalent to 39.3 per cent of GDP. Net outflows in the capital account rose to KD3.76 billion in 2000 from KD1.52 billion the year before. This moderated the effect of the much-improved current account on the balance-of-payments, which nonetheless rose to KD695 million, equivalent to 5.9 per cent of GDP, compared to KD282 million in 1999.

# OMAN

Table 10.8
Oman: main economic indicators

| | 1995 | 1996 | 1997 | 1998 | 1999 | 2000 |
|---|---|---|---|---|---|---|
| Nominal GDP (OR million) | 5307 | 5874 | 6075 | 5457 | 6003 | 7323 |
| Nominal GDP ($ million) | 13,608 | 15,062 | 15,577 | 13,992 | 15,392 | 18,778 |
| Nominal GDP growth | 6.8% | 10.7% | 3.4% | −10.2% | 10.0% | 22.0% |
| Real GDP growth | 4.8% | 2.9% | 6.2% | 2.9% | 3.7% | 4.6% |
| CPI inflation | −1.1% | 0.3% | −0.4% | −0.5% | 1.2% | 1.2% |
| **Fiscal indicators (OR million)** | | | | | | |
| Total revenues | 1852 | 1990 | 2267 | 1846 | 1798 | 2091B |
| Total expenditure | 2331 | 2254 | 2307 | 2222 | 2264 | 2440B |
| Current deficit | −479 | −264 | −40 | −376 | −466 | −349B |
| (as percentage of GDP) | −9.0 | −4.5 | −0.7 | −6.9 | −7.8 | −4.8 |
| Foreign debt ($ billion) | 2.9 | 3.1 | 2.8 | 3.4 | 3.7 | 4.0 |
| (as percentage of GDP) | 21.3 | 20.6 | 18.0 | 24.3 | 24.0 | 21.3 |
| **External indicators (OR million)** | | | | | | |
| Exports | 2333 | 2825 | 2934 | 2118 | 2775 | 3830 |
| Imports | 1684 | 1818 | 1996 | 2240 | 1846 | 2050 |
| Current account | −263 | 131 | −22 | −1134 | 70 | 550 |
| (as percentage of GDP) | −5.0 | 2.2 | −0.4 | −20.8 | 1.2 | 7.5 |

*Sources: Central Bank of Oman and Jordinvest estimates*

## *ECONOMIC OVERVIEW*

Until 1967, Oman's economy was largely based on agriculture and fishery. In the mid-1970s, the oil sector became the backbone of the economy and its main source of income, accounting for around 40 per cent of GDP, 80 per cent of exports and 75 per cent of government revenues. During the past decade, Oman has achieved strong economic growth, supported by a steady increase in oil production and exports and an expanding and dynamic private sector.

Oil remains the principal source of budget revenues and export earnings. The need to diversify the economy and build up reserves for future use is much more pressing in the case of Oman than in other GCC countries, given the country's relatively short horizon of proven and commercially viable oil reserves (16 years at the current rate of extraction).

The collapse in oil prices in 1998 highlighted the lingering structural weaknesses that constrain the economy's long-term growth potential. In 1998, the budget deficit amounted to 6.9 per cent of GDP, compared to 0.7 per cent in 1997, while the current-account deficit shot up to OR1134 million from OR22 million in 1997. However, the authorities must be credited for their immediate implementation of a number of revenue-raising and cost-cutting measures that contained the size of the 1998 fiscal deficit.

To reduce reliance on the oil sector, the Omani government has placed a great emphasis on the diversification of the economic base by expanding natural gas and non-energy industries. Its Vision 2020 plan, announced in the mid-1990s, aims to reduce the contribution of the oil sector to GDP to 20 per cent, from just under 40 per cent at present. Central to this plan is the development of the gas industry, which flourished in April 2000 with the completion of the Oman LNG (liquefied natural gas) venture. The development and promotion of gas-based industrial projects will greatly enhance Oman's non-oil revenues.

Privatization is another central pillar of Oman's economic policy. As a result of the emirate's rapidly expanding population, the government can no longer afford to provide all public services, as has been the case in the past, and budgetary strains will encourage the sale of more public assets. Over the coming few years, the government is likely both to sell some of its existing assets and pave the way for the private sector to participate in providing services previously dominated by the public sector. Further foreign involvement will also be encouraged in the electricity sector, as the country struggles to meet growing demand for power. In 1999, the government approved a programme for private sector participation in the power sector. Rapidly increasing demand and the substantial capital costs required for the expansion of capacity have led the government to focus on the electricity sector. A comprehensive proposal for the privatization of the sector is in place, and already a contract for a large independent power project (IPP) was signed in mid-2000. Furthermore, the government is considering privatization of Seeb and Salalah airports and the country's telecommunications provider, the Oman Telecommunications Company (Omantel).

Oman has also been actively liberalizing its trade and investment regimes in order to meet WTO requirements. The government plans to reduce taxes on foreign-owned businesses in order to boost foreign investment. Foreign offices with 100 per cent ownership will now only pay a maximum 30 per cent tax rate instead of 50 per cent, and foreign companies with investments in other companies will be exempted from paying tax on profits earned from their subsidiaries. The new tax amendments will enter into effect from January 2001. From April 2001, Oman allowed foreign firms to open representative offices in the country without local sponsorship, and from January 2001, raised the ceiling on foreign business ownership from 49 per cent to 70 per cent. From January 2003 the government will also allow 100 per cent foreign ownership in some financial services, such as banking, insurance and brokerage. In parallel, the Trade Ministry has said that foreign participation in projects that contribute to the development of the national economy can be lifted to 100 per cent provided that the capital invested is not less than OR500,000 ($1.3 million). Other incentives provided to encourage investment are exemption from custom duties on equipment and essential material for factories for a period of up to five years, with a possible 10-year renewal period.

In February 2001 Standard & Poor's up-graded Oman's sovereign credit rating from BBB-minus to BBB, the first up-grade since the sultanate was given a rating in February 1996. Standard & Poor's said that it believed the Omani government would continue to pursue prudent fiscal policies, as outlined in the 2001–5 five-year plan and the 2001 budget. It also said it expected the government to post strong surpluses in 2001 and 2002, rather than the deficits forecast in the budget.

In its rating, Standard & Poor's identified several issues that could constrain Oman's economic growth and credit rating in coming years unless the sultanate moves to address them. Other than the ever-present risk that oil prices could fall, growing pressure on Oman's labour market could hinder its economic progress. There is also an apparent skills shortage in the labour market. Some labour-market regulations, such as minimum-wage requirements, have discouraged the private sector from absorbing adequate numbers of Omani job-seekers.

Overall, the prospects for the Omani economy are promising. A strong privatization drive, the implementation of market-friendly reforms, membership of WTO in 2000 and the initiation of major industrial projects based on Oman's gas resources should trigger new inward investment flows, higher real growth and faster job creation over the next few years. The country has implemented several far-reaching reforms in its bid to obtain full membership in the WTO, including lifting restriction on foreign investment. It is expected that Omani firms will have to merge in order to meet the challenges of globalization and strong foreign competition.

## *ECONOMIC GROWTH*

Following an average rate of expansion of 5 per cent during the 1991–5 period, real economic growth slowed down by 2.9 per cent in 1996, before picking up to 6.4 per cent in 1997. Real growth dropped to 2.9 per cent in 1998, amid a slump in oil prices and the contagious effect of the Asian crisis. The Omani economy recorded positive real GDP growth of 3.7 per cent in 1999 and 4.6 per cent in 2000. The solid growth was triggered by high oil prices, a strong privatization drive, the implementation of market-friendly reforms, the country joining WTO and the initiation of major industrial projects based on Oman's gas resources. Real growth is estimated at 3.5 per cent in 2001.

## *INFLATION*

During the past few years, the Central Bank's prudent monetary policy has succeeded in achieving price stability, despite fluctuating economic growth. From 1991 to 1993, inflation averaged approximately 1 per cent, before becoming negative in the 1994–8 period. The inflation rate rose to 1.25 in 1999 and 2000. In line with the fifth development plan, Oman is expected to sustain a benign inflation environment, with the average annual rate hovering around 1.5 per cent.

Figure 10.1
Oman: CPI inflation

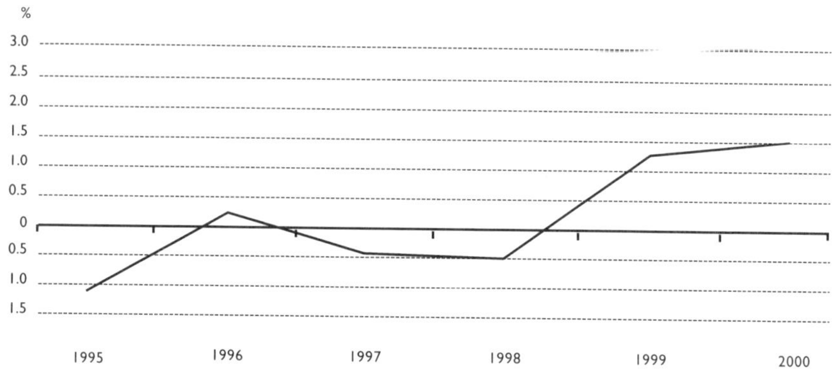


*Source: Central Bank of Oman*

## *EXCHANGE RATE*

Oman's cautious monetary policy stance has served over the years to ensure exchange rate stability. Since 1986, the riyal has been officially pegged to the dollar at 0.3845. The recovery in oil prices and faster economic growth amid an environment of mild inflation would alleviate any concerns surrounding the stability of the riyal. The Central Bank is committed to its policy of maintaining the current exchange-rate peg, even at the expense of draining foreign exchange reserves.

## *FISCAL POLICY*

Oman has been running successive budget deficits since the late 1980s, despite concerted efforts to cut spending and reduce dependence on oil revenues. To this effect, the authorities have financed these deficits largely by drawing on reserves from the state general reserve fund (SGRF) and by borrowing locally through issuing development bonds. The budget deficit dropped from 10.8 per cent of GDP in 1993 to just 0.7 per cent in 1997. Fiscal restraint was achieved amid higher oil revenues (19 per cent increase in 1997) and containment in public expenditures, a 2.4 per cent increase, as well as retrenchment of around 11,000 civil servants. In 1998, the weakening of economic activity and the collapse in oil prices depressed government revenues and widened the budget deficit to 6 per cent of GDP.

The 1999 budget, which was based on a pessimistic assumption of oil prices at $9 per barrel, forecast a budget-deficit-to-GDP ratio of approximately 11.4 per cent. However, the actual figures revealed better-than-expected results. According to the Central Bank, the actual fiscal deficit widened to OR466 million ($1210 million) – equal to 7.8 per cent of GDP, from OR376 million ($974 million) in 1998, but significantly less than the OR631 million ($1639 million) projected in the budget. Total revenue receipts fell by 2.6 per cent to OR1798 million ($4670 million) since net oil revenues were lower than in 1998 as a result of higher allocation to the SGRF. In fact, if all oil revenue were included in the budget, then the deficit for 1999 would have been less than OR30 million, significantly lower than in 1998. Expenditure rose by 1.9 per cent in 1999 to OR2264 million ($5881 million). The 1999 budget included several measures aimed at expanding the revenue-base. Among these were increases in custom duties on imports of vehicles to between 10 per cent and 15 per cent. Corporate taxes were raised from 7.5 per cent to 12 per cent, and taxes on luxury items were increased from 5 per cent to 15 per cent.

Table 10.9
**Oman: government budget, 1997–2000 (OR million)**

| | 1997 | 1998 | 1999 | 2000 | 2001B |
|---|---|---|---|---|---|
| Total revenues | 2267 | 1846 | 1798 | 2091 | 2495 |
| Oil revenues | 1749 | 1240 | 1202 | 1507 | 1875 |
| Gas revenues | 57 | 63 | 58 | 70 | 74 |
| Other revenues | 462 | 543 | 538 | 514 | 546 |
| **Total expenditure** | 2307 | 2222 | 2264 | 2440 | 2812 |
| Current expenditure | 1815 | 1666 | 1804 | 1899 | 2215 |
| Defence | 698 | 643 | 687 | 673 | 926 |
| Civil | 898 | 833 | 940 | 1027 | 1096 |
| Interest on loans | 120 | 101 | 99 | 120 | 110 |
| PDO | 99 | 89 | 78 | 79 | 83 |
| Investment expenditure | 356 | 432 | 426 | 489 | 525 |
| Subsidy to private sector | 95 | 16 | 34 | 52 | 72 |
| **Budget deficit** | –40 | –376 | –466 | –349 | –317 |
| (as percentage of GDP) | –0.7 | –6.9 | –7.8 | –4.8 | – |

*B: Budget*

*Source: Central Bank of Oman*

In 2000, higher natural-gas export revenues helped narrow the budget deficit considerably. In its 2000 budget plan, the government predicted a decline in the deficit from the previous year to OR349 million, relying mainly on higher oil revenues. Jordinvest is forecasting a budget surplus in excess of OR110 million in 2000, based on an average oil price of $29 per barrel for Brent crude and a 10 per cent increase in total expenditure. According to the 2001 budget plan, announced in January 2001, the deficit for the year is expected to be 9 per cent below the forecast deficit for 2000, mainly due to higher revenues from sales of oil and natural gas. The 2001 deficit is forecast at OR317 million ($823.4 million), with revenues up 19.4 per cent to OR2.495 billion in 2001 and expenditure up 15.2 per cent to OR2.812 billion. The budget was based on an oil price of $18 per barrel. About 75 per cent of forecast budget revenue for 2001 is expected to be raised by oil sales, while approximately OR260 million are expected to be raised by natural-gas sales. The government also intends to revive the privatization programme following a lull in 1999 and 2000.

## *EXTERNAL BALANCE*

In 1998, lower receipts from oil and non-oil export and increased expatriate remittances combined to impact adversely Oman's external balance. The balance of trade dropped from OR938 million in 1997 to a deficit of OR122 million in 1998, a situation magnified by dwindling oil revenues. With remittances continuing to expand gradually, Oman registered substantial current-account deficits, ranging from 8.2 per cent of GDP in 1993 to a phenomenal 20.8 per cent in 1998. Reserves draw-down and a manageable increase in the external debt have been the main sources of funding the domestic and external imbalances. Foreign exchange reserves fell from $1.5 billion in 1997 to approximately $1 billion in 1998, providing just over two months' import cover.

1999 witnessed a strong turnaround in the country's external account, with higher oil revenues raising the trade balance into credit. The trade balance rose to a surplus of OR929 million, creating in the current account a modest surplus of OR70 million, equivalent to 1.2 per cent of GDP. A further improvement in the country's external balances is expected in 2000, given the continued strong oil prices throughout the year.

Table 10.10
Oman: trade balance and current account (OR million)

| | 1996 | 1997 | 1998 | 1999 |
|---|---|---|---|---|
| **Trade balance** | 1007 | 938 | –122 | 929 |
| Exports | 2825 | 2934 | 2118 | 2775 |
| Imports | 1818 | 1996 | 2240 | 1846 |
| **Services balance** | –876 | –960 | –1012 | –999 |
| **Current account** | 131 | –22 | –1134 | 70 |
| (as percentage of GDP) | 2.2 | –0.4 | –20.8 | 1.2 |
| **Balance of payments** | –31 | 265 | –583 | – |

*Source: Central Bank of Oman*

## *EXTERNAL DEBT*

Oman's external debt stock grew from $3.1 billion in 1996 to $3.4 billion in 1998 and an estimated $3.7 billion in 1999, accounting for approximately 26 per cent of GDP. Although the debt-service-to-export ratio has increased over the past few years from 7.4 per cent in 1995 to an estimated 11 per cent in 1999, the country's level of external debt remains acceptable by international standards. In 1997, the Omani government tapped the international bond market for the first time, issuing $225 million-worth of five-year eurobonds.

## QATAR

Table 10.11
Qatar: main economic indicators

| | 1996 | 1997 | 1998 | 1999 | 2000 | 2001 |
|---|---|---|---|---|---|---|
| Nominal GDP (QR million) | 32,976 | 41,124 | 37,330 | 44,397 | 53,276 | 57,538 |
| Nominal GDP ($ million) | 9059 | 11,298 | 10,255 | 12,197 | 14,636 | 15,806 |
| Nominal GDP growth | 11.3% | 24.7% | –9.2% | 18.9% | 20.0% | 8.0% |
| Real GDP growth | 4.8% | 10.5% | 2.5% | 3.5% | 7.0% | 5.0% |
| Inflation | 4.9% | 4.9% | 2.9% | 2.2% | 2.7% | 3.0% |
| **Fiscal indicators (QR million)** | | | | | | |
| Revenues | 10,797 | 13,397 | 12,354 | 14,098 | 12,617* | 18,057* |
| Expenditures | 13,747 | 16,387 | 15,660 | 14,353 | 15,400* | 17,560* |
| Deficit | –2950 | –2990 | –3306 | –255 | –2783* | 497* |
| (as percentage of GDP) | –8.9 | –7.3 | –8.9 | –0.6 | 5.2 | 0.8 |
| External debt ($ million) | 7181 | 9026 | 10,796 | 11,196 | 11,700 | 13,000 |
| (as percentage of GDP) | 79.3 | 79.9 | 105.3 | 91.8 | 79.9 | – |
| **External indicators (QR million)*** | | | | | | |
| Trade balance | 4546 | 3143 | 7134 | 18,062 | 22,875 | – |
| Exports | 13,952 | 14,036 | 18,311 | 26,258 | 32,875 | – |
| Imports | –9406 | –10,893 | –11,177 | –8196 | –10,000 | – |
| Current account | –4537 | –6111 | –1658 | 7903 | 10,375 | – |
| (as percentage of GDP) | –13.8 | –14.9 | –4.4 | 17.8 | 19.5 | – |

* *Budget figures*

*Sources: Qatar National Bank*

### *ECONOMIC OVERVIEW*

Since 1950, the oil and gas sectors have become Qatar's main source of income, accounting for around 33 per cent of GDP. In 2000, Qatar's GDP stood at $14.6 billion and per-capita income was approximately $24,000, among the highest in the world.

To reduce its dependence on the oil sector, and limit the country's vulnerability to fluctuation in oil prices, the Qatari government has placed a great emphasis on the diversification of the economic base by expanding natural gas and non-oil sectors. Since 1994, Qatar has embarked on a massive investment programme to exploit the large natural-gas reserves in the form of LNG and related products. In terms of the size of its total reserves of natural gas, Qatar is third only to Russia and Iran. The government and foreign participants have between them spent approximately $9 billion on the development of Qatar's huge natural-gas export capacity.

Huge investment in the oil and gas industries and an ambitious array of export-oriented downstream projects is still being made. This, together with higher oil and gas revenues, will support the rapid expansion of the economy. The Qatari economy has posted record growth rates in 2000 and 2001, some of the highest globally.

The upturn in oil and gas revenues will also allay fears about the ability of the government to meet annual repayments of over $1 billion for the period 2002–2005. The country's total external-debt burden had quickly risen from $4.5 billion in 1995 to $13 billion at the end of 2000. However, a substantial portion of the debt is related to gas-sector projects, and external leverage is projected to decline as debt is paid back with project cashflows. Qatar's long-term competitiveness has been enhanced by the development of the country's gas resources, which is likely to increase government revenue streams.

The recovery in the price of oil, the accelerated development of natural gas projects, the sustainability of the privatization programme and continual investments in the non-oil sector will be the key catalysts in Qatar's growth in the foreseeable future. Qatar has now passed the most risky phase in its debt-driven development programme. Although external debt is expected to increase in the short term, debt ratios (such as debt-to-GDP and debt-to-exports) would be likely to improve due to sustainable economic growth driven by growing natural-gas export revenues. The fiscal balance should then improve, with increased privatization proceeds and higher revenues from LNG projects.

Qatar plans to keep a tight rein on spending, despite high oil prices and rising gas revenues, striving to cut its debt burden and replenish foreign-exchange reserves rather than to inject cash into the economy. An expansionary budget is expected for the fiscal year 2001/02, while the spending increase in the 2000/01 budget was limited to 7.3 per cent. The 2000/01 budget should show a healthy surplus, with oil prices almost double the $15 a barrel estimated. Qatari crude averaged $27.7 a barrel in 2000.

In November 2000, Crown Prince Shaikh Jassem Bin Hamad al-Thani issued a decree allowing up to 100 per cent foreign ownership in certain local projects. It also permits foreigners to lease Qatari land for up to 50 years. The decree aims to attract foreign investment and technology to the non-oil sector, allowing fully owned projects in the infrastructure development, health, tourism, and small and medium-scale industries sectors. The law excludes sectors such as hydrocarbons, banking, commercial agencies, property and insurance. In the small- and medium-scale industries sector, the country plans to set up ferro-silicon, acetic-acid, plastic-manufacturing, urea-formaldehyde and super-urea plants. In the power sector, Qatar is offering a 55 per cent share to a foreign developer of the independent water and power project at Ras Laffan.

In 2000, Qatar broke new ground in the international bond markets by becoming the first Middle Eastern country to raise a 30-year bond. The $1.4 billion eurobond reflects both the government's desire to extend its borrowing maturities and its need to raise money to meet a debt repayment requirement in which almost $4 billion has to be repaid during the period 2001–4. The bond has also enabled the country to expand its investor base with around 70 per cent of the money raised from US investors and the remaining raised mainly from Middle East and European investors.

In 2001, Standard & Poor's raised its long-term foreign-currency issuer credit and senior-unsecured debt-ratings on Qatar from BBB– to BBB+, and its long-term local-currency-issuer credit rating from BBB+ to A–. Standard & Poor's also raised its long-term foreign-currency-issuer credit rating on Qatar Petroleum in line with the sovereign, its sole shareholder. The outlook on the long-term ratings was revised from 'stable' to 'positive'. At the same time, Standard & Poor's raised its short-term foreign-currency-issuer rating to AA from AAA and affirmed its short-term local-currency-issuer credit rating at AA. The up-grade reflects the prospect for continued fiscal prudence, which, together with high oil and gas prices, are helping to reduce the public external debt burden. The agency also indicated that the ratings could be raised again if the government strengthens its political system and institutions, enhances the transparency of its finances, rationalizes further its current expenditures and restarts the stalled privatization programme using the proceeds to reduce its largest debt.

## *ECONOMIC GROWTH*

During the past decade, Qatar has achieved strong yet uneven economic growth, due to its heavy reliance on the production and export of petroleum related products, which by nature correlate with the fluctuation of oil commodity prices. For instance, in 1996 nominal GDP grew by a phenomenal 11.3 per cent alongside an 18.5 per cent increase in oil prices, although in real terms GDP growth was lower at 4.8 per cent. Real GDP growth rose to 10.5 per cent in 1997, but fell to 2.5 per cent in 1998 amid weakening domestic demand and the negative effects of the Asian crisis.

In 1999, real growth in the Qatari economy recovered to around 3.5 per cent, due to both a recovery in economic activity and stronger oil prices. In 2000, Qatar recorded the highest real growth in real GDP in the region, at 7 per cent, as substantial investments in oil and gas started to bring returns. The economy grew by 20 per cent in nominal terms in 2000, however, nominal growth in 2001 was substantially lower due to the decline in oil prices. Real GDP growth in 2001 is estimated to be around 5 per cent.

## *INFLATION*

During the past few years, the Central Bank's prudent monetary policy has succeeded in achieving price stability, despite fluctuating economic growth. During the 1993–5 period, the inflation rate averaged approximately 1 per cent. The inflation rate increased markedly in 1996/97 to 4.9 per cent, mainly due to the imposition of charges for the provision of healthcare services to expatriates; it then fell to 2.9 per cent in 1998, and to 2.2 per cent in 1999. The inflation rate is estimated to be 2.7 per cent in 2000 and 3 per cent in 2001.

## *EXCHANGE RATE*

Qatar's cautious monetary-policy stance has served over the years to ensure exchange-rate stability. The riyal, which is formally linked to the IMF's special drawing right at a rate of QR4.76, with a fluctuation band of 7.25 per cent, has in practice been pegged to the dollar at the rate of QR3.64 since the mid-1980s. The Central Bank is expected to maintain the exchange-rate peg for the near future, helped by the recovery in oil prices and the gradual movement in gas exports.

## *FISCAL POLICY*

Qatar has been running successive budget deficits since the late 1980s, amid a strong emphasis on project development and maintenance of a generous welfare system for nationals. Both internal and external borrowing has financed the deficits. Direct revenue from oil proceeds accounted for approximately 60 per cent of total government revenues, while indirect revenues through the collection of dividends on the profits of Qatar General Petroleum Corporation (QGPC) add another 15 per cent, bringing the contribution of the petroleum sector to approximately 75 per cent of total revenues.

Qatar's 2001/02 budget provides for a total spending figure of QR17.5 billion and projects that total revenues will exceed this amount at QR18.06 billion, generating a budgetary surplus – the first in 15 years – of QR497million. The budget aims to diversify the economy's income sources, boost the quality of education, health and other social services, reduce the debt burden and strengthen state reserves.

The 43 per cent projected rise in budgetary revenues compares to the more conservative 14 per cent projected increase in expenditure and reflects the cautious policy stance of other GCC states despite the surge in oil prices in 2000 and 2001.

Qatar's budget plan for 2000/01 was decidedly more optimistic than for 1999/2000, with a 50 per cent increase in oil-price assumption from $10 per barrel to $15 per barrel, still well below the actual oil price for the year – an increase in oil revenues by almost 20 per cent to QR12.6 billion and a 39 per cent rise in capital expenditures. The 2000/01 budget projected a deficit for the year of QR2.8 billion, down 23 per cent on the previous year's budget forecast.

Table 10.12
Qatar: budgets, 1998/99–2001/02 (QR million)

| | 1998/99 | 1999/2000 | 2000/01B | 2001/02B |
|---|---|---|---|---|
| Revenues | 12,354 | 14,098 | 12,617 | 18,057 |
| Expenditures | 15,660 | 14,353 | 15,400 | 17,560 |
| Current spending | 13,926 | 13,166 | 13,378 | 14,400 |
| Capital spending | 1734 | 1187 | 2022 | 3160 |
| Deficit | 3306 | 255 | 2783 | 497 |

*B: Budget*

*Source: MEES*

## *EXTERNAL DEBT*

Qatar's LNG investment programme, financed by a huge stock of external debt, led to the reversal of the country's position at the end of 1994, from a net creditor to a debtor. The country's external debt (including government guaranteed debt and QGPC debt) had reached $11.2 billion by 1999, accounting for 98 per cent of GDP and over 170 per cent of total exports.. A new $500 million sovereign loan was launched in September 2000 following Qatar's second eurobond issue, which raised $1.4 billion in mid-June. Qatar's foreign-currency debt stock is considerably higher than those of similarly rated sovereign credits; however, debt ratios should improve considerably in the medium term, following the completion of several LNG projects, with exports nearing full capacity, in spite of additional external debt accruing in the short term. Debt-to-GDP and debt-to-exports ratios are likely to improve beyond 2001, due to sustainable economic growth driven by growing natural-gas export revenues.

Qatar was awarded two sovereign ratings from major credit-rating agencies. Standard & Poor's and Moody's assigned a BBB and a Baa2 rating to Qatar's external debt, the equivalent of an investment grade. The ratings reflected both the country's sizeable oil and natural resources and the government's successful role in managing the economy. The ratings were, however, constrained by a strong reliance on the energy sector, the heavy external debt burden, the continuity in the large fiscal deficit, and the country's sensitivity to regional shocks.

## *EXTERNAL TRADE AND BALANCE OF PAYMENTS*

Qatar has registered hefty current-account deficits since 1993, which have escalated from 8.6 per cent of GDP in 1993 to 26.5 per cent in 1995, before dropping to an estimated 4.4 per cent in 1998. Despite a high merchandise trade surplus, a current-account deficit remains, due primarily to services and private transfers throughout most of the 1990s. In 1999, the current account improved drastically to record a surplus equivalent to 17.8 per cent of GDP due to higher oil and LNG exports and significantly lower imports.

Table 10.13
Qatar: balance of payments (QR million)

| | 1997 | 1998 | 1999 | 2000 |
|---|---|---|---|---|
| Trade balance | 3143 | 7134 | 18,062 | 32,224 |
| Exports | 14,036 | 18,311 | 26,258 | 42,224 |
| Imports | −10,893 | −11,177 | −8196 | −10,000 |
| Services and transfers | −9254 | −8792 | −10,159 | −12,500 |
| Current account | −6111 | −1658 | 7903 | 19,724 |
| (as percentage of GDP) | −14.86 | −4.44 | 17.80 | 37.02 |
| Net capital transfers | 4336 | 1483 | 1043 | 1250 |
| Balance of payments | −1775 | -175 | 8946 | 18,747 |

* *Middle East Economic Digest estimates*

*Source: Qatar National Bank*

Despite the drop in oil prices in 1998, the trade balance more than doubled to QR7.1 billion, from QR3.14 billion in 1997. Although the merchandise trade surplus rose to 19 per cent of GDP in 1998, the current-account deficit stood at 4.4 per cent, due to a substantial deficit in the services and transfers account. The trade balance witnessed a further improvement in 1999, rising to QR18.1 billion. Higher oil and LNG exports in 1999 were accompanied by a 27 per cent fall in imports as a result of the decline in LNG-related capital imports. The much-improved trade balance pushed the current account into credit for the first time in years, with a positive balance of QR7.9 billion, equivalent to 17.8 per cent of GDP.

The sharp increase in oil and gas exports in 2000 had a striking effect on the country's external balances. Total exports rose to an estimated QR42.2 billion, up from QR26.3 billion in 1999, which was more than double the figure achieved in 1998. Import growth was more modest, rising by an estimated 22 per cent to QR10 billion, leaving a trade surplus of QR18.1 billion. The current-account surplus is estimated to have increased to QR19.7 billion, equivalent to 37 per cent of GDP. The outlook for Qatar's external balance is positive. Growing LNG exports over the middle to long term should help to curb the reliance on crude-oil exports.

## THE UAE

### *ECONOMIC OVERVIEW*

Prospects for the UAE are supported by strong economic and financial fundamentals. Proven oil reserves are equivalent to 100 years' production at current levels of output.

Table 10.14
UAE: main economic indicators

| | 1996 | 1997 | 1998 | 1999 | 2000 | 2001 |
|---|---|---|---|---|---|---|
| Nominal GDP (AED billion) | 175.8 | 184.5 | 173.1 | 190.5 | 229.4 | 238.5 |
| Nominal GDP ($ billion) | 47.9 | 50.3 | 47.2 | 51.9 | 62.5 | 65.0 |
| Nominal GDP growth | 12.1% | 4.9% | –6.2% | 10.1% | 20.4% | 4.0% |
| Real GDP growth | 10.10% | 2.0% | –1.0% | 4.0% | 6.5% | 3.5% |
| Inflation | 3.2% | 3.3% | 2.1% | 2.1% | 2.0% | 2.5% |
| **Fiscal indicators (AED billion)** | | | | | | |
| Expenditure | 18.25 | 19.86 | 21.39 | 22.91 | 23.12* | 22.63* |
| Revenue | 17.40 | 18.87 | 19.63 | 20.43 | 20.68* | 20.43* |
| Budget deficit | –0.85 | –0.99 | –1.76 | –2.48 | –2.44* | 2.24* |
| (as percentage of GDP) | –0.5 | –0.5 | –1.0 | –1.3 | –1.0 | –1.0 |
| External debt ($ billion) | 18.8 | 20.3 | 20.2 | – | – | – |
| (as percentage of GDP) | 39 | 40 | 43 | – | – | – |
| **External indicators (AED billion)** | | | | | | |
| Exports | 121.95 | 125.49 | 111.7 | 128.88 | 159.0 | 1300 |
| Imports | 94.83 | 97.7 | 105.9 | 112.65 | 117.3 | 1150 |
| Current account | 22.52 | 22.69 | –0.39 | 10.23 | 33.80 | 15.00 |
| (as percentage of GDP) | 12.8 | 12.3 | –0.2 | 5.4 | 15.1 | 6.2 |

* *budget figures*

*Sources: UAE authorities and IMF*

The current account has been in surplus for several years – with the exception of 1998 – while reserves and foreign assets of the public sector are reported to be in excess of $180 billion by the end of 2001, and of high quality.

Although the oil sector still dominates much of the economy in the UAE, a concerted move towards diversification has been underway for some time now. Careful planning and big investments in infrastructure, backed by growing manufacturing and financial sectors, helped develop the economy as a regional trading hub. The non-oil sector contributed over 75 per cent of total GDP in 2000, compared to just 40 per cent in 1980. Nonetheless, much of the non-oil economy remains largely dependent on the public sector, and public spending is directly related to oil revenue.

It is against this scenario that the government will have to formulate its policy over the short term. An intensification of fiscal consolidation will be needed, along with further diversification away from oil through more investment in the private sector.

Cost-cutting measures, while important for addressing internal and external imbalances, will have to be concentrated more on reducing current expenditure instead of merely halting project spending. With an extensive infrastructure already in place, it would be possible to reduce capital outlay on this. Also, capital outlay on productive projects should be rigorously screened to ensure profitability. A broadening of the revenue base and a strengthening of the tax system – which remains largely rudimentary – is also needed. The government will have to increase revenue from fees for services or utilities, and try to reduce the unconditional financial support that has been available to UAE nationals.

Reining in capital costs will most definitely have to involve the private sector. But a greater role for the private sector will require structural improvements focusing on economic reforms and a broader public divestiture programme. The direct sell-off of government assets has so far been limited. But the process is likely to accelerate, particularly as the official stock market gains added depth.

The role of FDI is expected to expand rapidly in the near future, particularly in Dubai, where diminishing oil reserves have added urgency to the reform process. Foreign-ownership restrictions are likely to be lifted in non-strategic sectors of the economy, but the upstream oil sector will remain under state control. Dubai is leading the way in reform, having already taken several steps towards easing restrictions on foreign-majority ownership.

Abu Dhabi has been pursuing an innovative privatization programme in the utilities sector, and has tapped into project finance for major capacity-expansion schemes. The economy of the UAE is also highly diversified, with activities in Dubai increasingly moving away from oil into such activities as tourism, conventions, re-exports, banking and IT. The private sector has taken a prominent role in three high-profile schemes in Abu Dhabi: the Saadiyat island-development project, the Dolphin project and the Thuraya Satellite Telecommunications Company.

Dubai is adopting a slightly different approach, with the establishment of the Dubai Internet City (DIC) in 2000. The aim of establishing the DIC as the regional hub for e-business reflects Dubai's ambition to be the region's trading centre. Dubai's dwindling oil reserves will effectively be exhausted by 2010, creating an urgent need to develop a diversified economy large enough to sustain further growth. However, unlike Abu Dhabi, the government has not seen privatization as an option. Instead a form of corporatized government has been selected as the best way to create a business-friendly environment.

The financial sector in the UAE also witnessed many developments in 2000 and 2001. Most noteworthy is the fact that the UAE now has three share markets: the over-the-counter market, the Dubai Financial Market (DFM), launched in the spring of 2000, and the Abu Dhabi Financial Market (ADFM), following in mid-November. A formal link between the DFM and the ADFM was established in 2001.

The increase in oil prices and a more aggressive private sector should reflect positively on the UAE's economic prospects in the near term. The dirham is pegged to the dollar at AED3.67, and the risk of devaluation remains minimal. Interest rates will continue to track US rates and inflationary pressures will remain relatively subdued, helped by limited imported inflation and the fixed exchange rate.

## *GROWTH*

The UAE's economic growth has mirrored fluctuations in the price of oil since the early 1970s. The recovery in oil prices in 1999 drove the economy up by 10 per cent in nominal terms and GDP reached AED192 billion ($52.3 billion), more than making up for ground lost in 1998, when nominal GDP contracted 6.2 per cent as the collapse in oil prices reduced government revenues by around 33 per cent. The combined effect of lower revenues and government expenditure, the recessionary effects of low prices on the other Gulf economies, and economic turmoil in Russia, resulted in a fall in the value of re-exports. Real GDP growth picked up to 4 per cent in 1999, following a contraction of 1 per cent in 1998.

According to official estimates, the UAE economy grew in nominal terms by 20.4 per cent in 2000, due mainly to strong oil prices and increased crude exports. Real GDP, at 6.5 per cent, recorded one of the highest growth rates in the region that year. Growth in 2000 was supported by a number of new projects, including the DIC and oil- and gas-investment projects of Abu Dhabi National Oil Company. Real GDP growth remained strong in 2001, estimated at 3.5 per cent, as the benefits of two years of strong oil prices filtered down and new industrial capacity came on line. High oil revenues resulted in higher government spending by individual emirates, which in turn boosted private-sector confidence, investment and overall economic activity in the country. Moreover, concentrated efforts to attract FDI provided a further impetus to private sector growth.

The UAE has been successful in reducing its dependence on the oil sector from 46 per cent to 26 per cent in the nine years to 2000. Non-oil GDP has recorded a growth rate of 9 per cent per annum over the period 1990–2000. The manufacturing, construction, agriculture, mining and quarrying, electricity and water sectors posted average annual growth of 8.75 per cent during this period, and the sectors' share of GDP increased from 19.3 per cent to 27.05 per cent. Over the same period the services sector grew at an annual average of 8.46 per cent, its share of GDP rising from 34.66 per cent to 45.13 per cent. Manufacturing has been the fastest growing sector, with average growth of 10.59 per cent over the period, its share of GDP rising to 13 per cent in 2000 from 7.74 per cent in 1990, mainly due to the surge in the sub-sector of petroleum and petrochemical products.

## *MONETARY POLICY*

The central objective of monetary policy in the UAE has been officially to peg the dirham to the dollar. This has been achieved primarily through regulating domestic liquidity under an open exchange and payments system. The Central Bank's sale and purchase of foreign exchange is the principal instrument used in adjusting the stock of domestic liquidity. This exchange arrangement, coupled with a restrained domestic-credit stance, has contained inflation and kept domestic interest rates closely linked to those on the dollar. The dirham deposit rates ended 2001 below 2 per cent, in line with dollar rates.

## *INFLATION*

According to official estimates, inflation stood at an estimated 3 per cent in 1997, although unofficial data estimated it to be 5 per cent. With negative GDP growth in 1998, inflation remained subdued at approximately 2.1 per cent. Weaker Asian currencies and a strong dollar lowered the price of imports and helped ease inflationary pressures. In view of the openness of the economy, inflation developments largely reflect movements in import prices. The inflation rate for 1999 and 2000 remained stable at 2 per cent, rising slightly to 2.5 per cent in 2001. Nonetheless, the stability provided by the exchange-rate peg, the openness of the economy and the Central Bank's ability to absorb excess liquidity are likely to keep inflationary pressures at bay.

## *EXCHANGE RATE*

Since 1987, the dirham has been officially pegged to the IMF's special drawing rights at the rate of 4.761 with a margin of fluctuation of up to +/-7.25 per cent. However, in practice the dirham has been *de facto* pegged to the dollar at an exchange rate of AED3.67. As a result, dollar fluctuations against other major currencies have a considerable impact on purchasing power and inflation. While commercial banks are free to engage in foreign-exchange transactions, in practice rates have been close to those quoted by the Central Bank. Given that oil prices are denominated in dollars, the government can be expected to retain the current exchange system in the foreseeable future. The currency peg is supported by current-account surpluses and a build-up in reserves and assets. In addition, the strength of the dollar will ensure that the dirham remains strong against other currencies.

## *FISCAL POLICY*

The 2001 federal budget projected a deficit of AED2.238 billion. This is 8.3 per cent lower than the AED2.44 billion deficit budgeted in 2000. Government spending is forecast at AED22.63 billion, against revenues of AED20.43 billion. The 2000 federal budget set total expenditures of AED23.12billion ($6.299 billion) and total revenues at AED20.68 billion ($5.634 billion).

Analysis of public finances in the UAE is made difficult by the lack of information at the individual emirate level, which includes vital sectors such as oil and defence. It is estimated that the individual emirates together spend about twice as much as the central administration. At the federal level the budget is largely financed by cash contributions from Abu Dhabi, an act seen by many as a way to distribute oil wealth to the poorer emirates, since the constitution stipulates proportionate contributions by all seven emirates. Oil revenues account for up to 70 per cent of total government revenues. Interest income on overseas assets contributes another 20 per cent, and provides a comfortable and reliable cushion against fluctuation in oil prices.

Table 10.15
UAE: federal budget (AED billion)

| | 1998 | 1999 | 2000B | 2001B |
|---|---|---|---|---|
| Expenditure | 21.39 | 22.91 | 23.12 | 22.63 |
| Revenue | 19.63 | 20.43 | 20.68 | 20.23 |
| Deficit | −1.76 | −2.48 | −2.44 | 2.24 |
| (as percentage of GDP) | −1.00 | −1.30 | −1.00 | −1.00 |

*B: Budget*

*Source: MEES*

Whereas the deficit in the federal budget remains manageable, fluctuating around 1 per cent of GDP over the past few years, the consolidated budget of the seven emirates tells a different story. While data on the consolidated budget is limited, the volatility of the revenue stream, together with the maintenance of generous social spending, has contributed to the accumulation of budget deficits in the last few years. The deficit rose to a high of AED28.8 billion, or 16.5 per cent of GDP, in 1998, due to lower oil revenues, and was reduced only marginally to AED28.2 billion in 1999, equivalent to around 14.6 per cent of GDP, on account of lapses in the assessment and payment of taxes and royalties. Despite the oil revenue windfall, fiscal expenditures were kept under control in 2000, resulting in a substantial reduction in the deficit to an estimated AED4.1 billion, less than 2 per cent of GDP.

A closer look at the country's fiscal position reveals some serious structural weaknesses. The revenue base is relatively narrow and highly dependent on oil, as UAE nationals do not pay personal or corporate taxes. Non-oil revenues reflect receipts from health services, electricity tariffs for commercial users and customs duties. On the other hand, sizeable current expenditure commitments, a large wage bill and a high level of government subsidies make the budget inflexible.

## *EXTERNAL DEBT*

The federal government has been able to finance growth and maintain high standards of living without having to resort to external borrowing, helped by regular current-account surpluses and sizeable net overseas assets. As a result, the government has no sovereign loans and has no domestic debt in the form of bills and bonds. The UAE's total external debt, including debt to foreign institutions and private creditors, is estimated at around $20 billion by the end of 2001. Two-thirds is short-term and related to trade finance activities, reflecting the importance of commerce in the economy. The remainder includes financing of joint ventures with foreign companies and other productive investments. Debt owed to official creditors accounts for less than 7 per cent of the total. The UAE has been a net creditor to the world, and has extended aid to a number of developing countries. It is unlikely that the federation will resort to international loans or bond issues in the foreseeable future.

## *EXTERNAL SECTOR*

The UAE has traditionally enjoyed a substantial trade surplus, however, developments in the trade and current accounts have largely reflected the variation in oil export receipts which make up approximately one-third of total merchandise exports and re-exports.

The UAE's current-account balance has closely mirrored peaks and slumps in oil exports. After recording surpluses of AED22.5 billion and AED22.7 billion in 1996 and 1997 respectively, the current account fell into a deficit of AED0.4 billion in 1998. This was a direct result of a 30 per cent decline in crude-oil exports that year to AED34.6 billion from close to AED50 billion the year before. However, the capital-account balance recorded a surplus in 1998, resulting in a higher balance of payments.

**Table 10.16**
**UAE: balance of payments (AED billion)**

| | 1997 | 1998 | 1999 | 2000 |
|---|---|---|---|---|
| Total exports* | 125.49 | 111.65 | 128.88 | 159.00 |
| Crude oil | 49.10 | 34.60 | 45.40 | 70.10 |
| Re-exports | 39.08 | 42.38 | 45.06 | 46.90 |
| Total imports | 97.70 | 105.94 | 112.65 | 117.25 |
| Trade balance | 27.79 | 5.71 | 16.23 | 41.75 |
| Current account | 22.69 | –0.39 | 10.23 | 33.75 |
| (as percentage of GDP) | 12.30 | –0.20 | 5.40 | 15.10 |
| Capital account | –21.49 | 3.15 | –4.61 | –23.34 |
| Balance of payments | 1.20 | 2.76 | 5.62 | 10.41 |

** including re-exports*

*Source: Central Bank of UAE*

The rise in oil prices in 1999 returned the current account to a surplus equal to AED10.23 billion, or 5.4 per cent of GDP, but still considerably below its pre-1998 levels. The balance of payments strengthened further in 1999 to reach AED5.6 billion, reflecting modest capital outflows. With higher oil prices in 2000, the trade more than doubled to AED41.8 billion, from AED16.2 billion in 1999, and the current account surplus more than tripled to AED33.8 billion, accounting for 15 per cent of GDP. As oil prices declined in 2001, the UAE's external balances adjusted lower, with a current-account surplus of AED15 billion. The trade balance over the next few years will be supported by continued growth in non-oil exports and re-export activity.

## BAHRAIN

Table 10.17
Bahrain: main economic indicators

| | 1996 | 1997 | 1998 | 1999 | 2000 | 2001 |
|---|---|---|---|---|---|---|
| Nominal GDP (BD million) | 2294 | 2387 | 2325 | 2489 | 2996 | 3145 |
| Nominal GDP ($ million) | 6037 | 6282 | 6118 | 6595 | 7939 | 8334 |
| Nominal GDP growth | 4.3% | 4.1% | –2.6% | 7.1% | 20.4% | 5.0% |
| Real GDP growth | 4.1% | 3.1% | –2.0% | 4.3% | 5.3% | 4.2% |
| Inflation | –0.2% | 0.2% | –0.4% | 0.5% | 1.7% | 1.5% |
| **Fiscal Indicators (BD million)** | | | | | | |
| Revenues | 614.4 | 705.7 | 554.0 | 566.0 | 572.0 | – |
| Expenditure | 627.3 | 703.5 | 704.5 | 726.0 | 732.0 | – |
| Deficit/surplus | –12.9 | 2.2 | –150.5 | –160.0 | –160.0 | – |
| (as percentage of GDP) | –0.6 | 0.1 | –6.5 | –6.6 | –6.0 | – |
| **External sector (BD million)** | | | | | | |
| Exports | 1768 | 1648 | 1230 | 1557 | 2143 | – |
| Imports | 1607 | 1514 | 1240 | 1304 | 1644 | – |
| Trade balance | 161 | 135 | –11 | 253 | 499 | – |
| (as percentage of GDP) | 7.0 | 5.6 | –0.5 | 10.4 | 18.6 | – |

*Source: Commercial Bank of Bahrain and other international sources*

### *ECONOMIC OVERVIEW*

In 1999 Bahrain witnessed the first change in leadership in 38 years, which brought renewed vigour to economic reform and greater confidence in the economy. The country is the Gulf's main financial and banking hub, hosting more than 70 banks – including 45 offshore banking units – and the largest concentration of Islamic banks and institutions in the region. However, Bahrain's service industry is facing tough competition from Dubai, and accelerated reform is needed to allow the industry to expand its market share and capitalize on new opportunities within the wider Gulf region.

Bahrain derives less direct benefit from rising oil prices than its Gulf neighbours given its limited hydrocarbon resources. The indirect benefits of the regional upturn in 1999 and 2000 are evident in the services sector, including tourism and offshore-banking activities. The country also benefits from other GCC states' willingness to provide grants and budgetary support. Activity in the tourism and the offshore-banking sectors began to expand in the second half of 1999 and through 2000 and 2001, stimulating growth in the economy.

More importantly, the Bahraini government has capitalized on the higher regional growth to open up the economy further, gaining for itself international recognition as one of the most open economies in the world. The Heritage Foundation, which ranks countries by the degree of economic freedom, found Bahrain to be the fourth-freest economy in the world in 2001. The country allows GCC nationals to own up to 100 per cent of a stock listed on the Bahrain Stock Exchange, and foreigners to own up to 49 per cent of a local stock. All GCC nationals are now allowed to own property in Bahrain, where previously only citizens of Saudi Arabia, Kuwait and the UAE were entitled to do so.

Another promising development is the issuance in April 2000 of an Amiri decree providing for the creation of a Supreme Council for Economic Development. The Council, to be chaired by Prime Minister Shaikh Khalifah bin Salman Al Khalifah, will devise a strategy for developing the country's economy, emphasizing policies to promote economic growth and foreign investment. Although the country boasts a more diversified economy than many other GCC states, one which provides some shield from the vagaries of the oil market, significant vulnerabilities persist in the economy that could once again be exposed by a decline in oil prices. Bahrain still depends on oil for around 60 per cent of state revenues and a slightly higher percentage of exports.

Since oil receipts have dwindled as a result of the depletion of the country's already-limited resources, Bahrain needs to focus on developing its services and non-oil manufacturing industries to meet greater competition from both within and outside the region. Attracting more foreign investment by providing investors with the right working environment will be a key element in the country's economic policy over the next few years.

## *GROWTH*

The Bahraini economy recorded real growth of 5.3 per cent and 4.2 per cent in 2000 and 2001 respectively, as there has been continued strength in the oil market and moves to open the economy further to foreign investment have started to bear fruit. This followed real growth of 4.3 per cent in 1999. In nominal terms the economy expanded by 20.4 per cent in 2000 and 5 per cent in 2001. The regional upturn, which relies heavily on oil prices, has translated into both higher foreign demand and financial support for the country.

## *MONETARY POLICY*

Bahrain has long adopted a conservative and conventional approach to monetary policy and the Bahrain Monetary Agency has developed a wide range of tools to manage monetary growth and interest rates, maintaining a small margin between domestic and dollar-rates.

## *INFLATION*

Inflation has not been a problem in Bahrain, averaging approximately 1–2 per cent over the past two decades. The Bahraini authorities have so far adopted a gradualist approach in phasing out subsidies, successfully avoiding jumps in the CPI. As a result, plans to privatize state utilities and raise user charges are unlikely to have a substantial effect on consumer prices in the near future. However, enhanced spending power within the region brought about by higher oil prices has resulted in increased spending in Bahrain by both nationals and visitors from the region – namely Saudi Arabia – which has led to higher inflationary pressures. The inflation rate rose to 1.7 per cent in 2000, compared to 0.5 per cent in 1999, and was marginally lower in 2001, at 1.5 per cent.

## *EXCHANGE RATE*

Preserving the value of the fully convertible dinar is the principal concern of the monetary authorities. In 1978, the local currency was officially pegged to the SDR at a rate of 0.476 inside a plus or minus 7.25 per cent band, however, the dinar in reality has been pegged to the dollar at an exchange rate of BD0.376. The peg came under some pressure during the Iraqi invasion of neighbouring Kuwait; however, speculation on the currency markets quickly subsided as the Bahrain Monetary Agency continued to provide dollars at the predetermined rate. The exchange-rate peg is expected to remain stable in the foreseeable future, especially in light of the improved prospects for Bahrain's external and fiscal accounts.

## *FISCAL POLICY*

The oil-price crash of 1998 demonstrated that despite Bahrain's successful pioneering efforts at diversification compared to other GCC states, the government remains heavily dependent on oil income for budget revenues, making the budget very prone to external shocks when oil prices fall. Oil revenues typically account for approximately 60 per cent of government revenues in the Bahraini budget. Consequently, the oil-price crash of 1998 reduced government revenues by over 20 per cent, as a result of which the budget balance fell from a modest surplus of BD2 million to a deficit of BD151 million, equivalent to 6.5 per cent of GDP.

The recovery in oil prices of 1999 and 2000 has provided considerable fiscal respite, especially as the original budgetary projections for 1999 and 2000 were cautiously based on an average oil price of $12 per barrel. With actual oil prices well above this level, it is likely that the actual deficit was way below the BD160 million set out in the two-year 1999–2000 budget draft. The 1999 revenues were initially forecast at BD566 million, of which BD260 million was from oil and gas revenues. Jordinvest estimates that the government earned at least BD100 million more in oil revenues and, assuming expenditures remained more or less in line with budget projections, this would have reduced the deficit to around BD60 million, possibly less.

**Table 10.18**
**Bahrain: government budget (BD million)**

| | 1998 | 1999* | 2000* |
|---|---|---|---|
| Oil revenue | 259 | 260 | 256 |
| Non-oil revenue | 295 | 306 | 316 |
| **Total revenue** | **554** | **566** | **572** |
| Current expenditure | 560 | 596 | 602 |
| Project expenditure | 144 | 130 | 130 |
| **Total expenditure** | **705** | **726** | **732** |
| Deficit/surplus | −151 | −160 | −160 |

* *1999–2000 two-year draft budget*

*Source: Bahrain Monetary Agency and international sources*

The same can be said about the 2000 deficit, which was also projected at BD160 billion. Brent crude averaged around $29 per barrel in 2000, pushing oil revenues further above 1999 levels. Some increase in spending above that of the budget was recorded; nonetheless, the budget balance showed a surplus in 2000 for the first time in years.

Bahrain's two-year budget proposal for 2001 and 2002 projects a deficit equal to BD314 million ($833 million), 1.9 per cent lower than the deficit in the previous two-year plan. The budget outlines an 18.1 per cent increase in revenues to BD1344 million ($3565 million) for the period. Higher revenues will to some extent be offset by a 13.7 per cent rise in expenditure to BD1658 million ($4398 million). The breakdown of expenditure into current and capital expenditure has remained stable, with 81 per cent of total spending allocated to current expenditure.

Over the past few years the Bahraini government has demonstrated its ability to contain expenditures successfully in the face of revenue constraints. However, the government must address the budget's vulnerability to fluctuation in oil prices by raising non-oil revenue sources. The desire to maintain the country's status as a tax-free economy limits room for fiscal manoeuvre. The government is heavily involved in the economy, accounting for some 70 per cent of economic activity, leaving much room for privatization. There is also a lot of scope to increase charges and fees on utilities and public services.

## *PUBLIC DEBT*

The government follows a policy of strictly minimizing its official debt to foreign financial institutions. To date, it has financed its budget deficit through dinar-denominated treasury bills, development bonds, direct loans from domestic banks and concessional loans from various Arab development funds and the Islamic Development Bank. In April 1998, Bahrain ventured into the local capital markets for the first time with a BSE-listed 6.25 per cent five-year BD40 million bond that was well received. The government may forge ahead with other similar issues to replace maturing development bonds. In 2001, the government also pioneered a debt instrument that conforms to Islamic standards. Total public debt at the end of 1999 is estimated to be 22 per cent of GDP.

## *EXTERNAL SECTOR*

Bahrain generated a trade surplus of BD253 million in 1999, well ahead of its performance in 1998, when the trade balance had showed a deficit for the first time in years. The deficit in 1998, equal to BD11 million, was mainly due to the 65 per cent decline in oil revenues to BD664 million. As a result, oil income in 1998 comprised just over 50 per cent of exports, compared to 62 per cent in 1999.

Bahrain is not an OPEC member, and therefore oil production is not tied to any quota. However, the limited size of domestic oil resources and the arrangement with neighbouring Saudi Arabia for the provision of crude oil for refining in Bahrain leaves the county with little leeway to increase output and compensate for lower oil prices.

**Table 10.19**
**Bahrain: current account, 1998–2000 (BD million)**

| 1998 | 1999 | 2000* | |
|---|---|---|---|
| Current account | –292.30 | –128.10 | 42.50 |
| Trade balance | –10.70 | 252.70 | 499.00 |
| (as percentage of GDP) | –0.46 | 10.35 | 18.58 |
| Exports | 1229.60 | 1556.80 | 2143.40 |
| Oil exports | 664.40 | 1035.60 | 1577.80 |
| Non-Oil exports | 565.20 | 521.20 | 565.60 |
| Imports | 1240.30 | 1304.10 | 1644.40 |
| Oil imports | 334.90 | 528.00 | 838.30 |
| Non-oil imports | 905.40 | 776.10 | 806.10 |
| Services (net) | 27.40 | 38.20 | 55.30 |
| Income (net) | –60.90 | –110.90 | –139.50 |
| Current transfers (net) | –248.10 | –308.10 | –372.30 |

* *provisional figures*

*Source: Bahrain Monetary Agency*

The surge in oil prices in 1999 drove exports up by 27 per cent to BD1.56 billion. The trade position was further boosted by a fall of 14 per cent in non-oil imports to BD776 million, reflecting a decline in both volume and average import prices. As a result the trade balance moved back into positive territory with a surplus of DB252.7 million, equivalent to 10.4 per cent of GDP. The current account remained in debit, although it did improve from a deficit of BD292 million in 1998 to BD128 million in 1999.

In 2000, exports rose by 38 per cent to an estimated BD2.1 billion, driven by higher oil revenues, while imports rose at a lower rate of 26 per cent to BD1.6 billion, raising the trade surplus to BD499 million (18.6 per cent of GDP), its highest level in years. The improvement in the trade balance brought the current account into positive territory with a modest surplus equal to BD42.5 million.

# 11

# THE ARAB WORLD: A VISION FOR GROWTH

The vision for growth presented here seeks to reflect a pragmatic, action-oriented sense of the possible. Now is not the time for sterile debates about conflicting data, nor is there a need to engage in elegant theorizing about the relative merits of alternative approaches to economic development. Global trends are clear enough. Globalization is here to stay and the region must embrace this dynamic process. We should stop the political, economic and cultural collapse that lies at the roots of Arab rage. We should make the case to Arab people that Islam is compatible with modern society, and that faith cannot be a substitute for political realities and economic prosperity. The Arab youth desperately need the skills and knowledge to find a place for themselves in a modern, interconnected world. This book reflects on the experience of other countries that have had economic success in recent years, and presents several strategies aimed at ensuring a more prosperous future for Arab nations.

Arabs and Israelis should struggle to reach a comprehensive peace agreement sooner rather than later. Israel cannot claim to be a democracy and continue to occupy and militarily rule three million people against their will. It is bad for Israel, bad for the US and bad for the rest of the world. Without a lasting peace, the whole region will continue to suffer from the cloud of uncertainty hovering over it. The Al Aqsa *Intifada* is not simply an episode that will gradually fade away. It is a widespread movement against lingering Israeli occupation that is likely to continue until a final peace is attained. The longer the unrest in the Palestinian territories lasts, the more Arab governments will be under pressure to react. This will raise the risks of conducting business in the region and will reflect negatively on Arab stock markets, with the region's tourism sectors and investment flows suffering most.

After averaging $28.80 a barrel for Brent crude in 2000 and $23 a barrel in 2001, oil prices in the future are expected to trade in a lower range of $18–28 a barrel. Oil revenues for the Gulf states are forecast to average $80–100 in the near future, compared to $150 billion in 2000. This will still be sufficient to help support strong economic growth in both the oil and the non-oil sectors. For the first time in years governments are introducing practical measures to liberalize the business arena, and are implementing new reforms aimed at greater private-sector participation and bringing in more foreign investment. The non-oil Arab countries will benefit from spillover effects of higher growth prospects in the Gulf through remittances, tourism, exports and investments.

Jordan and Oman joined WTO in 2000 and 2001 respectively, and Saudi Arabia is likely to join in the near future. As most of the Arab countries will become members of WTO, this will necessitate less protectionism, stricter enforcement of property rights and greater liberalization. In a region in which more than 50 per cent of the 275-million-strong population are under the age of 24, and in which unemployment is conservatively estimated at 14 per cent, governments will have to strike a balance between promoting economic efficiency and tackling social inequalities and rising unemployment. All Arab countries have a common aim of raising the real GDP growth rate past annual population growth rates.

Parliamentary elections in Jordan, Lebanon, Egypt, Tunisia and Morocco and the rising importance of consultative bodies in the Gulf countries, suggest that increasingly democratic practices will be introduced and government organizations will become more accountable. Nevertheless, the dilemmas of freedom versus security and globalization versus tradition will not be easily resolved. There will always be conflict between globalizers and localizers, between those who want to embrace change and those who are worried that change will destroy their culture and rob them of their traditions.

The region needs a reformation in the practice of Islam that makes it move forward without necessarily weakening religious beliefs. What most preachers tell you today is how to go back a millennium. Very few are reinterpreting Islam in light of modernity, an innovation that would bring the religion to the people in the language of their own specific era. The deadly cycle that produces extremists, religious antimodernism, political suppression and obsolete educational system, should not be allowed to perpetuate.

The strict and consistent enforcement of the rule of law is a basic prerequisite for growth and development. It gives the region's private sectors the confidence that the state will ensure that their rights will be protected if they invest locally, and that the law will be enforced equally on all. People should feel that society treats all its members equally, and that rich and powerful citizens do not enjoy special privileges.

Policy-makers should convince the private sector that they are serious in implementing the required reform policies. Credibility is the key to reform, especially in countries that follow a gradual approach. The sustainability of reform policies can foster private-sector confidence by reducing concerns about policy reversal. If a sufficient number of firms delay investing until a more positive assessment can be reached, this could lock the economy into a low-investment, low-growth equilibrium. In contrast, policies perceived as credible, consistent and unlikely to be reversed may induce private investors to move money into the region, thereby boosting growth and reducing the cost of adjustment.

The Arab countries should start by developing the infrastructure of the new economy, by putting in place an efficient speed-data communications network and Internet services accessible to the majority of the population at affordable prices, reducing telecommunications costs, eradicating the illiteracy of the Internet, and subsidizing PC use.

The region needs to adapt its educational system to the new economy by putting more emphasis on computer-literacy and English teaching from a young age. Tomorrow's literacy rates will be defined in terms of computer literacy. In order to create a generation of creative and imaginative graduates, Arab teachers need to train students on how to think, rather than what to think. The problem of creating free thinkers in authoritarian regimes is obvious. Institutionalizing democratic practices would go a long way towards creating the right atmosphere for free enterprise and risk-taking. Arab schools should teach innovation rather than 'memorization', creativity rather than conformity.

With few exceptions, educational systems in the region produce civil servants and corporate employees to do routine jobs, rather than creative workers who can adapt to new technologies and work in occupations that may not yet exist. This clearly should change in order for there to be the human-resource base needed for the new economy. Adapting to technological change has become a life-long activity.

The region needs to develop an entrepreneurial culture that fits today's information age. Some deep cultural shifts must take place to encourage entrepreneurship in societies where caution and risk-aversion are virtues, and where public-sector-led initiatives and corporate hierarchies are still preferred over free markets.

The Arab countries have so far produced very few creative entrepreneurs. The start-up culture of tireless, low-paid work for a common and vague promise of future riches is still alien to today's Arab youth. High-school and university graduates often opt to work in established organizations rather than take the risks of start-up companies. The availability of innovative employee-ownership schemes, including stock options that allow founders to share the growth potential of new companies, will go a long way to encourage entrepreneurs to take risks and start their own businesses.

We need to develop venture capital and IPO markets to aid innovative companies, since shortage of venture capital is a major obstacle facing start-up companies in the IT field. US venture-capital spending doubled to more than $60 billion in 2000. According to the Harvard Business School, a dollar of venture capital produces three-to-five times more patents than a dollar of research and development. The number of start-up companies In South Korea doubled in 1999 to 4700, and the market capitalization of Korea's KOSDAQ market jumped 13 times, to $100 billion in 1999.

It is very difficult for innovative companies in our region to bypass traditionally cautious commercial bankers and go straight to investors with IPOs. Without an exit mechanism, investors will not put their money into venture-capital funds targeting regional IT sectors. Companies wishing to list their shares on local exchanges are required to show three years of profit; this law must be changed, as most start-up companies in the IT sector are not immediately profitable, and sometimes need new investors before they have revenues.

The region needs to add something of a high-tech flavour to its stock markets, or, better yet, establish a regional NASDAQ-type exchange providing a friendlier atmosphere in which to list IT-related companies. This will help attract home part of the capital that has been invested in new-economy shares abroad.

Arab countries need to put in place the right legislative infrastructure to facilitate the growth of new economy industries and protect intellectual property rights. When e-commerce transactions take place, there is no record on paper testifying to the reliability of the legal particulars of that transaction. New functional laws need to be developed which call for the admission of e-mail as evidence in commercial lawsuits. Following the recent introduction of new copyright laws in Jordan, Kuwait and Lebanon, most Arab countries now have anti-piracy legislation in place. This is necessary, but not sufficient to encourage international firms to transfer e-business activity to the region. This legislation must be strictly enforced.

By implementing e-government applications, countries in the Middle East are moving in the right direction. Pioneering initiatives such by Dubai's DIC, and the emphasis on IT in Egypt, Jordan and Lebanon, indicate that the region is creating e-governments, a positive move. This, however, requires the reinvention of government, involving major restructuring, the integration of current organizations, and an adherence to cultural changes in the way the government and the public interact with each other, as well as the automation of manual procedures so that they can be made available online.

Ultimately, the e-government trend will make a dramatic change in the relationship between governments and the public in the Arab world. The use of Arabic in the whole process is crucial. The elements of success for e-government include selecting the right business partners, understanding and accepting change, overcoming security issues, providing a user- and language-friendly environment, and creating easy information access through the Internet, mobile phones and other devices.

There is no 'silver bullet', no single action that by itself will expand economic opportunity and ensure prosperity. Real and lasting change will only come about as a result of the cumulative effect of many small steps, each one part of a broader and more comprehensive economic vision about what the region could look like in 20 years. The enormity of the challenge is clear: we can and must break from the past and embark on a new course, one that takes advantage of the opportunities presented by the global economy, without being overwhelmed by its many challenges.

Governments can choose, through the policies they implement, whether to be prosperous or poor. Those Arab countries which integrate into the world economy, empower their private sector and change the role of the government from player to referee, while maintaining political stability and the rule of law will be winners in today's global markets. Those nations which fail to implement reform, or do so slowly and hesitantly, will remain stuck on a slow growth path.